Chicken Soup for the Soul®

for the Soul®

Hope
&
Miracles

D0401826

Chicken Soup for the Soul: Hope & Miracles
101 Inspirational Stories of Faith, Answered Prayers & Divine Intervention
Amy Newmark, Natasha Stoynoff. Foreword by John Edward

Published by Chicken Soup for the Soul Publishing, LLC www.chickensoup.com
Copyright © 2015 by Chicken Soup for the Soul Publishing, LLC. All Rights Reserved.

The publisher gratefully acknowledges the many publishers and individuals who
granted Chicken Soup for the Soul permission to reprint the cited material.

Front cover photo courtesy of iStockPhoto.com/Atropat (© Atropat).
Back cover and interior photo courtesy of iStockPhoto.com/dsteller (© dsteller).
Photo of Amy Newmark courtesy of Susan Morrow at SwickPix.

Cover and Interior Design & Layout by Brian Taylor

Distributed to the booktrade by Simon & Schuster. SAN: 200-2442

Publisher's Cataloging-In-Publication Data
(Prepared by The Donohue Group, Inc.)

Chicken soup for the soul : hope & miracles : 101 inspirational stories
of faith, answered prayers & divine intervention / [compiled by] Amy
Newmark [and] Natasha Stoynoff ; foreword by John Edward.

pages ; cm

ISBN: 978-1-61159-944-2

1. Faith--Literary collections. 2. Faith--Anecdotes. 3. Miracles--Literary collections.
4. Miracles--Anecdotes. 5. Prayer--Literary collections. 6. Prayer--Anecdotes. 7.
Anecdotes. I. Newmark, Amy. II. Stoynoff, Natasha. III. Edward, John (John J.) IV.
Title: Hope & miracles : 101 inspirational stories of faith, answered prayers & divine
intervention V. Title: Hope and miracles

BL626.3 .C45 2015
204.2/02   2014956833

PRINTED IN THE UNITED STATES OF AMERICA
on acid∞free paper

25 24 23 22 21 20 19 18 17 16 15   01 02 03 04 05 06 07 08 09 10 11

Chicken Soup for the Soul

Hope & Miracles

101 Inspirational Stories of Faith, Answered Prayers & Divine Intervention

Amy Newmark & Natasha Stoynoff
Foreword by John Edward

CSS

Chicken Soup for the Soul Publishing, LLC
Cos Cob, CT

Chicken Soup for the Soul

Changing lives one story at a time™
www.chickensoup.com

Contents

❶
~Messages from Heaven~

❷
~Miraculous Healing~

❸

~Touched by an Angel~

❹

~Against All Odds~

❺
~Divine Intervention~

❻
~Answered Prayers~

❼
~Think Positive~

❽

~Dreams and Premonitions~

❾

~Mysterious Miracles~

❿
~Miraculous Reunions~

Foreword
Allowing Miracles

I f you ask people to define what a "miracle" is, odds are a lot of them will describe an epic, Cecil B. DeMille movie moment, like Moses raising his staff to the sky as God parted the Red Sea or Jesus of Nazareth bringing Lazarus back to life four days after he'd been dead and buried.

These are the kind of larger-than-life miracles that are described in the Hebrew and Christian bibles—and in the scriptures of other religions, as well—stories that capture people's attention big time. As far as defining miracles go, these dramatic, God-like moments are at the top of the list.

But the list doesn't end there, thousands of years ago in faraway lands. Miracles don't only happen to people we will never know who are long gone.

Today, we hear about all sorts of modern-day miracles. Everyone's heard about the mother who, in a burst of adrenaline, can lift a 3,000-pound car to save her child pinned underneath. Recently, there was a story in the newspaper about a ninety-one-year-old woman in Poland who was dead in the morgue for eleven hours before coming back to life in a body bag, leaving doctors stunned.

In *Chicken Soup for the Soul: Hope & Miracles—101 Inspirational Stories of Faith, Answered Prayers & Divine Intervention*, you will read about all sorts of miracles that happen every day to people you may know: A woman who takes ill while driving feels the hands of a deceased friend take over the wheel for her; A little girl badly burned in a campfire sees her burns heal overnight after a prayer vigil; A teenager hears a voice that tells her to take a walk outside, and it leads her to an area where she saves a woman's life.

Some miracles of life are so common that people take them for granted. A baby coming into the world is a miracle, as is someone passing away and crossing to the Other Side. Every year when spring arrives and the trees in my back yard begin to bud, I'm amazed. To me, these small miracles are just as awe-inspiring as the larger-than-life ones of the old days and the modern ones we hear of today, and I'm grateful for each and every one of them.

The point is, miracles come in all shapes and sizes, and this book is filled with a wide variety of them. The personal stories you'll read here about hope, faith, answered prayers and divine intervention are to me all about one thing—our connection to a higher power or divine source.

It's a connection we all have, and recognizing that is the first step to allowing miracles, big and small, into your life.

In the work that I do as a psychic medium, that is the most important truth I try to convey. At my events all over the world, the question I'm most often asked no matter what country I'm in is: "How can I get a stronger connection with the spirit world and how can I do what you do?"

I always correct people who insist that I have a "gift." I don't look at it that way. I have an ability—it's something I've had since childhood for as long as I can remember. But it's an ability we all have to some degree, one that everyone can tap into and strengthen if they choose to. It's all about noticing, embracing, and welcoming it into your life.

"There is an energy out there," I explain to audiences, "and you are made of this energy. You can call it 'chi' or you can call it 'prana.' You can call it a higher power or you can call it 'God' or 'Yahweh' or 'Allah.' I don't care if you call it 'Sam.' It doesn't matter what you label it. It just matters that you acknowledge that this unseen energy is there."

Once you make that connection, miracles await you like a new world awaiting discovery. When Christopher Columbus set out across the Atlantic Ocean, he didn't know for sure what he would find. But he had to have hope and faith that a new world was out there in order to find it.

It wasn't a blind faith, mind you. I'm not a fan of the kind of faith in which people believe everything they are told and don't question anything. People are surprised when I describe myself as a "healthy skeptic" in my approach to life, but I am and always was.

So while I'm not a fan of blind hope, I am a fan of what I call "inspired" hope.

In this book, in the story "Never Walk Again?", doctors tell eighty-nine-year-old Beulah Dobson that she won't be able to walk after breaking her vertebrae in a fall. But she refuses to give up hope that she will, and her hope is not unfounded. She doesn't lie in her bed waiting for an impossible miracle to happen. She senses the possibility of it and prays and works hard exercising, willing her feet to move a little at a time each day until she helps to make her miracle happen, until she walks again. She was hopeful, but also inspired.

Prayer is a way for us to invite divine intervention into our lives.

I pray every day, sometimes using a rosary but not always. In my book, *Practical Praying*, I talk about praying with intention. It doesn't so much matter what prayer you say or if you get on your knees when you do it or walk the dog around the park as you do it. What's important about the act of praying is that just *in the doing of it*, you are stating an intention to the universe, to the higher or divine source.

In "Jesse in the Sky" Scarlett Lewis prays with heartbreaking intention as she cries in a bathroom stall in the Orlando airport. When she leaves the airport, the answer to her prayers is written in the sky — literally.

Praying is like setting the thanksgiving table before the guests come. When you say a prayer, you are welcoming the miracles into your house to sit at your dinner table. Prayer is a way for us to imagine the undiscovered land we hope to find before we even see it.

Maybe in today's world, we don't expect seas to part or water to turn into wine. But as this inspiring collection of stories shows us, we can hope for miracles when we need them. And sometimes, they arrive when and how we least expect them.

~John Edward

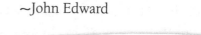

Editors' note: John Edward is one of the world's foremost psychic mediums. His clientele has included people of the clergy, law enforcement agencies, and people from everyday life. For thirty years he has used his abilities to connect people with loved ones who have passed on—in private readings, at public events all over the world, and on his internationally syndicated talk shows, *Crossing Over with John Edward* and *John Edward Cross Country*.

He is the author of the critically acclaimed New York Times best sellers *One Last Time*; *What If God Were the Sun*; *Crossing Over: The Stories Behind the Stories*; *After Life: Answers from the Other Side*; *Final Beginnings*; *Practical Praying: Using the Rosary to Enhance Your Life*; *Infinite Quest*, and his most recent novel, *Fallen Masters*.

Introduction
Divine Timing

Life calls the tune, we dance.
~John Galsworthy

Amy: *Natasha and I are running late finishing this book. But we're used to that. Because we're writers, and perfectionists, and we always take on too much! I was always this way. I was even born sixteen days late according to my mother, but hey, perfection takes time, right?*

Natasha: I, on the other hand, arrived in this world early. Minutes ahead of my twin brother, I was born on December 31st in the year The Beatles first appeared on Ed Sullivan, and two months premature of my March due date.

But that was the first and last time I've ever been early — or even on time — for anything in my life. Since my birth day, I've been late for school exams, family weddings, court duty, surgeries, flights to Paris, and interviews with A-list celebrities whom I kept waiting on their yachts, to the exasperation of all who know me, love me, or hire me.

"You're cursed," they tell me.

"Maybe," I shrug. "But one day, I'll be crazy lucky."

Because if my rudimentary calculations are correct, at one point in my life when I least expect it… all my stars will align like never before, and in a sublime act of supernatural intervention saved up for that one moment, my tardiness will save my life.

Amy: *It may sound like rationalization, but we both have great stories about times when being late, through some kind of divine intervention, actually saved lives.*

Natasha: My theory begins with my grandfather on my father's side, Stavro Shaumanduroff, who was famously late for a boat once.

It was the spring of 1912 and he was a handsome, strapping man of eighteen preparing to voyage across the ocean to America. The family had recently fled their home village of Smurdesh, Macedonia, after various invasions and uprisings. A relative of my grandmother, Vasil Chekalarov, was a fierce, legendary revolutionary until Greek troops captured him and chopped his head off, parading it through the village as a warning to others.

The family transplanted to Sofia, Bulgaria with a plan: Stavro would set sail for New York with a third-class ticket and two boyhood friends, work long hours there on a factory assembly line for several months, then return with pocketsful of coveted dollars.

The future of the family, his father told him, was in Stavro's strong, Slavic hands.

Apparently, it was also at the bottom of his coffee cup.

Before the journey, his mother, Stoyanka, served her son some *Турско Кафе*, then peered into his drained cup to read the coffee grains settled on the bottom. The family gathered around as she squinted.

"*Neh*," she said, shaking her head back and forth, pointing to the broken line of sludge in the cup. "Not good. Stavro, you no go this time."

Her pronouncement caused an uproar. The Shaumanduroff women were respected for their fortune-telling abilities, but this was news no one wanted to hear. Never mind the coffee grinds, he was going!

Stavro took a train to Southampton, England, to meet his buddies and catch the boat. On the morning of April 10th, he stood on a dock looking up, up, up with eyes as wide as the donkey-cart wheels back in Smurdesh.

The *Titanic* was humongous, shiny and beautiful, and he couldn't wait to get on her. But as the hundreds of passengers boarded the luxury liner, Stavro couldn't find his friends; they had missed their train to Southampton. He waited until he heard the triple-blast horns at noon signaling final boarding, then raced to the boat with his father's words ringing in his ears:

"The future of the family depends on you. You are our hope."

He reached the vessel just in time to see the lines cast off and *Titanic* freed from land.

"You're too late," a dockworker said. By twenty minutes.

Amy: *Later on in this volume, you'll read about Natasha's other grandfather, who also made it to the U.S. from Eastern Europe and brought his family over through a series of fortuitous coincidences and lucky breaks. I'm glad it all worked out since it has been such a pleasure putting together this collection of jaw-dropping stories with Natasha. She has shared many of her own stories in this book, and I think you'll have trouble putting it down. I have come away from working on* Chicken Soup for the Soul: Hope & Miracles *even more convinced that there are good reasons for hope, that good things do happen to good people, and that our lives can be filled with miracles if we stay open to them.*

Natasha: I've come away more convinced, too. And I have a second story of divine intervention to share! Let's skip ahead sixty years to a cloudy fall morning in 1972 in the Windy City, one week before the U.S. Presidential Election. The mood in the Democratic campaign headquarters was somber. The Watergate break-in had happened a few months earlier but the young staffers, including my friend Jamie — a recent Columbia University grad — still knew that George McGovern stood no chance against Nixon.

Jamie's job in the Chicago press office was to write news releases and distribute campaign schedule updates to the Woodward-and-Bernstein-types covering the election in their smoke-filled newsrooms. The Xerox telecopier transmitted copy at a speed of six minutes per page!

Once in a while, the twenty-two-year-old was given top-secret assignments. Like the time he was instructed to fetch a list of grocery items and hand-deliver them to McGovern's hotel. The list included a bottle of Jack Daniel's, Hershey bars, and an orange (the senator had a cold, he was told, off the record).

On the night of October 29th, the staffers worked especially late. With Marvin Gaye and The Temptations playing in the background, they stuffed envelopes until their fingers ached and it was well past midnight. Jamie got back to his apartment, set his alarm for 6:30 a.m. so he could catch the 7:20 a.m. train, and passed out. Every morning he took the same train on the Illinois Central commuter line. He picked it up at 53rd Street and rode it along Lake Michigan past Soldier Field football stadium.

That morning, Jamie's alarm clock didn't go off. He overslept until 8 a.m., then rushed to get ready... turning on his clock radio to the all-news AM station WBBM as he got dressed. That's when he heard:

"....breaking news...in what may be the worst train wreck in Illinois history, one commuter train rear-ended another at approximately 7:40 a.m. this morning near the 27th Street platform, killing dozens and injuring hundreds of passengers..."

It was Jamie's train. The final death tally was forty-five with over 300 injured. The crash occurred two stops and twenty minutes away from Jamie's apartment.

Amy: *And now let's advance the calendar again, to the afternoon of December 21, 1988, when the phone rang and I learned that my father's flight home from London, Pan Am flight 103, had mysteriously crashed in Lockerbie, Scotland, only thirty-eight minutes after taking off from London's Heathrow Airport.*

My father worked in London part-time and was flying home that day to join the family for Christmas. With one phone call, everything changed for us. Of course, we were filled with dread, but it all seemed so unbelievable that I rushed to reassure my mother and grandmother, who were panic-stricken, that we really didn't know anything yet.

Our only hope was that my father was somehow not on the flight.

Remember back then, when you could miss your flight and use your ticket on a later flight or even on another airline?

But if my father had missed the flight, why hadn't he called us to tell us that he was okay? After all, it was already nighttime in London.

We left messages on the answering machine at my father's house for hours but there was still no word. We grew increasingly worried, but I held onto a little hope. After all, we were the family that was always late!

Finally, when it was very late in London, my father called us to report that he had missed the flight and gone out to dinner, with no idea that his flight had crashed and that his horrified family was waiting for news back in New York. Dad had finally noticed the blinking light on his answering machine and listened to our increasingly frantic messages. He was very shook up when he learned that all 259 people on his flight were killed, along with eleven people on the ground. He came home a couple of days later and we had quite a meaningful Christmas that year. We were all counting our blessings, and I have valued every day with my father since then.

We were relieved to learn as well that Pan Am 103 was not full, meaning that some other poor soul didn't take my father's place on standby. Dad's seat remained empty, so humanity was up one that night!

Natasha: Good thing we're both from a family that's always late. As we've said, lateness can be divine. A little more than a decade after your father's missed flight, my former roommate, Alessandra, was pacing back and forth in her Upper East Side loft in Manhattan.

The babysitter was supposed to arrive at 8 a.m. to look after Ale's eight-month-old son, but she was twenty minutes late and Ale was anxious. She was the CEO of the family-owned shipping company and because they had offices all around the world, it was crucial she be downtown at her desk every day by 8:30 a.m. to field incoming calls from various time zones.

When the apologetic sitter arrived, Ale raced down five flights in her high heels and ran to catch the express subway going south. Her office on the 46th floor at One World Trade Center had magnificent views of the Statue of Liberty and the Hudson River.

She got off the subway just before 9 a.m., stepped onto the platform, and smelled smoke. Without any hesitation, Alessandra immediately crossed the platform and got on the train going north, back home to her baby. She had no idea that the first plane had hit her office tower less than ten minutes earlier. But she'd smelled smoke here before—in '93 when terrorists planted a bomb that detonated. So when she smelled smoke, she smelled trouble. She got out of there on one of the last subway trains running. A few minutes later, the second plane hit.

A sinking ship, a train wreck, and two acts of terrorism—all narrowly missed. You can call it coincidence, luck, or fate. We prefer to think the odds are with us that we each get one fabulously epic and divine intervention in our lifetime that saves us.

We plan to be fashionably late for ours.

~Natasha Stoynoff and Amy Newmark

Chapter 1

Hope & Miracles

Messages from Heaven

Jesse in the Sky

When love is lost, do not bow your head in sadness;
instead keep your head up high and gaze into heaven for that is
where your broken heart has been sent to heal.
~Author Unknown

Since the day my six-year-old son Jesse was killed, I've prayed a million prayers. I've prayed that there is a heaven and that Jesse is there playing with his favorite rubber ducks. I've prayed that his brother, J.T., and I would survive our broken hearts and smile again. And I've prayed, over and over, that the world become a less violent, more loving place.

Jesse was murdered on December 14, 2012, when a young man shot his way into Sandy Hook Elementary school in Newtown, Connecticut, and opened fire — killing six adults and twenty children, Jesse included.

My little boy was a hero in his final moments. When the gunman's rifle jammed for a few seconds as he stood in the first grade classroom, my sweet Jesse yelled to his classmates hiding in the bathroom across the room: "Run! *Run now!*"

His last words saved their lives, but he couldn't save his own. The young man with the rifle was blocking Jesse's escape path and a moment later, he shot my boy in the head as my son faced him.

Jesse's act of bravery doesn't surprise me a bit.

Every night in his bubble bath, he would surround himself with superhero ducks and his collection of toy soldiers—"my army men," he'd call them—lining them up along the porcelain tub's edge. On Saturday afternoons, he'd go "on patrol" at our farm. First, he'd get in uniform: his green army helmet and camouflage-patterned snow boots. Then, he'd stick his water pistol in his waistband and go stand guard by our front gate, pacing back and forth, ready to squirt harmful intruders who dared approach.

He wanted to keep us safe and happy. That's the part of Jesse that called out to his classmates to run, and it's the part that answered my prayer one day when I was on my knees in grief.

Some people say we can receive "signs" from our loved ones who are on the "Other Side" after they've passed—and I believe it.

Since Jesse's been gone, J.T. and I and the rest of the family have been comforted by dozens of little "signs" from him—flickering lights when we call out his name or notes we've found in Jesse's handwriting when we're desperate to hear his voice. Some may think these signs are coincidental, but we feel they are much more than that. To us, it's Jesse saying hello and letting us know he's watching over us. They are little, intimate moments that we recognize—we don't need big billboards in the sky to let us know he's there.

But one day, that's exactly what we got.

About two weeks after the shooting, J.T. and I had to get away. The grief in our town was so all-consuming that we were drowning in it. We boarded a flight to Orlando in hopes that a few days in the warmth would help us begin the healing process, if that was even possible.

On the flight south, we had more signs from Jesse. When I tried to listen to different genres in the in-flight music selection, the songs kept skipping to a favorite of Jesse's—and then, one for his mama who was a teen in the Eighties—Rick Springfield's "Jessie's Girl." I sat back in my seat with a big smile, ecstatic to hear from my boy and, as always, hungry for more signs that showed he was with me.

Arriving at the Orlando airport, I checked my iPhone. I'd sent a text hours earlier to a psychic I'd recently met, detailing the signs I'd been getting from Jesse and asking for her input.

Her response devastated me: *Maybe Jesse is lingering here and not moving onward because he wants to make sure you and J.T. are okay. Spirits do that sometimes.*

I didn't want J.T. to see my distress, so I told him, "Wait for me at the car rental, I'll be right back." I raced to the ladies room, locked myself in a stall, and burst into the most gut-wrenching tears I'd cried so far—and that's saying a lot. I was horrified that I'd lost my boy, and in such a tragic way. Now was I keeping his spirit from moving onward due to my own selfishness? Was Jesse hanging around in some kind of limbo just to give his mother the signs I had come to depend on?

I cried even harder at this possibility, and I knew what I had to do. Jesse had been unselfish and brave in his final moments, and I had to be that now, too.

"Jesse, you've been so precious," I said aloud, "to send us such sweet messages to comfort us and let us know you're okay. But you have to listen to your mama now. We are going to be okay—J.T. and I. You can go to Jesus now, do you hear me, sweet boy? Go to Jesus, we will be okay. Always know how much I love you."

I dried my tears and returned to J.T., giving him a big hug.

"Everything's going to be all right now," I told him, and we hopped into the rental car and sped off down the highway. We'd only been driving for a few minutes when I saw it.

High up against the open blue sky, a small plane was soaring across. It had just spelled out something in smoke:

JESSE & JESUS. TOGETHER FOREVER.

Except the "J" in "Jesse" was backwards—the same way Jesse used to write his name.

Was I imagining this? I looked over at J.T. and saw him looking up. Did he see it, too?

"Mom, look!" J.T. yelled, excited. "Jesse's with Jesus!"

We pulled over to the side of the road and sat in awe and silence, staring at the sky. Then J.T. quickly took some photos of the message as it began to dissipate.

We were stunned. What a miraculous affirmation, I thought. I had no doubt that Jesse heard my tearful plea in the bathroom stall, and was telling his mama not to worry, that he was fine and indeed, in the arms of Jesus.

Jesse! Thank you, thank you, thank you! And thank you, Jesus... please take good care of my sweet boy!

I had no idea who the skywriting pilot was and I never attempted to find out. To me, it would be no less of a miracle if I solved that mystery. Only a handful of people knew where we were flying that day, and our departure time had changed three times due to bad weather, so how could anyone have timed a skywriting message to appear at the exact moment we were driving down the highway?

Nearly two years after we got our message in the sky, a friend read an article in the *Miami Herald* about two Christian pilots in Florida who started a "sky ministry" and used their bright-yellow crop duster, dubbed "Holy Smoke," to write inspirational messages to people at 10,000 feet. On a clear day, you could see their Jesus writings from thirty-five miles away.

"God is the one strategically putting those messages there," one of the pilots was quoted as saying, "we're nothing more than the pen. These are God's love letters to his children."

I have yet to call and confirm if the Holy Smoke pilots were the ones who wrote my Jesse message, but I will someday.

Until then, I consider whoever was up in the Orlando sky that day a messenger from heaven and Jesse. He was God's helper, answering my prayer when I needed it the most.

~Scarlett Lewis with Natasha Stoynoff

Embracing a Second Chance

The most important thing in illness is never to lose heart.
~Nikolai Lenin

It was the end of July and Orlando was hot and humid. We sighed with relief as we settled into the air-conditioned three-bedroom rental. Lorenza and I claimed the master suite, his mother and sister, Michele, unpacked in their adjoining studio, and our young son asked, "Is it time to eat?" He grabbed his favorite toy and disappeared into the bedroom he would share with my mom.

Summer heat didn't bother Christopher. He was elated to be on vacation with his aunt and both grandmothers. Summer break would soon end, but entering the sixth grade was the least of his concerns. We were close to the theme parks, so all he could think of was a fun-packed week.

While my husband returned the luggage cart to the lobby, Michele and my mother-in-law studied a pile of slick travel brochures. Mom joined me in the kitchen to prepare dinner and we talked about our itinerary. We would spend two days at Disney's Animal Kingdom, shop for souvenirs, and attend a dinner theater. The rest of our time would be spent leisurely relaxing around our resort.

That night, everything changed. Everybody else slept as I tried to doze off, but that wasn't an easy task. It had been two years since I was diagnosed with aortic stenosis. Up to then, I was unaware that

I had a congenital heart defect. My cardiologist forecasted two more years until open-heart surgery, but lately I had noticed a discernible change in my condition. I propped myself up on a mountain of pillows to breathe easier, but I could still hear congestion in my lungs. How would I navigate the amusement park without collapsing? I moved to a wide bedside chair, elevated my feet on the ottoman, and leaned back against a pillow, thinking I'd rent a scooter.

The next morning, I knew I couldn't go with my family. My feet were swollen, I felt breathless, and I was spitting up blood. "I'm staying here," I told them, refusing to ruin their day with the details of my night.

"No, Momma!" my son said with disappointment. "I want you to come!"

I squeezed his arm gently. "I need a nap, son… maybe another day."

"Are you sure? We can go tomorrow." My husband studied me, concern evident in his eyes.

My ever-vigilant mother was determined to take care of me. "I'll stay with her. Take Chris to the park and have fun."

I gave my husband a kiss, then my son. "Don't worry. I'll rest today, and we'll go to dinner tonight."

I hid my tears until they walked out the door. I was discouraged about giving up time with my family, but I was even more distressed about what I had discovered by surfing the Internet on our laptop. I was experiencing the warning signs of congestive heart failure.

When we returned home, I made an appointment with my cardiologist. Lorenza sat beside me in the examining room, holding my hand. I had told him my suspicions, but I hoped I was wrong. I still had not resigned myself to the prognosis because I'd felt pretty normal until recent months. The symptoms had manifested slowly and I'd adjusted my life accordingly. Except for driving my son to and from school, I stayed home most days and I had gradually curtailed my normal routine.

Following an echocardiogram, Dr. Moore joined us. "The valve has narrowed so much that it's severely obstructing blood flow. I'm referring you to a surgeon."

"When will that be?" Lorenza asked.

"As soon as possible."

I cried.

The doctor gave me a consoling hug. "You'll feel better after surgery."

I should have been hopeful but I felt fearful and anxious instead. I was frightened that I would die. That possibility sent my mind reeling. Even though I knew I had no choice, and that I certainly wouldn't survive without a new heart valve, my anxiety got the best of me. I remembered what I'd been through years earlier when I had gallbladder surgery. Would surgery be painful? They'd have to stop my heart! How could this be happening to me? My father had died from cardiac arrest when he was fifty. Would I die young too?

We discussed all the possibilities with Christopher because it was unfair not to tell him what everybody else knew. "Daddy and I need your help now," I told him. It's amazing how little kids will step up when necessary. He assisted his dad with household chores without complaint. Lorenza did all the cooking. They were always loving and tender, and I needed their comforting words more than ever as I fought depression. My mother had moved to Florida the year before to be closer to my little family. While I knew she wanted to be by my side through this turmoil, I also realized she had come to help take care of our son while I was sick… and in case I didn't make it through surgery.

I wanted Chris to remember our time together fondly. We went to movies, we packed picnic lunches, and one day we drove to St. Augustine Beach where Lorenza parked on the hard sand so I could watch my guys swim in the ocean.

We went to my mother's house one Sunday for dinner. By then, I was overwhelmed. No matter what my husband and mother said to calm my nerves, it was never enough. I prayed fervently, asking God to take all of it away from me. I wanted a miracle.

I went out on the porch and immersed myself in that peaceful moment as a bald eagle swooped over the marsh. It was high tide, my favorite time of day. "Help me, God. Tell me what to do."

I was surprised by what I heard but I recognized the message immediately. "I never had a chance. You do." My dad had died more than thirty years before, when heart procedures weren't so advanced. At that moment, I realized I had been selfish — so self-absorbed that I hadn't acknowledged that a mechanical valve was a gift. I had an opportunity to live a longer, more fulfilling life.

I walked back into the house and announced, "I am ready for heart surgery."

Mom and Lorenza were astonished. I smiled, knowing they were puzzled yet relieved.

My husband embraced me. "What happened?"

"God told me I'll be okay," I answered. "I'm going to get well now."

The morning I went to the hospital for surgery, Chris woke up early and surprised his dad with a breakfast omelet prepared in the microwave. "I'm taking care of him," he said proudly.

That day I felt serene and hopeful. When I said goodbye to him at the door, he gave me a gigantic hug. "I'll see you soon, Momma."

I was so proud of my little man, and I was no longer fearful of leaving him. "I'll call you tonight, son, when I wake up," I promised.

And I did.

~Claudia McCants

A Feather from Heaven

Death is not extinguishing the light;
it is putting out the lamp because dawn has come.
~Rabindranath Tagore

After I got the call from my sister in Florida that our mother was in intensive care, I was on a plane within the week. I knew she was very ill—double pneumonia, congestive heart failure and anemia due to internal bleeding somewhere—but Mom had battled most of these health issues before and had triumphed. Nearly eighty-one, she was our family's indomitable Energizer Bunny. So when the pulmonologist broke the news that our mother was not going to make it, my brother, sister and I were stunned and heartbroken.

I looked down at my vibrant, funny, bossy, inexpressibly lovable mom and wondered how anyone so alive could be terminally ill. There she was, hooked up to beeping machines and wearing a CPAP with the highest saturation rate of oxygen available. But unlike the other patients in ICU, she was her usual silly self, making faces, teasing the nurses, joking and laughing.

Even after the doctor had explained the dire prognosis to her, her irrepressible attitude didn't falter. "You know," she told us, "I would've thought that hearing I was going to die would make me a basket case, but strange as it seems, I'm really at peace about this." We, her children, of course, were not. "Don't cry," she said, wiping our tears. "I know where I'm going after all. Heaven's going to be wonderful." We did our best, but heaven seemed so far away.

Throughout her days in the hospital, Mom had a positive spirit that became infectious. She entertained and inspired family, friends, neighbors and beloved members of her church; each visitor was treated to her off-the-wall sense of humor and uplifting faith. As long as her pain was kept under control, she was the sassy, often hilarious life of the party. The rules in the intensive care unit limited callers to two at a time, but there were rarely less than six in Mom's room. The wonderful staff, captivated by this high-spirited, anything-but-ordinary patient, smiled and looked the other way.

One afternoon, Mom's best friend and longtime comrade-in-shenanigans, Janet, came for her daily visit. She brought her twelve-year-old granddaughter, Kimberly. Janet and Mom tossed insults and droll comments back and forth as Kimberly and I alternately laughed and rolled our eyes. After a few minutes of this though, Janet grew serious and handed Mom an envelope. "Here, I brought you something," she said. "Open it and read the note."

Mom smiled, drawing out the folded sheet of paper, and began to read out loud a lovely little poem about angels. "Oh, that's sweet," she said, when she finished.

"Now, look in the envelope," Janet instructed. Pulling it open, Mom peeked inside and chuckled. "It's a feather!" She held the tiny white plume up for us to see. "Must have been a small angel, huh?"

Kimberly and I laughed.

Janet, smiling through suddenly teary eyes, leaned forward and grabbed Mom's hand. "Listen, you—this feather is important. When you get to heaven, I want you to send it to me to let me know you got there."

Mom laughed. "You don't want much, do you? Okay, I'll see what I can do."

During the week to come, our family and Mom's dearest friends stayed close by her side, treasuring every second, cherishing every wisecrack, every laugh, every tender, reassuring hug. Each of us was imprinting on our hearts the moments spent with her.

Much too soon, however, the day came when I had to return to Portland. Saying goodbye was agonizing. How could I leave knowing I wouldn't see her again? Mom though, with her unshakable faith, hugged me and whispered, "I love you. This isn't goodbye, sweetheart, it's see you later." My last memory of my mother is of her grinning her irresistible grin and blowing me kisses through her oxygen mask.

Early the following Monday morning, I got the call: surrounded by her children, grandchildren and dearest sister and brother, Mom had slipped gently from their arms into God's.

On Tuesday afternoon, my phone rang; it was Janet. We had been checking in with one another throughout the weeks leading up to Mom's death, so I assumed she was calling to see how I was doing. Instead, her voice brimmed with excitement. "I have something to tell you," she said. Intrigued by her unexpected tone, I asked, "What's up?"

"My granddaughter, Kimberly, stayed with me last night," she said. "We finished watching a movie and were just sitting there on the sofa, when I looked over and saw Kimberly's arm go up in the air. 'What on earth are you doing?' I asked her. She turned to me and held out her hand, 'Grandma, look!'"

Janet's voice dropped to an awed whisper. "It was a little white feather, Tina. Right out of thin air!"

My arms broke out in goose bumps and I smiled as I pictured my mother entering Heaven, pointing to the nearest angel's wings and saying, "Hey, I need to borrow one of those feathers!"

"Oh Janet," I said with a lump in my throat. "She made it! I never doubted that she would, but what a sweet miracle you've been given—we've all been given. Thank you, Lord."

Janet sniffled back, "Amen Tina, Amen."

~Tina Wagner Mattern

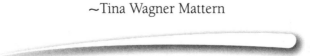

Find Your Rainbows

God puts rainbows in the clouds so that each of us—in the dreariest and most dreaded moments—can see a possibility of hope.
~Maya Angelou

always enjoyed the magic of seeing a rainbow. I was mesmerized by the vibrant colours and the allure of the promised pot of gold at the end of it. Truth be told, I never realized there was much more to rainbows than what meets the eye.

But rainbows can also be a sign. They have the ability to be a sign of hope as well as a gateway connecting us with our precious loved ones who have passed.

My difficult journey of loss started when my beautiful daughter Maddie was diagnosed with bone cancer when she was only twelve. She began the greatest battle of her life. With incredible courage she fought as hard as she possibly could, but after three years, her warrior body was ravaged beyond repair. Knowing she would soon die, Maddie's mission became to take care of us as we dealt with her impending death. She used her precious energy to ensure we would not suffer after she was gone. Her father, my husband, had lost his battle to ALS when she was only six. Although only a child then, she was like an old soul, sensitive to the grief and struggle Stephen's death had brought to our family.

At age fifteen, she courageously proclaimed her gratitude for the life that she had. She told us she was not afraid to die. Her final message to us was, "I love you but you must promise me you won't be sad when I'm gone. I will be okay." She truly became our hero. Soon after that brave conversation, Maddie passed away in my arms.

I didn't believe I had the strength to go on, but I had to for the sake of my eleven-year-old son. I searched in vain for answers. Why Maddie? She was so young and so kind. I was debilitated by grief and I needed some kind of continuing connection with my daughter. I begged her to send me a sign, to assure me she was okay.

The messages started to come right away, first to Vicki, Maddie's best friend. Vicki kept all her friends' phone numbers on little sticky heart notes on her bedroom wall. The day after Maddie passed away Vicki entered her room and found a sticky heart note that had fallen off the wall and was lying by the bed. She flipped it over and her heart skipped a beat when she saw Maddie's name and number on the note! She couldn't believe it. Maddie was saying goodbye to her. The next day she put the heart in Maddie's casket, her way of letting Maddie know that she understood; they would stay connected.

Then one day my niece Teela sent me this e-mail: "After Maddie left us I had a dream. I saw her in a rocking chair. I asked her what she was doing here; she was supposed to be dead. She told me it was a mistake! She hadn't gone anywhere and was still with us. I sat down and put my head in her lap and cried. She just repeated over and over that everything was going to be all right, that it was a mistake, she was still with us! She sent this message to help me stop being so sad."

Although I tried my best to be positive, I had a few emotional meltdowns where I would question myself and my decisions. What if I could I have done something different to save Maddie? On one particular occasion I came across an old homemade Mother's Day card from Maddie. It read, "Mommy, I can't think of anything you could have done better. You are the world's greatest mom!" It was as if she somehow knew these words would one day heal my wounds.

On the first anniversary of Maddie's death, our family and friends gathered around her grave to celebrate her life. We released 100 coloured balloons into the sky. Laughter and small talk filled the air till we heard a gasp, then more gasps. Someone pointed upward; we looked up and followed the balloons' path in the sky. We were stunned to see two beautiful rainbows above us. It was a cloudless sunny day, so where did those rainbows come from? We watched the balloons dance up and through the rainbow archway. It was as if heaven opened its gates to receive them. After all, the cemetery was called Gates of Heaven. I knew Maddie was sending me a sign and I could hear her voice whispering in the wind, "It's okay Mommy, I'm okay."

We have received many letters and stories from people about dreams and signs they've received over the years from Maddie. She is still held close in all their hearts. We lovingly named this phenomenon "The Magic of Maddie."

Recently, Maddie's beloved dog Winston, a neurotic roly-poly Pug, passed away. He was old, diabetic, and had been having seizures. He was in distress so my son Derek and I took him to the veterinarian's clinic and were with him when he took his last breath.

I couldn't bear going straight home without Winston so I asked Derek to take a walk with me. It was a hot summer's day so we headed to the beach. I kept telling Derek, "I need a sign." I needed some comfort.

Derek consoled me, "Mom, it's alright. Don't worry. Maddie will take care of Winston."

I was too upset to listen. "Derek, we need a sign, I wish Maddie would send us a sign, like she did last time!" I looked up in the sky, expecting to see a rainbow, but all I saw was the bright afternoon sun.

Derek was patient but hungry and went to a kiosk buy French fries for lunch. Then we sat on a blanket by the water. I lay back on the blanket and looked up at the sky. My heart raced at what I saw. I tapped my son frantically on the shoulder. "Do you see what I see?" I exclaimed in shock.

Derek's head followed my gaze, his French fry frozen in mid-air. "You mean that big rainbow above us?" he said. He saw it too. Thank God! I was not losing my mind! I stared at the rainbow for the longest time, wanting to memorize every detail. Without a doubt it was a sign from Maddie. She was saying, "Got him, Mom. Winston is okay too!"

I'll never look at a rainbow the same way again. They are powerful symbols that affirm our bonds cannot be broken, not even in death. The universe is always sending us signs. No matter how difficult life gets, these signs, like rainbows, are gifts that remind us we never lose our connections to the people we love. Keep your faith, open your heart and look up, way up. Find your rainbows!

~Sharon Babineau

The Last Dance

You can dance anywhere, even if only in your heart.
~Author Unknown

My parents married on June 27, 1942 in a beautiful stone church in upstate New York. The bride was seventeen, the groom twenty. After promising to love and to cherish until parted by death, they danced at the reception. They kept these promises and continued to dance for seventy years.

During their courtship and their entire married life they enjoyed big band music. They were beautiful dancers, commandeering a dance floor with style and grace. We kids grew to love the sound of Glenn Miller and Tommy Dorsey, conjuring up images of our parents gazing into each other's eyes as they glided across the floor.

I was the oldest, followed by my brother Terry and three sisters Judy, Gail, and Joni. We grew up in a house filled with love and a strong sense of family. The radio was always playing music and at the first strains of Glenn Miller's "In the Mood" or "Sentimental Journey" our parents rolled the living room rug back and we sat cross-legged on the sofa to watch the magic happen. The hardwood floors of the farmhouse became a grand ballroom as we watched them move as one. Each of us grew up loving music of all types and dancing of all styles.

Tragedy struck in 1976 when our brother Terry was killed in a horrible accident. He was thirty and left behind a young wife and three-year-old daughter.

Having suffered rheumatic fever and subsequent heart damage as a child, Mom was beginning to have cardiac problems. Three months after Terry's death, our mother had her first open heart surgery at age fifty. She recovered from surgery without a single complication in spite of grieving the loss of her only son.

She had heart surgeries again in 1992 and 2002, and Dad was her devoted caregiver. By her side day and night, he was her dance partner and referred to her as his Princess.

In spite of health issues, Mom and Dad's dancing days weren't over. Their love for big band music continued, but they could only hold each other and sway in time to the music. They both longed to twirl around the floor as in earlier years, but settled for the gentle swing and sway.

When my father, who had always been the hearty one, got sick, we steeled ourselves. The doctors at Duke Medical Center diagnosed aortic stenosis and at the age of ninety, Dad had open-heart surgery. For two days, Mom didn't leave his side. She looked drawn and pale. We knew Mom was tired, but we didn't know she was starting to have kidney failure.

On the third day of Dad's post-op recovery, eighty-seven-year-old Mom was hospitalized. Our hearts were heavy. It was the end of an era. Despite the seriousness of each of their conditions, the Lord was not done with them. Their love and devotion would show the rest of the family the meaning of the words "for better, for worse, in sickness and in health."

A week later, both parents, weak and tired, were discharged to my sister Judy's home. Timing was critical for the surprise we planned. I had arrived with Mom and gotten her settled in bed when Judy came through the door with Dad. With her assistance, he headed for the bedroom.

Judy steadied Dad as he paused, gazing at Mom in their bed. He bent over and kissed Mom on the cheek. "Is it really you, Princess?"

She reached up with her hand and cupped it around his head. "Yes, it's me. Are you really here?"

He answered by getting in bed with her. They nestled into each other's arms as Judy and I stood in the doorway crying. We didn't know how long we'd have either of them, but we knew we'd do our best to keep them together.

Six weeks later, Mom had a setback and died after a few days in the hospital. The family was devastated. It was as if we had the wind knocked out of us.

Living without her was a struggle for Dad. They had been married seventy years. A year after Mom's death, Dad fell ill and began his downward spiral. Two months later, as he lay dying, he turned to me and announced in a weak voice, "I'm going to be with your mother for our anniversary on June 27th. We are going on a cruise and we'll dance to big band music."

It was one of the last conversations we had. He passed peacefully the evening of June 26th, right on schedule for their anniversary the next day.

Mom and Dad were both cremated. They requested that their ashes be combined and spread on my brother's grave and then be committed to the waters in front of our summer vacation house. We honored their request, but added touches we thought they would both love.

For the entire four-day weekend we honored their memory. We gathered as sisters and our husbands along with Terry's widow, experiencing the closeness that our parents had instilled in us.

Having combined Mom and Dad's cremated remains, we returned them to a heart-shaped biodegradable box provided by the funeral home. We sealed it shut with superglue, as directed, preparing for a water burial.

On a beautiful sunny day in early September, we left the dock in two kayaks and a fishing boat, slowly moving into the deeper water of the Bay. Our youngest sister Joni paddled one of the kayaks, our brother-in-law Jeff accompanied her in the other. The rest of us were in the boat. Mark turned the stereo system on and big band music played. Strains of "Moonlight Serenade" followed by "Sentimental Journey" wafted across the water.

Gently resting the container on the gunwale of the boat, each sister placed a hand on the heart-shaped box for the last time. We said a prayer as we prepared to commit our parents' ashes to the body of water that they loved so dearly.

Joni, sitting low in her kayak, received the box and reverently placed it in the water. It began to sink in exactly four minutes, as the directions said it would. We watched until it sank out of sight. "Sentimental Journey" was into the chorus.

Suddenly, two identical whirlpools rose to the surface side by side and moved in perfect syncopation across the surface of the water toward the main house. All of us watched in stunned silence as tears streamed down our faces. We looked at each other and said, "Did you see that?"

Dad had told me they were going on a cruise and would be dancing to big band music. He was absolutely right. At that moment, each one of us knew it was a sign from our beloved parents, a joyous sign of a couple in love gliding across the surface of a new dance floor in their last dance.

~Nancy Emmick Panko

A Note from Heaven

Grandmas hold our tiny hands for just a little while, but our hearts forever.
~Author Unknown

can still remember the feel of her hand the last time I held it. She lay very still in my mother's bed, her kidneys failing. My thumb lovingly stroked her thin translucent skin. Her old wrinkled hands told a lifetime of stories: of cradling her children and grandchildren, preparing hearty warm Thanksgiving and Easter meals, skillfully handling dental tools, crocheting and tatting yarn into beautiful lace and flowers, and rubbing the sore back of a frail husband. I smiled as I saw the soft apricot nail polish on her long right thumbnail. Only yesterday I had knelt at her feet, oiling her dry legs and giving her a manicure. She was so proud of that long nail, holding it up and smiling, and with a wink, warning me not to file it down too much.

It was time to go back to Boston, to say goodbye forever. "I love you Gram, more than I can say. Mom will take good care of you," I whispered into her ear. I rested my head against her shoulder, gently embracing her with my arm across her chest. How do you let go? How do you pull away when you know it will be the last time? I memorized the pattern on the bedspread tucked around her, the sound of her breathing, the feel of her touch, the smell of her Estée Lauder perfume. I wanted to keep those memories with me for a lifetime.

Two weeks later, 1,000 miles away, I received the call. "Gram is in heaven," my mother said softly. Tears filled my eyes.

As the days unfolded, my mother asked me if I would sing at Gram's funeral. I was honored, agreeing to do anything I could to help make this easier for her. I set aside my own grief to prepare the hymns, the music that would comfort all of us.

After my flight back, I walked into the house and felt drawn to the room, the bed, and the place where I had last held her hand. The same pattern on the bedspread, the same quiet now filled only with the sound of my own breathing. I knelt on the floor and gripped her pillow and breathed in, searching for a little bit of the familiar Estée Lauder perfume. But there was none and I wept.

Seeing my despair, Mom quietly came over and slipped her hand in mine, leading me into another room where a shrine of sorts had been set up in my grandmother's memory. The green marble urn containing her ashes sat on a table surrounded by her red rosary, the faceted beads worn by years of prayerful touch. There were pictures of Jesus welcoming someone to heaven and lovely images of Gram in healthier days. I stood quietly taking it in.

The funeral went as well as could be expected. I made it through the emotional hymns, keeping myself together, and doing what had to be done while my mother cried her tears of loss and gratitude. After the service, I rode in the car with my dad and uncle to the store where we shipped my grandmother's ashes to Chicago to be buried next to my grandfather. My uncle and I added a single rose next to her urn before the box was taped shut.

As I flew home I watched the palm trees and beaches shrink below me as we soared over the sparkling ocean water. I felt closer to Gram, to heaven, as we slid through the white clouds.

Walking into my house, I set my luggage down and was greeted by gentle hugs from my family. As everyone dispersed, I headed downstairs to be alone.

Suddenly in the quiet of the basement, I felt overwhelmed. I fell to my knees near a closet under the stairs where I kept boxes of old photos and mementos waiting to be sorted someday. It's the kind of place where you could not put your finger on something even if you wanted to. There is no rhyme or reason, just cards, negatives and photos thrown in random boxes for "someday."

My grief bubbled to the surface at last and all the goodbyes poured out on the floor in my tears. "I miss you so much, Gram," I sobbed out loud, bringing my hands to my face. As the pain of missing her filled my heart, I called out to God, "I know she is happy being with you in heaven, and I wouldn't want to take that away from her, but I miss her so much…." I cried as I had never cried before.

Suddenly, an unexpected wave of complete, warm peace moved through my body from head to toe like a wave. I sat up on my knees and caught my breath. My shoulders relaxed as I brushed the tears and damp hair from my cheeks. I heard a whisper: "Reach into the closet."

Still on my knees, I reached for the handle, twisting it slowly. I slid it open just wide enough to slip my hand and arm into the dark. Reaching into a box I could not see, I grasped the first thing I felt, a piece of thin paper. I slowly withdrew my hand. I was holding a fragile yellowed piece of paper I had never seen before. The edges were torn but the words were intact: "Cathy. I love you! Gram." Somehow, my dear grandmother had reached out across the universe to send a message to comfort a hurting soul.

~Cathy Stenquist

A Spirit of Hope

All that is in heaven… is also on earth.

~Plotinus

When my husband, Steve, and I lived in Dallas, Texas, we spent a lot of time visiting and caring for my mother, Ethel M. Marsden. Ethel lived in a nearby nursing home, and after years of declining health, she eventually passed. We laid her to rest in her longtime home of St. Louis, Missouri.

A few months later, as a thank you gift for his support and assistance during that difficult period, I bought Steve a beautiful painting of a dragonfly. Dragonflies were not particularly significant to either Steve or me. But the painting was created by our favorite artist, and he had used our favorite colors—purple and blue—so we both loved it.

Immediately after purchasing that painting, we discovered that in many circles the dragonfly is considered to be a symbol of transformation. Certain Native American tribes, in fact, believe dragonflies carry the souls of the departed. We had no idea how significant that information would become!

You see, both Steve and I were present at the time of my mother's transition, and I was having a very hard time letting go of that final, painful image of my mother's lifeless form. One day, I felt divinely guided to visit the gravesite of another loved one buried right there in Dallas… far from my mother's final resting place in St. Louis. As I stood by the grave, a fluttering motion caught my eye. It was a couple of dragonflies hovering over a headstone a number of rows away. A few minutes later, those two dragonflies had been joined by ten more. And later still, dozens had gathered at this single spot in the cemetery.

I was just about to leave the cemetery—and was, in fact, in my car—when I noticed in my rearview mirror that even more dragonflies had now converged at this one place on the grounds. That's when I distinctly "heard" a still, small voice urging me to go over there. Strongly sensing that something very important was happening, I backed up my car, got out, and walked over to the headstone where the dragonflies had assembled. And guess what name was etched in the granite? Ethel M. Out of hundreds and hundreds of graves in this huge, metropolitan cemetery, I had been drawn by a group of dragonflies to the one headstone that bore my mother's name.

As the dragonflies swirled all around me, I immediately understood the message. My mother was no longer sick and withered. She was—as the dragonflies symbolized—transformed! As Spirit, Ethel was now dazzlingly beautiful and flying free! And I was now free, too—free of that disturbing, lifeless image that had been haunting my thoughts for so long.

Were those dragonflies actually my mother letting me know that—as Spirit—she still existed, and that she was once again happy and whole? That's for you to decide. All I know for sure is this: That miraculous occurrence lifted an emotional burden that had been weighing me down for a long, long time. And I am grateful.

~Carol Marsden Taylor

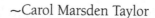

8

Paradise Cove Revisited

When someone you love becomes a memory, the memory becomes a treasure.
~Author Unknown

When John died, a part of me died with him. Though we knew each other for only eighteen months and lived on opposite coasts, we had fallen deeply in love and entered into a long-distance relationship. John Crawford was a retired actor in Los Angeles, best known for his role as Sheriff Ep Bridges in *The Waltons*, and I was a widow with two children in Maryland. I had written him a fan letter, which had unexpectedly led to a romantic relationship. I loved visiting him in California and being a part of his world. After he crossed over, I longed to be close to him again, so I went back to L.A. a year later and revisited many of the places where we had been together. But the glow was gone, and I found it all achingly empty. I soon realized that it was John who had given everything we shared its magic, and John was no longer there.

One special place I went back to was Paradise Cove in Malibu, where John had first introduced me to the Pacific Ocean. I ate dinner outdoors at the beachside restaurant, surrounded by the same magnificent panorama of sea and sky that I had shared with John, but instead of feeling comforted, I felt even more lonely. Memories only intensified the pain of losing him.

I finished my meal and wandered along the beach, looking for something, anything, that would signal John's presence. The weather had been an odd mix on that last day of September, but the sun had finally managed to break through the clouds and showers. As I gazed out over the ocean at a beautiful late afternoon sky, deep blue with gold- and rose-tinged clouds, a rainbow formed—no, two rainbows in two completely different places, but they weren't your typical rainbows. They were more like pieces of rainbows, carefully arranged. I took pictures of them, and they were so unusual that they were reported on the local TV news that night. Maybe it was wishful thinking, but I couldn't help but believe that those unique and lovely rainbows were somehow a sign from John.

A few more months passed and I still longed to be close to John, so I made an appointment to see a psychic for the first time. Irene Richardson knew nothing about me, much less John, and she didn't even know why I was coming to see her until I walked into her shop and sat down. After nervously telling her that I wanted to connect with someone who had passed, I was careful not to feed her any information other than what she asked for: name and date of birth for John and me.

She immediately connected with John's spirit and asked me if he had been a writer. I said yes, because John was indeed a writer as well as an actor, with a book and an award-winning screenplay to his credit. He was a wonderfully talented artist as well, and his oil and acrylic paintings were hauntingly beautiful. He had given me one that had been in storage, but I was always admiring the special ones that adorned the walls of his home. I often wished that he had left one of them to me, but I didn't tell Irene any of this.

A little later, Irene asked me if John had been famous. Hiding my amazement, I simply said yes and didn't elaborate. She saw him associated with classic Hollywood. Another bull's eye. She continued to tell me things that she couldn't have known beforehand about John and me. Then she asked if I had recently visited a beach that I had been to with John. I said that I had. Had I seen a rainbow directly in front of me, out over the ocean, in the shape of a cross? I almost stopped breathing for a moment. I hadn't thought about it that way before, but that was exactly what the rainbow over the ocean had looked like: a bright, colorful cross, brushed across a canvas of blue sky. Had I seen another rainbow at the same time, back and to my left? I had, just over my left shoulder, towards the cliffs. I got goose bumps as this woman I had just met accurately described the unusual rainbows I had seen on that September day in Malibu.

What Irene said next completely blew me away. "John is saying, 'I was there with you that day. Forget about the other paintings; those rainbows were my painting for you.'"

When I got home, I looked again at the photos I had taken of the rainbows, and they were just as Irene had described them. On God's canvas, John had painted a masterpiece for me.

We can sense a loved one's presence beyond the veil, but we don't often get the tangible evidence that we crave. I got mine that day in Paradise Cove, and I have treasured it ever since.

~Elizabeth S. Kline

Spiritual Connection

Other things may change us, but we start and end with the family.
~Anthony Brandt

was lucky to have a very close relationship with my parents. I was an only child, and we did everything together. On winter evenings we used to sit by the fire playing card games. Dad often read favorite books aloud while Mom and I knitted or sewed. We loved going to the theater and always had season tickets. After I got married, my career and family kept me very busy, and I sensed my parents felt somewhat abandoned, as if they had never thought about me growing up and leaving them. So we began buying theater tickets again, just for the three of us.

The years passed happily, but by the time Dad reached eighty-five he had become quite frail. He began having seizures and we started spending time in emergency rooms and doctor's offices. Then he fell in their bathroom, hit his head on the sink, and was never the same again. Mom and I spent every day with him in the hospital, but as the days turned to weeks, we began to visit separately.

One dreadful day, I got a phone call from the hospital. "Your mother slipped on ice and fell on the way to visit your father, and now she is in the Emergency Department." I raced to the hospital. Her hip was broken, but they had quickly put her on strong painkillers and surgery was booked for that night. The surgeon assured me she was in excellent health and would make a full recovery.

I went upstairs to Dad's room. His nurse had already told him about Mom's fall, and he was sitting up in bed, eyes wide with fear and confusion. "Do you blame me?" he asked, as tears spilled down his cheeks.

"No, of course I don't!" I assured him with a hug.

"I heard the weather was bad, but I insisted she come anyway. It's all my fault!" he cried.

"She's not in any pain, and it could have happened any day, Dad. And Mom wouldn't have missed a day with you anyway, you know that." Then I told him all the reassuring details from the surgeon, and how confident he was about everything. "And soon I will be able to bring Mom to see you, so we can still all be together!" The relief on his tired old face was heartbreaking.

Mom's surgery was completely successful and she was transferred to rehab for six weeks of therapy to ensure a full recovery. Thankfully it was in the building next door, so I was able to take her to see Dad every day. I trundled her wheelchair through basement corridors and up elevators, and their faces lit up the moment they saw each other. I kept a lot of hankies on hand!

In a strange way, those six weeks became very pleasant. The three of us laughed and chatted, Dad read the newspaper aloud and we played our card games like old times. But as Mom grew strong and healthy again, Dad slipped farther away. He became forgetful, confused and belligerent, and the staff struggled to cope with his refusal to accept his medications. He even began to forget who Mom and I were.

The doctors, who had tried so hard to keep Dad well, eventually took Mom and me aside and told us that there was nothing more they could do for him. They planned to transfer him to a separate palliative care facility, where he would receive the proper care until the end. It was the most dreadful thing to hear, but we had known for a while that his time was near. Mom was just one week away from her release date from rehab, so it wouldn't be long before we could resume our daily visits. And since he slept most of the time by then, we hoped he wouldn't miss us too much. I saw him whenever I could, and I telephoned his nurses twice a day. They always assured me that he was comfortable and peaceful.

The day before Mom was scheduled to go back home, I cleaned and prepared her house as instructed by her doctor. I had to remove all scatter rugs and anything she might trip over, install a raised toilet seat and various other safety items, as well as clear out the fridge and restock it with easy meals.

All the time I worked, I felt uneasy. I felt as if I was struggling, frantic, fighting for something, searching for something. I kept getting short of breath and felt the need to stop working and gasp for air. Then finally everything was done and ready for Mom. I glanced at the old hall clock, hoping I would beat the traffic going home. It was just coming up to 3:00 p.m. I wanted to call Dad's nurse, but I was anxious to get home.

Suddenly—I breathed. Deeply. I felt as if I hadn't taken a good deep breath in hours. As the old clock chimed three times, I sighed and slumped, exhausted.

When I got home, there were three phone messages from Dad's nurse. I called immediately.

"Are you sitting down?" she asked.

I was.

"I am very sorry to tell you that your father passed away."

I had been expecting and dreading that call for a while, but it was still a shock.

She went on to say, "Alan had been restless all day, getting more and more anxious and agitated, struggling and short of breath. Then suddenly he gasped, breathed in deeply, and then he was gone. I was bathing the man in the other bed, so I was right there when it happened."

"Can you tell me what time that was?" I asked.

"Yes, it was exactly 3:00 p.m.," the nurse answered. "I checked my watch."

Then I made the worst phone call of my life, to my mother. I gently told her what had happened, without mentioning anything about my experience at their house.

Her first question was the same as mine: "What time was it?"

"Exactly three o'clock this afternoon."

She didn't say anything for a moment. Then she began hesitantly, "I hope you won't think I am crazy, but I had just returned to my room from physiotherapy, so I knew it was three o'clock. I felt so restless and anxious. I opened the window, as I felt I couldn't breathe. Suddenly a gust of wind blew in my face, and I immediately thought of Alan. I gasped a deep, deep breath. It felt as if your father was right there with me."

Was Dad trying to contact both of us at that last moment of his life? Did we all share his last breath, even though we were far apart from each other? Can souls reach out to the people they love? We will never know for sure, but I do believe that somehow, spiritually, we were all together at that last moment of my father's life.

~Julia Lucas

Mom's Garden of Three

The soil is the great connector of our lives,
the source and destination of all.
~Wendell Berry

When my mother passed away, many of my closest friends gave me spring blooming bulbs as gifts because they knew that my mom and I had shared a love of gardening. Mom could happily spend hours working in her garden and she'd passed on to me her delight in welcoming old flower friends each spring, and also planting new ones. We both adored that sense of renewal and liked nothing more than to put on our gardening clothes and get our hands into the dirt.

My mom had died rather unexpectedly in the cold, grey month of February. My heart felt broken—like it too had a heavy cover of snow, and I just couldn't imagine how or when it would thaw. It was too cold to plant the lovely basket of bulbs from her friends, so I set them aside in my cold storage, thinking to myself that I would plant them in the fall and dedicate one of my beds as a special "memory garden" to honor my mom.

My mother was an amazing person—she was one of three triplet girls born to Scottish immigrants in 1927 in Brantford, Ontario. And let me tell you, those three girls were a handful! They were all extremely creative, social and more than a little mischievous—they loved playing tricks and surprises on their friends and families.

During the spring following my mother's death I spent many hours working in my garden. It was one of the things that lifted my spirits. I was trying to decide where I should create her memorial garden. I am lucky to have a large beautiful yard with many lovely spots and I just couldn't decide. Should it be back by the fence where I could see it from the kitchen window? Or should I put it close to the house so I could feel her near me? There were so many places I could choose from and I just couldn't make up my mind. I decided to wait for inspiration to hit.

One day I noticed a mysterious plant that had somehow "appeared" in an empty garden bed right under my bedroom window. It looked oddly familiar. I knew it wasn't a weed, but I also knew I had not planted it. I was completely puzzled so I decided to just let it grow and see what developed. Day by day the little plant flourished. One Saturday afternoon as I was working in my yard, I realized that it had done something unusual—it had separated into three different stalks of the same plant. I knew I had seen it before, but couldn't remember where. I ran inside to look in a gardening book and saw that it was a plant called "four o'clocks." And then I knew why it had seemed so familiar. It was one my mom had planted many times—we had always had them in the garden at our family cottage at the lake, and also in the flowerbeds of our family home in London, Ontario when we were growing up. But I hadn't seen one in years and had certainly never purchased one. So how could it be growing right here—when I knew I hadn't planted it?

I felt a shiver run up my spine—and then I got it. I smiled as I said out loud, "Okay Mom, I get the trick. You helped me decide, didn't you?" I truly believe that my mother sent me this little "tri-plant" as a sign to tell me, "I'm still here. This can be my garden and I will always be just a glance away if you need me." She chose a four o'clock because it had a history with our family so I knew it could only have been sent from her. And she had made it separate into three, like those mischievous and marvelous triplets—so I couldn't possibly miss the symbol—or the surprise! My decision had been made. I knew where to plant her garden and where to add the bulbs from her friends.

And the messages didn't stop there. That first Christmas, my mom's absolutely favorite time of year, we had the whole family over to our house for dinner. I had inherited two of her African violets when she passed away. I had never had luck with violets before, but I repotted them, put them on my table and hoped that they'd survive. On Christmas Day, while we were opening presents, I suddenly heard my husband say, "Beckie! Take a look. There are flowers on your mom's plants!" I glanced over and both African violets were blooming. And guess what? Three little blooms on each!

Over the years there have been other signs too numerous to mention, the last one being a few summers ago. I had taken a much-needed, short holiday at a friend's cottage and we were creating a garden for her. The island where the cottage sits is mostly rock so we had to bring in dirt and plants and create gardens out of the stone at the water's edge. At one point, as we were hauling large rocks out of the water and were up to our elbows in dirt, my friend said, "That's weird—there are daisies here—how can that be? We never had flowers here!" I looked over and sure enough, there were three little daisies—my mom's all-time favorite flower. I knew again in that moment she was watching over me. I'd hardly ever had the time to take a holiday just to rest and relax because of my job and she'd always been telling me to slow down and take time to smell the flowers. She would have been so happy to see I was doing this for me.

But my first sign is still the best—her little memory garden under my bedroom window. How fitting that she wanted it there—where I can see it every day all spring, summer and fall, and think of how much she loved me, and how much I'll always love her.

Thanks, Mom.

~Beckie Pruder

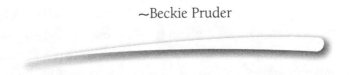

Fleur-de-lis

Old as she was, she still missed her daddy sometimes.
~Gloria Naylor

After some success as a writer over the last five years, I had been chosen as a contributing author to *Chicken Soup for the Soul: Miraculous Messages from Heaven*. It was a wonderful day when the first copies of the book finally arrived. I took my time, carefully opening the package and removing the top book. The house was quiet and the afternoon was slipping into evening. I went into the bedroom, removed my shoes, and settled into the massive pillows on the bed to view my story.

Opening the book for the first time, I found the table of contents, and ran my fingers down the page searching for my name, my story. I didn't get far. Finding a story called "Hi, from Dad," I stopped, my finger holding its position. The title caught my breath; it captured my attention. Almost without thought I opened the book to its page and read the story. Simply enough, it was an eloquent story of a young woman who had lost her father and received a message from him in a miraculous way.

Memories of my dad flashed in my mind. Closing the book, I found myself reliving the difficult days of his illness and the grief of his passing. Here it was three years later, and I still found myself doubting some of those tough decisions, hoping that in the end he knew I provided the best care I could under the circumstances.

Similar to the author of the story I had just read, I wanted to know whether my dad was all right and if love extended past this physical life into the next. But my fear and my doubts until now had stopped me from looking for any continuing connection. I had been afraid to ask and have silence as my only answer.

Reading this story encouraged me. Perhaps it was time to request a sign from my dad. Just a small sign, I told myself. Something clear that I would understand. Looking around the bedroom, my eyes settled on a brown metal box with a large fleur-de-lis on it.

Perfect. My dad was from New Orleans and the fleur-de-lis, the lily-shaped flower, was a decorative symbol found throughout the city. "Okay, Dad," I said in the quiet of the room. "Please send me the sign." Closing my eyes, I sent my request to the heavens.

Over the course of the next few days I followed suggestions provided by the Chicken Soup for the Soul publicists and arranged a book reading at Changing Hands Bookstore in Tempe, Arizona. They welcomed the chance to feature local authors and even encouraged me to see if another author featured in the book might want to join. Making arrangements with my contact at Chicken Soup for the Soul, I soon connected with one.

She was a young woman, excited to join me.

"What's the name of your story?" I asked as we exchanged information over the phone.

"'Hi, from Dad,'" she told me.

"What story?" I questioned. Softly she repeated it.

How could that be? Of all the authors in the book, I spoke with the one who had inspired my quest. What a strange coincidence.

The following morning I turned on a local TV news station to catch the weather, but they were in the middle of a sports report. The New Orleans Saints' helmet flashed on the screen, prominently displaying the fleur-de-lis symbol.

Leaning forward, I immediately thought of my request for a sign from my dad. There it was on the screen in front of me!

"Coincidence!" I proclaimed to the empty room. Simply that. Dismissing it as invalid, I turned it off. After all, signs don't come through your television. But my small inner voice wondered. What did I know of signs? Until now I had been too reluctant to ask for one. And despite the appearance of exactly the requested sign, I just couldn't believe that was it. Refusing to give it any more consideration, I pressed on to other issues and put any thoughts of the fleur-de-lis aside.

Determined to make the book reading a success, I designed a colorful invitation and made arrangements with friends and colleagues to help me pass out the cards. One of my last places to drop off the invites was the small salon where I'd had my hair cut over the last few years. The owner had been kind enough to offer to display some of the invitation cards in the shop. She immediately stopped working to look over the cards and announce my event to the women in the salon.

I quickly added that a second local author, Laura Johnston, was going to join me. "Laura Johnston?" said a questioning voice from the corner waiting area. I turned to respond to her question, but no words came out. I stood frozen in disbelief, looking in the woman's direction, not making a sound. On the wall around her hung magazine racks displaying the latest hairstyles and issues of *People*. But it wasn't the magazines that caught my attention; it was the design on the racks themselves. They were decorated with an assortment of fleurs-de-lis.

My sign! I gasped. Not one fleur-de-lis, but a collection of them! Rushing forward I placed my hand on the rack, my palm resting on a fleur-de-lis, trying to collect myself. In his quest to make sure I truly got his sign, my father had also added a bit of irony. The fleurs-de-lis were on magazine racks. My dad, during his younger years, had lived in New Orleans on Magazine Street, a house we had driven by so many times with him during our visits.

"Okay Dad, I get it," I said to myself, my eyes tearing, my emotions confused, unsure. Then I understood; one clear emotion had found its place inside me. Gratitude. It overwhelmed me. Looking upwards I sent words of gratitude for the sign and gratitude for our life together. Above all, gratitude to my dad, that through it all, his love remains.

~Diana Creel Elarde

Brotherly Love Bridges the Gap

The great men of earth are the shadow of men, who, having lived and died,
now live again and forever through their undying thoughts.
~Henry Ward Beecher

After my father died, my brother George persuaded me to leave South Carolina and attend college in Virginia so he could keep an eye on me. He said, "You know, the eyes are the windows of the soul." Right—because when I goofed up, he saw through my eyes and through my lies, all the way to my soul. Oh, the sermons he delivered during my liberal-thinking, beer-drinking, buck-naked streaking Sweet Briar College days.

And yet, George was my "Google" before the Internet, my confidant before I had wise friends, and my best cheerleader, whatever the endeavor. Being fifteen years my senior, he showed me the meaning of perseverance, resourcefulness, integrity, temperance, humility, hope, humor and happiness. As the twig is bent, the tree's inclined, so I learned to enjoy life to the best of my ability from his book: The Joy of George.

I loved my big brother the moment I was born, and I love him now and every minute in between. He gave a meaning to my life that I had no right to expect, that no one can ever diminish. I never knew a world without him in it, and I never wanted to. So even in death, George found ways to connect with me.

I've been blessed to hold the hands of many people as they drew their last breaths, but my brother is the only one who continued to communicate after death. I don't pretend to understand how it happens—whether ESP, or God, or George's sheer will.

George collapsed while dressed to attend a funeral. My sister-in-law, Margie, performed CPR while waiting for the ambulance. He lived three unresponsive days on a respirator with no brain waves, according to the tests. I couldn't understand or accept the irony. How could my brother, a neurologist, be without brain activity?

My husband, Ed, and I traveled 500 miles and reached George's side on the third day of the nightmare. As Margie led me to his room, she told me to talk to him because he could hear me. The sight of my brother with tubes and wires attached sent such a wave of hopelessness through me that I couldn't speak. Not to George, or anyone.

How could this healthy, slender, seventy-three-year-old man be dying? His cardiologist said he didn't have a heart attack; his heart just stopped. I asked myself how a man's heart could be beating, beating, beating—and just stop? Then I remembered.

I'd asked George years ago if he jogged. "No, I don't," he said. "I believe a man has just so many heartbeats allowed him, and I'm not going to waste one of them on jogging!"

When the doctor said he could do nothing else, my heart broke. George had made the decision in a living will to discontinue ventilator use, so the family gathered to say goodbye. After the doctors removed the equipment, Margie, Ed and I went back in his room.

He looked better, more approachable, without the wires and monitors. There was no beeping. Margie laid her head on George's right shoulder and said her last words to him.

I inhaled deeply and leaned up to his left ear. "George, I need you to know how much you've meant to me. You've been there at every fork in the road, helping me make good decisions. Everything a brother should be, you have been. Your example has made me want to be a better person. All that I am, and ever hope to be, I owe to you. I will miss you and everything about you, and I'll love you till the day I die."

With her head down, Margie didn't see George open his right eye. Thinking it was part of the dying process, I reached over to close it. But he opened it again. When he opened his left eye, a huge tear rolled out onto the pillow beside me. He took one last breath, then resolutely closed both eyes. I gasped and covered my mouth to stifle a cry. Awed, I looked at Ed who whispered, "He heard you."

George's action appeared volitional — one last attempt to convey love, one final farewell among the living — and it turned out to be a promise of things to come as well.

• • •

Making our way home through the Shenandoah Valley the day after George's funeral, Ed and I saw a deer standing off the highway — right in the sunshine. Bucks don't tend to come out in broad daylight, but since George had been a wildlife commissioner and one of our last outings was a hunt, it struck me that this deer could be a sign from him.

After returning to South Carolina, we plugged in the Christmas tree lights. Later those lights went off for no reason, but the electricity never blinked in the rest of the house. It surprised us when the Christmas lights came back on by themselves an hour later.

That evening another enigma astonished us. My daughter brought a piece of paper downstairs that had just come through my office printer: my brother's eulogy — which I'd written in Virginia. The document didn't exist on the computer upstairs, but on a flash drive in my pocket. I hadn't been upstairs since coming home. We still have no explanation.

More events shocked my rational mind that week. George might truly have been communicating with me. So I addressed him in a loud voice, begging him to come to me in a dream if he was responsible for these happenings. I demanded it be that very night, none other.

Never one to be late, George showed up right on cue! He and I were in a small room with our backs to each other. Turning around we both understood we weren't in the same realm — his spiritual, mine physical. Yet reaching out, we touched. Realizing I could feel his physical body, I wrapped around him like an octopus—as I did when I was five and he was twenty. Knowing it might be our final chance, we said things one rarely says in this life. After a while someone tapped my shoulder. I heard, "Time's up." I cradled George's face in my palms and gazed into the sky blue windows of his soul one last, long time.

Despite my lifelong skepticism of the supernatural, every intuitive bone in my body tells me that George, our Renaissance Man, has discovered yet another field of proficiency—a miracle in my estimation—love strong enough to bridge the gap from The Great Beyond.

~Janet Sheppard Kelleher

Send Me a Penny

Death ends a life, not a relationship.
~Jack Lemmon

"A penny for your thoughts." That's what I used to say. Before. That old, lovely saying has now grown even richer and more personal for me and my family. It has become, for all of us, "A penny to let you know that I am thinking of you."

It was August 2001. That day was an early morning workday like any other. I got up, poured a cup of coffee and a bowl of cereal and sat at the counter to read the newspaper. When I got to the "Dear Abby" column, there was an article about pennies from heaven. Without thinking much about it I said under my breath, "Send me a penny, Daddy."

My father was the apple of my eye. He was crotchety and opinionated and my two sisters and I loved him like crazy. He had been a widower for twenty years, and so our lives, our friends, became his. He was my best garage sale buddy. He had lived at one time with both of my sisters, in California and North Carolina, respectively. He now had a senior living apartment near my home in Oregon. Dad had injured his lungs severely ten years earlier torching what he didn't know was lead paint off the exterior of my cousin's house. He was now seventy-six years old and had adapted well to his limitations and continued to do most things he loved, if at a slower pace.

That was why his telephone call to me at work the Friday of

Memorial Day weekend was so frightening. When I answered the phone he said weakly, "Mo, I don't feel well. Something is wrong." I don't think I had the phone in the cradle before I was running out the door. Dad had been on a trip to visit both of my sisters in the last month and to see a new great-grandson. He had fun but came back exhausted and nursing what he thought was a bad cold. I worried it had turned to pneumonia, as his weakened lungs were susceptible.

I called ahead to let the emergency room know we were on our way, and within ten minutes we were pulling up and being met by a nurse with a wheelchair. I was stunned, after my father's initial workup, to be told that he was having a heart attack. Later that day he had a stent placed and he was admitted to a regular room for observation. He was discharged to my care two days later on Sunday. He complained he still did not feel well, but his doctor assured us that this was to be expected after a heart attack. Once I got him home, he said to me, "I am so glad I have you girls to look after me." The next morning, I walked into his room to discover that he had a second heart attack earlier that morning. Although I tried to revive him with CPR, it was too late.

That was the worst day of my life. I had so much guilt and remorse. I was paralyzed with pain. So, when I flippantly mentioned three months later on that August morning that I wished he would send me a penny, it was because I longed to connect with him again. I felt like I had let him, and my entire family, down by not protecting him. I was struggling mightily with the loss and not moving forward very well at all. So even though I asked for a penny, honestly I did not expect a response!

I finished breakfast and went upstairs. I went into the walk-in closet and took out my clothes for work. I walked a few steps back into the bathroom to get ready for a shower, talking to my husband about mundane stuff. I turned around to grab something else from the closet, and there, centered right in the middle of the carpeted floor was a penny. I gasped so loudly I scared my husband. I started to cry and knelt down and clutched the penny to my chest. I had just been in the closet seconds earlier and the penny was not there. I would have seen it. It was not near any coats or purses from which it might have fallen. It was, indeed, a penny from heaven. I sobbed and sobbed and through the tears I knew I had been visited by a miracle.

I had that penny made into a necklace I cherish. The most wonderful thing now is that every time anyone in my family finds pennies in odd places, we say, "Hi Daddy," or "Hi Grandpa." We find them all the time now. My niece was showering one day, heard a plunk in the shower and looked down to see a penny in the tub! I was using my iPad one day, set it down and came back later and a penny was sitting on top of it. These occurrences happen so often that we all see it as the norm in the most personal, spectacular, inclusive way.

I never try to convince others of how these pennies make there way from heaven to my family and me. I have no idea myself. All I know for certain is that it happens at those times when our hearts crave the connection the most, and we know it is not a coincidence. The most delightful part is that we aren't consciously expecting them, we are living our lives and they just seem to appear when our need is the greatest.

My father's passing left huge holes in our hearts. Every time a penny arrives, we remember him and the love of family he left behind. That is a legacy, a miracle, that my family knows we are blessed to have, and we cherish it every time we are visited by his spirit of love.

~Maureen Buckley

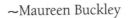

Chapter

2

Hope
&
Miracles

Miraculous Healing

Never Walk Again?

When the world says, "Give up," Hope whispers, "Try it one more time."
~Author Unknown

As I lay in my hospital bed after surgery, I tried to comprehend the doctor's verdict. "You will never walk again." Never walk again? It sounded like a death sentence. Even though I was already eighty-nine years old, I was not ready to stop living a full life. I turned on my side and cried out to God for mercy. "Please, Lord, I need a miracle."

Two weeks earlier I had gone to my great-nephew's wedding in California. While leaving the hotel pool area one day, I tried to push open a door to the hallway, not realizing that it was locked. That's when I suddenly fell backwards onto the cement floor. Pain seared through my body. My niece and nephew rushed to my side. "Are you okay?" they asked. I was too stunned to answer just then, but I was hoping that I had not been seriously injured. Quickly, they helped me up and took me back to my hotel room. Since I could still move around, I wasn't too concerned and believed I would be fine for the wedding in two days.

Even though I had to sleep in a chair, I managed with some help to make it to the rehearsal dinner the next day. The following day, I was still able to attend the wedding. Yet after the reception I couldn't get up from the chair. I knew something was seriously wrong and I needed to get back home to see my own doctor.

My daughter took me back to my hometown and rushed me to

the local hospital. My pain was so severe by that time that the medical staff couldn't get me into the correct position to take an X-ray. After keeping me in the hospital overnight for observation, the doctor, unable to determine a cause, sent me home. However, the next few days I was in so much pain I had a hard time getting out of bed.

"Lord, what's happening to me?" I cried out again and again. "Please, heal my body."

When the pain continued to worsen, my daughter had an ambulance take me back to the hospital where an X-ray revealed that I had fractured three vertebrae. Right away I was transferred to a larger hospital where a specialist advised immediate back surgery. "It's a delicate surgery and at her age she may not survive," the doctor had told my family. Yet I had survived, although the surgery had not improved my condition. That's when the doctor had told me that I would never walk again. "Am I to live the rest of my life in a wheelchair as an invalid?" I now agonized. Somehow I couldn't accept that verdict. There had to be a way that I could walk again, even at my age.

I believed that God was a God of miracles and I knew God could heal my body. But I realized that I also had to do my part, so right then I determined to at least work at trying to walk again. Rehabilitation exercises taught me to stand. I worked hard at holding onto bars, hoping my feet would move just a little on their own. But they didn't. At first I was somewhat discouraged. Should I just give up and accept the medical prognosis? Then, these words from the Bible suddenly popped into my mind and filled my heart with renewed faith and hope: "Everything is possible for one who believes" (Mark 9:23, NIV).

"I'll walk again. I'll show everyone," I told my visitors. They smiled but they didn't seem to believe me. They prayed for me, mostly that I would accept life in a wheelchair. But I kept praying that the Lord would give me the strength to keep trying to walk again.

How I longed to go outdoors, to walk along the streets, to do all those things I had been able to do before the accident. What would my future be like not being able to walk? My imagination ran wild, but I didn't want to dwell on it. I had to be positive about my future.

I had had my share of challenges, but none as formidable as this and I was not one to give up easily.

Determination to walk again filled me with energy. I worked hard during my exercises each morning. As I willed my feet to move little by little, I finally was able to push my feet forward while standing in a walker. I was so encouraged that I tried even harder. My faith and courage soared as week by week I felt some improvement. Within a few months I could take one step at a time when holding onto my walker. Then two steps. Now I knew that if only I would work at it hard enough, I would achieve what the doctors thought was impossible. A year and four months after the accident, I was finally able to walk around the room holding onto a walker. How excited I was, knowing this was the first step toward a normal lifestyle.

Today, two years after the accident, I can walk well even outside on the street holding onto a walker. The broken vertebrae have healed. Now I am looking forward to the future with hope and a thankful heart. "A miracle," the staff told me. I agreed. I knew that with faith, determination, courage, and hard work anything is possible.

~Beulah Dobson

A Glimpse of Heaven

If we have died with Him we shall also live with Him; if we persevere we shall also reign with Him.
~2 Timothy 2:11-12

The assignment was to "draw heaven." I took out my prized box of perfectly sharpened crayons and searched for my favorite sky blue crayon. I carefully drew a large sky, dotted with puffy white clouds, separated in the center by a beautiful, arching rainbow. On each cloud, I drew tiny angels; some with harps and others singing and dancing.

At the top of the rainbow, I tried my best to draw God's face with deep brown, loving eyes and a long flowing, white beard. His loving arms were outstretched. I tried to position the rainbow so that it reached from God's face to connect with the earth He had created. His domain contained pastel-colored tulips, trees and people of all ages and backgrounds.

I was a child then, and I saw heaven as far away, connected to us by one of God's exquisite rainbows. Since then, I have often wondered about heaven, not as much about its appearance, but rather what kind of life I needed to live to be worthy. What would it be like to experience eternity and timelessness? What would it actually be like to come face to face with God?

The same year as that assignment, my life turned upside down. My dad, my hero, suffered a massive stroke. He was hospitalized for several weeks and then spent three months in a rehabilitation facility.

In what seemed like an instant, my dad's life dramatically altered. He went from being a highly successful lawyer and a vice president of a major corporation to being unable to utter even one word. His right side was completely and permanently paralyzed and he would need to work for years to regain some of the expressive language skills that had been his forte.

Despite the daily struggles he faced, my dad was the epitome of kindness, love, compassion and fairness. He treated everyone with respect and dignity. He never let the effects of his stroke affect his ability to give and love completely. He never complained of his immense struggles or how even simple tasks such as eating, writing or extending his hand for a handshake needed to be renegotiated using his left hand.

For seventeen years following his stroke, I held my breath as he labored up and down the stairs in our colonial home. I would watch as he clutched the mahogany banister with his strong left hand. Then he positioned his left leg on a step and with effort, pulled up his right leg until his legs were side by side. Step by step, in a slow, methodical rhythm, he would repeat this process until he reached the next floor. It was that way every day for seventeen years.

That was until June 30, 1981, two weeks after my dad had gall-bladder surgery and the surgeon explained that they had "almost lost him several times on the operating table." His heart and body were unable to withstand the time needed to complete the surgery so they brought him out of anesthesia without being able to close his bile duct. Day after day, my dad coughed up bile, grew weaker and was filled with pain. Despite all of his suffering, he approached life and everyone around him as he always had—with an amazing spirit and a genuine, loving, compassionate kindness for others.

On the morning of June 30, 1981, my dad couldn't move even a finger without excruciating pain. He never complained but I could see the effects in the creasing around his eyes and the slight groan he tried to conceal under his breath. After he tried several times to get up from bed, I tried to pull him up without hurting him. When he was finally able to sit upright, I looked into his eyes. Despite the significant struggle, he looked at me with gentleness and warmth, and he smiled.

After resting for several minutes, he leaned on me. Walking very slowly and in terrible pain, he made his way to the center staircase. Walking the twenty feet from the bedroom to the staircase took almost all of his energy.

He was supposed to go back to the hospital and my mom was getting everything ready downstairs. Dad had insisted that my sister go to work that day, but I still wish she had been with us to experience what happened. At the base of the staircase, my mom had a chair waiting for him just in case he needed to rest before heading to the hospital.

As my dad placed his left hand on the banister, as he had done countless times before, I noticed that the overcast day suddenly looked bright. There was a light like I've never seen before radiating from the window behind him, enveloping his face, body and the steps ahead of him.

I was reaching out to help him when I saw the pain in his face disappear. He was no longer holding onto the banister. As he began his descent, he virtually floated down the steps. His feet skimmed over the steps and he wasn't holding the railing. My mom and I watched in amazement.

His right leg and arm were no longer encumbered. He seemed free.

At the base of the steps, he fell into my mother's arms. My mother quickly asked me to call 911 as she attempted mouth-to-mouth resuscitation. Even with the paddles and considerable effort, the paramedics were unable to revive him. As they lifted Dad onto the gurney, one kind paramedic informed me that my father wasn't on this earth anymore. Maybe he knew what my mom and I knew already—my dad had gone to heaven.

So, now if I were asked to "draw heaven" I would try to describe it as a place where all physical limitations are lifted—a place where God's love and light heal and where people who have lived good lives are rewarded. Heaven is a place where there is only love—God's love.

If I am ever feeling discouraged or sad, I think back to the day when God gave me the gift of a glimpse of heaven. With my own eyes, I witnessed my dad gracefully floating from his place on earth to his well-earned place in heaven.

~Mary Ann Klein

The Healing Hand of God

The prayer that begins with trustfulness and passes on into waiting will always end in thankfulness, triumph, and praise.
~Alexander Maclaren

My husband and I had agreed to a weekend camping trip with our good friends, Doug and Kathy, fellow youth leaders from our church. Our three young children were just as excited about time at the beach as we adults. We had a great time swimming during the day and at night we decided to gather around a campfire.

We edged our lawn chairs closer to the fire pit as a chill settled over the day. While we were talking and roasting hot dogs and marshmallows on long sticks, I realized that our four-year-old daughter, Elizabeth, had wiggled her chair too close to the fire. I opened my mouth to instruct her to move back when the unthinkable happened. The chair tipped forward, dumping her onto the ground at the edge of the pit. She dropped onto a bed of smouldering coals.

All four adults reached for her. My husband and I grabbed her and ran to the nearby water tap. My first thought was to douse her smoking shorts. I hadn't considered the possibility of burns—until I saw her feet. Blisters swelled like balloons filled with water. Our daughter wailed out her pain. Adrenaline took over as we hustled to our vehicle. We covered Elizabeth's burns with a clean towel and, leaving our older children with Doug and Kathy, headed for the hospital in the nearby town.

"She has second- and third-degree burns on her feet and her hip." I wanted to cry for this innocent child who wept out pain she didn't understand. "You'll want to take her to your family doctor to keep an eye on them."

We headed home where Doug and Kathy waited with our other two girls. Elizabeth sat quietly in the car with me, her feet swaddled in white gauze, the burn medicine giving her temporary relief.

The next day we rented a small wheelchair. Our doctor informed us that Elizabeth would be off her feet for a few months and would likely undergo skin grafting. By Wednesday, an infection set in and Elizabeth's temperature soared. That evening, she hallucinated, experiencing an imaginary card game of Go Fish. We headed to the hospital again.

A child should never have to endure debriding. It is a painful process where the burnt skin is removed. Anaesthetic is useless since the nerves in the burned tissue are damaged. For the next week, our little girl underwent the removal of the decaying tissue while I held her and prayed for God to give us a miracle.

I was supposed to go to a women's retreat two weeks after our camping weekend. I called our group organizer and told her why I had to cancel. "Pray for Elizabeth. She's in so much pain. Pray for healing."

Unknown to us, that request went to the retreat leadership team. While the ladies from our church began their adventure in the Muskoka woods, I made daily trips to the doctor to have the bandages changed and new medication applied. Standing behind Elizabeth's chair, I waited patiently while new gauze and tape covered wicked wounds and I prayed. I prayed that God would heal our daughter and that he would use this moment in time to show his love.

Saturday morning came and I headed out into the countryside to our doctor's home. He'd been very concerned about the infection and insisted that the bandages be changed daily. Sunday morning showed no improvement in Elizabeth's feet. We went to church as a family, her little red wheelchair carrying her down the aisle. She played quietly until the service finished and we headed home. That evening, the phone rang and I made my way to the kitchen to answer it.

"The whole group prayed for Elizabeth." Our group organizer's voice hummed with excitement. "It was something. Over 200 women gathered together praying for a miracle. I can't wait to see what God will do."

Monday morning brought a warm September sun and the girls and I climbed into the van and headed to the doctor's house. He'd warned me the day before that he would not be in the office until Tuesday and to come to his house. We pulled up the long drive and parked. Lifting Elizabeth into her wheelchair, I instructed her sisters to remain in their seatbelts until I called them. I turned toward the porch and spied the doctor coming down the walkway.

"And how's my patient today?"

Elizabeth grinned and waited while he squatted before her and unwrapped her feet. I watched from my place behind the chair, the prayer for healing running through my mind. My heart lurched as his expression sobered. What was wrong? Were her feet worse? Had the infection spread?

"I don't understand." The words came out in a slight stutter.

I locked the chair brakes and moved to the front, leaning over the doctor's shoulder. There in his hand rested one of Elizabeth's feet, the skin beautiful and fresh and pink. Not a mark marred the skin that had been a pucker of scorched flesh the day before. I laughed—a single, shocked chuckle—and he glanced up at me, his eyes frightened.

"I guess that's what happens when 200 women ask God for healing." The words slipped from my mouth and I watched the fear turn to confusion.

"If that's what you want to believe."

I laughed again, this time in amazement. "Do you have a better explanation?"

The doctor shook his head and tried to pull on the mantle of professionalism. "I guess we don't need any more bandaging. Bring her in a week from now and I'll check it over again." I thanked him as he turned and headed for his house.

We sang songs as we drove home and then I spent the morning watching Elizabeth chase her sisters around the yard. Two weeks. She had suffered for two weeks and I pondered all that her suffering had accomplished. Because of it, our family's faith grew, a doctor saw the healing hand of God and 200 strangers learned the importance of prayer.

~Donna Fawcett

Walking the Talk

He performs wonders that cannot be fathomed,
miracles that cannot be counted.
~Job 9:10

will never forget the spring of 2003. Although I grew up in a very religious home, I became agnostic during my high school and college years. Eventually, as I entered the business world upon college graduation in 1989, through the guidance of an older, wiser, and more educated sister, I took some steps toward having not so much a religion about God but a relationship with God. Elizabeth was there for me when I needed her most, bringing joy out of sorrow during a difficult time in my life.

Although a few people I knew believed in miracles, I didn't. I had suffered from many unanswered prayers in seeking peace in the midst of many problems that caused me lots of pain along my path. Nevertheless, many years later, following more spiritual growth, I found myself serving as a former businessman turned Protestant minister in a role as an Associate Pastor for a very large church in Connecticut. I had already been married to a wonderful woman with whom I had been blessed to become a dad of two beautiful daughters, affectionately known as my "princesses."

One day in early spring of 2003, someone in the church brought to my attention another man who was also married to a beautiful wife with whom he had two wonderful girls. Described as a "man's man," William Cox was not only rough and tough, but also very hard working and capable in his role as a custodian. Unfortunately, he was very seriously injured while moving furniture. His prognosis was sobering. At best, he would spend the rest of his life in a wheelchair, most likely paralyzed from the waist down, never to walk again. At worst, he would die.

William's wife, Joann, invited me to join her and some other believers in praying for William at the ICU of Danbury Hospital on October 28, 2002. Little did I know that it was her birthday. This dear woman of faith recently revealed to me that she felt God had given her a list of those he wanted there that night.

In line with guidance found in the New Testament book of James, we anointed him with oil and prayed in the name of Jesus, the ultimate Wounded Healer, who stated that "with God all things are possible." When I laid my hand on William's head, I felt compelled to ask for what seemed to be the impossible. I was certain that as crazy as it may have seemed, given this man's current medical condition, I was to swallow all pride when it came to managing the perception of others and simply ask God to completely heal William. At that very moment, I felt a strange heat sensation I had never previously experienced running through my hand, which I had placed on William's head.

My foremost concern in that moment was learning William's wife and daughters had accepted Christ but he had not. Yet, like me, they wanted him with them—not only temporally on earth, but eternally in heaven.

While laying my hand on William's head, before I could even think, the following words came out of my mouth: "Lord Jesus, you've created the universe and blessed it with William who lies here not yet knowing you and your love for him. Please do not let him leave this earth without making a conscious decision as you have requested of all to accept you as his Savior and follow you as his Leader. Your Word tells us that with God all things are possible. Though these good earthly physicians have done all they can, we know that you, the great Heavenly Physician, can do what they can't. We beg you to go beyond medicine in fully healing William not only physically but also spiritually so that he can one day enjoy you eternally. We ask this in Your Name. Amen."

Several weeks later, on Tuesday, May 13th of 2003, at 3:00 p.m., William WALKED into my office! He looked at me and smiled. I was simultaneously astonished, excited, and amazed! Goose bumps, which I have since called "God bumps," ran up and down my arms while the hair on my arms and the back of my neck stood up. His only question for me, even though he had never previously spoken to me, was this: "What do I need to do to know God? I'm ready." As you can imagine, I ran with that! William understood that God gave him a second chance at life—and he took it! A man who at times had been bitter and resentful soon miraculously became better and peaceful. The peace that replaced his anxiety inwardly continues to shine through his life outwardly.

My wife, children and I eventually moved on to plant a church in Newtown, Connecticut, where we thankfully have witnessed God turn many trials into triumphs since the shooting tragedy of December 14, 2012. Although many years have passed since I've last seen William, not a day has passed when I don't believe in miracles, as he is a walking one.

~Jim Solomon

The Falling Air Compressor

Heal me, O LORD, and I shall be healed; Save me, and I will be saved,
for You are my praise.
~Jeremiah 17:14

As my husband Dave and his friends were positioning the eight-hundred-pound air compressor, it suddenly began to fall. Dave's friends stepped back but Dave, standing directly in front of it, reached out to steady it. The result? The air compressor went back into its proper position, and all seemed well for a few seconds until my husband doubled over in pain.

Dave wasn't one to complain about sickness or pain. He struggled into the house with the help of his friends and lay on the floor. He refused to see the doctor and, over the next several hours, muscle spasms began to run the full length of his spine.

Dave still refused to discuss the pain, but his facial expressions and the occasional tear that ran down his cheeks revealed the truth. By this time, he was unable to get off the floor. He finally agreed to go to the chiropractor, thinking that a spinal adjustment would ease the problem.

After my son and I managed to get him into the passenger seat of the car, I cautiously drove him the fifteen miles to the chiropractor, who had helped him through previous injuries. After an evaluation of Dave's condition, the doctor felt he could not help and suggested we go to our family doctor. That involved another agonizing trip in the car.

After several X-rays and other diagnostic procedures, we had the final verdict. Our family doctor had seen injuries like this before and knew that nothing but surgery would help. He asked if Dave wanted him to make an emergency appointment with a spinal surgeon so he could have the surgery as quickly as possible.

My husband had never had any type of surgical procedure—even a minor one—and he completely rejected the idea of someone cutting into his back. I wondered what in the world we would do at this point. He was still bent over in anguish, and he walked with a noticeable limp, which I assumed was from his continued "bent" position.

The week before all this occurred, we had contacted a local pastor to whom we knew God had given the gift of healing. Since our son had neurological difficulties that medications and doctors could not seem to adequately control, we had made an appointment with this pastor on behalf of our son. In spite of Dave's condition, which had only grown worse during the preceding two or three days, my husband insisted we keep the appointment with the pastor. Again, we managed to get my husband into the passenger seat while I drove.

We had been seated in the pastor's office for several minutes, explaining our son's situation while saying nothing of my husband's injury. Dave had a steel will and he was able to conceal most of his pain at this point. Since we did not personally know this pastor, we thought he assumed my husband's bent-over position was permanent for some reason.

As the pastor began praying for our son, he suddenly stopped, turned from our son, and looked at Dave. He paused for a moment and then quietly said, "I am being led not to pray for your son, but for you, Dave. The Lord has told me you have had a serious back injury. What happened?"

We looked at each other in astonishment, for we knew this pastor had no previous knowledge of my husband's situation. After we briefly explained the air compressor accident, the pastor said, "Stretch both of your legs out in front of you." I could see from Dave's expression that even this amount of movement caused great pain, but he did as asked. In astonishment, I looked twice at what I had difficulty believing the first time.

One of my husband's legs was a full two inches shorter than the other. Since this had not been the case before the air compressor accident, I knew that the terrible muscle spasms had drawn up his leg. That was the reason for his limp.

The pastor took hold of Dave's feet and began praying in the Lord's name that he receive a full healing. He prayed for the shortened leg to be restored to its normal length, that no lingering effects remain, and that God be given all the praise for the healing.

As the pastor continued praying, thanking God for the healing he knew was coming, a divine presence seemed to fill the room that made all of us look toward Dave's outstretched legs. We watched in amazement as the shortened leg slowly began lengthening, eventually matching the length of the unaffected leg. I had previously heard of healings such as this but had never witnessed one myself. Yet as I watched Dave's leg slowly "grow" to its proper length, I knew I was witnessing a miracle. As I looked toward my son, I saw that his eyes were as big as saucers, too.

During the next few days, the slight soreness that remained after the pastor's prayer completely vanished, and Dave's body was restored to its previous healthy condition. Never again did that injury cause my husband any problems!

~Carol Goodman Heizer

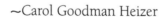

A Life Well Loved

Miracles, in the sense of phenomena we cannot explain, surround us on every hand: life itself is the miracle of miracles.
~George Bernard Shaw

would never make that choice. The medical and religious communities felt it was the right thing to do, but their reasoning made me even more resolute in my decision.

The surgeon appeared stricken. "Your thyroid cancer has spread to ten lymph nodes." It seemed he was delivering the message to himself rather than the patient sitting in front of him.

"You will need a radical neck resection, placing you under anesthesia for seven or eight hours. The four-month fetus you're carrying could be severely deprived of oxygen during that time so a therapeutic abortion is recommended. Otherwise, you could be delivering a child with multiple deformities or health problems."

Spreading cancer, abortion, deformities. This couldn't be happening. Why me? Why these horrible things for my child? The doctor exited the examining room and my husband joined me moments later to assure me that he would support any decision I made.

The nurse practitioner entered the room along with my parish priest and began a litany of reasons why a therapeutic abortion was being recommended. "Whenever there is a pregnancy involved, cancers spread more rapidly. You will need radiation immediately after surgery and it shouldn't be delayed for the four or five months until you deliver the baby. You are only twenty-four years old with four other children at home under the age of five. Who will raise them if you're gone?"

My parish priest, Father Bill, stepped gingerly into the conversation with tears in his eyes. "Shirley, if you're worried how the church feels in this situation, don't be concerned. Our church makes exceptions when a mother's life is in jeopardy."

I listened and went over each argument carefully in my mind. I believed in a good and loving God, not a cruel, punishing God. I would put him in charge of my health and my family. Believing this was best, I decided to carry my child to term no matter the consequences. He or she deserved all the love and opportunity I had been given by my mother.

"Schedule the surgery," I said to the nurse practitioner. "I'm keeping my baby."

My husband and Father Bill looked at each other with concern, but both knew I must be the one to make the decision.

After the surgery, the surgeons and obstetricians were surprised my pregnancy continued without problems. A beautiful baby girl, Nancy Ruth, was delivered and placed in my arms five months later.

Before we left the hospital, the pediatrician came in to tell us the status of our daughter. He explained that she appeared in good health, with no deformities of any kind. But there was a problem. My breathing stopped and I felt sure my heart must have stopped beating also.

"Her cries are shrill and piercing and she stays tightly curled in the fetal position. These are generally signs of spastic cerebral palsy. There is no cure for this condition and she will probably need lifetime care. It affects the nervous system, brain, and muscles. Every facet of her life may be affected: learning, eating, walking, talking."

The doctor's manner was detached and I felt he wanted to break the news and hurry from the room so he wouldn't have to deal with devastated parents.

"What caused this? How did it happen? Are you sure? Are there any tests we can run to be positive?"

I had a thousand questions and refused to let him get away until he answered all of them.

"No one knows for sure how it happens. Generally something goes wrong in the womb. Lack of oxygen to the baby's brain possibly," he answered.

The very second he ended that sentence, the guilt train arrived. How could I have been so selfish? What kind of life had I created for this child?

The next several weeks, I held and cuddled my baby, trying to assure her how much she was loved, how I would always take care of her and mostly, how sorry I was for being responsible for her condition. I was wracked with guilt.

When Nancy cried, it sounded like a shrieking noise. Her arms stayed pulled in close to her sides, with her little fists balled up. Diapering her was difficult. You had to pry open her little knees just to get the diaper on and secured.

One morning, after her bottle, I placed her in the crib on her side. She was lying in her usual tight fetal position. When I didn't hear her cries for attention after a couple of hours, I tiptoed into the bedroom to check on her. She was lying on her back, with her arms and hands open. Her legs were spread-eagled like a little frog. I was in a panic. My little girl must have died. When I grabbed her, and pulled her up to my chest, I realized she was smiling at me and her little fingers curled around mine for the first time. Tears poured from my eyes and I prayed this was not temporary.

A trip to the pediatrician gave us few clues as to why this could have occurred. He was astounded. It was suggested the replacement thyroid I need to take daily crossed the placental barrier causing hyper-thyroidism in my child, possibly explaining her spasticity. Not wanting me to expect too much, he advised there might still be problems and this could just be a temporary remission or anomaly.

I knew better.

My child was healed and God had granted us a miracle.

This special baby is now a special woman. She is a military veteran and has a college degree. She works as a vice president for a large financial conglomerate and has a grown son and daughter. She is a devoted wife, mother, daughter, sibling, grandmother, citizen and is devout in her faith.

God helps with our difficult decisions. Just ask Him.

~Shirley Irene Dilley

Mica's Miracles

For every mountain there is a miracle.
~Robert H. Schuller

"Thirty-seven... thirty-eight... thirty-nine... Yay, Mica! Woohoo!" Mica's excited barks rang out in the frozen stillness. Atop Blackhead Mountain in January, I stamped my feet and clapped my hands to stay warm and also to celebrate Mica's amazing accomplishment. Making it to the summit of Blackhead is no mean feat, as the trail ranges from steep to wickedly steep to holy-cow-you-have-got-to-be-kidding-me steep. At the summit, she planted her feet and pointed her nose skyward and barked thirty-nine times — once for every mountain she'd climbed since our beginning more than a year earlier.

Mica, a Belgian Malinois, came into my life in May 2012. I already had a pack of rescued dogs of my own, but when I heard that a senior dog had been dumped at a shelter, I turned to Iske, who was reading the computer screen over my shoulder. "Look, Iss," I said, "a dog your age, abandoned at the shelter. We'll foster her and help her find a family of her own." Iske's tail thumped against my chair as my heart raced and my eyes filled. Iske's approval meant a lot. After all, I may have adopted her, but she rescued me. Through a brutal breakup and single parenthood, illness and eviction, financial troubles and relationship meltdowns, Iske had been my rock. Rescue, I learned from Iske, is a two-way street.

Now it was time to give back, and Mica was clearly in need. She had spent the past eleven years bored, frustrated, lonely, angry, and frightened, alone on the end of a chain. Her potential went utterly unappreciated, the neglect all the more piercing due to her incredible athletic ability and intelligence. After eleven years, her family moved from their home and disposed of Mica as if she were just so much trash. From that first glance at her photo, there was no talking sense to me. I would make sure she was safe and comfortable, no matter what. A few e-mails and a transport miracle later, Mica arrived at my home.

Mica had a tough time adjusting to her new home. She refused to be petted, walking away from all affection. She didn't know any commands, pulled dreadfully when on the leash, and sought distance and solitude at home. She was not aggressive at all—just stiff and aloof, sad and uncomfortable. She missed her family and all that was familiar, as awful as it was. We loved her from the distance she maintained and hoped her heart would heal enough to let us in.

After being with us for a few weeks, I decided to take her into the Catskill Forest for a short hike. She had learned her name and came when I called her, so I weighed the risk against the potential joy hiking might bring her. After a half a mile or so on the trail I took off the leash. She pranced away and sniffed the ground. Then she raced, paws flying, leaping over fallen logs, wagging and barking, along the next three miles of trail. At the lookout, she posed upon a rock and surveyed the layers of hills dropping away towards New Jersey and beyond. And everything changed.

Mica's miracle unfolded over many more hikes. She tasted freedom and she loved it. Hiking became a way of connecting with me, as she came to trust that I would give her the freedom she valued above all else. She'd been with us just over six months and had settled in nicely when a run-in with a porcupine resulted in a vet visit. The vet and I examined every centimeter of her body with a fine-toothed comb, seeking any stray quills. And that was when we found it: a small ugly bump on her belly.

The bump grew quickly and surgery was scheduled. When I took Mica in for her post-op checkup, the vet sat me down and spoke in that horribly quiet tone reserved for the worst of news. Grade 3 mast cell sarcoma, very aggressive subtype, no clear margins, and in his brutally honest opinion—"six months at the most." We discussed all the options and he shook his head slowly, petting Mica's soft ears. "Just take her home and make her happy," he said. "Anything else will ruin what little time she has left. Just make her happy."

In the face of such heartbreaking news, I did what any reasonable person would do. I adopted her. No more foster status, I felt that for whatever time she had left she deserved to die with my last name, a full member of this family.

And then I took Mica hiking. We committed to completing the Catskill 35—the thirty-five highest mountains in the Catskill region. If Mica could live long enough to hike them all—and then repeat four of them again in the winter—she could earn a certificate and patch for doing so. Hiking the 35 gave me a goal that structured our hikes. It gave me something to focus on besides her cancer. It gave me hope. And it gave her profound joy to be loose and running free up and down the mountains of the mighty and ancient Catskills.

We took it mountain by mountain, hike by hike. I kept a tally sheet next to the computer, filling in the dates as I uploaded photos. Doing anything thirty-five times takes time, and I fussed and worried over Mica as we hiked the list. Her pack mates came along to lend a paw. At first I thought we'd never make it to the winter hikes. Predicted to survive six months at most, we hiked often, logging miles and mountains in good order. And miraculously, Mica did not sicken. She did not show any signs of illness or discomfort at all. In fact she looked vibrantly well. It would have been amazing for any senior dog to hike and climb at this level of intensity, but Mica bravely trotted up those mountains at age twelve with terminal cancer, thirty-nine times. I got choked up at least once on every hike, burying my face in her neck and tearfully telling her what an amazing girl she was.

We hiked with the forest ranger and we hiked with my human friends, but mostly we hiked alone, just Mica and her canine sisters and me, up and down mountain after mountain. We gained hope. We got more and more excited as the number of remaining climbs shrank. And then the day was upon us: more than one year after her surgery, we were making that final climb. From a hopeless and pitiful creature on the end of a chain to barking her thirty-nine barks upon the summit of Blackhead Mountain, Mica's spirit has shown me just what a miracle really is.

It's been six months since Mica finished. Her certificate hangs above my desk, testimony to her courage and strength. We still hike regularly, working on a new list now. At her last vet visit, we got more bad news: the shadow we saw on the X-ray is lung cancer. Not a problem. Mica and I know what to do. "The mountains are calling and we must go."

~Halia Grace

21

Chicken Soup for the Soul

The Amazing
Foul Ball

The other sports are just sports. Baseball is a love.
~Bryant Gumbel

Every three weeks for two and a half months, we drove the two hours to Lucile Packard Children's Hospital at Stanford. After morning tests, Ross's doctor or an intern would puncture his spine, withdraw fluid to be tested, and inject him with two powerful medications. Twelve hours of intravenous chemotherapy followed.

The resulting nausea made Ross feel even worse, but this is what we had to do to defeat the cancer in his lymph gland.

To distract us from our anxiety about our third visit, I bought the best box seats available for the San Francisco Giants/Montreal Expos baseball game. Ross, a seven-year-old baseball fanatic, slept in the back seat as my wife and I drove from Sacramento through sporadic drizzle.

In the fifth inning, I left to take a picture of Will Clark from behind the backstop. He was on deck when Willie McGee hit a hard, looping foul near our seats. "No way," I thought, and continued looking toward home plate. McGee doubled on the next pitch and then Expos' pitcher Dennis Martinez intentionally walked Clark.

As I returned to our seats I sensed something had happened. My first thought was that Ross or Stacey had been hurt, but people were smiling at me. Ross stood there grinning, proudly holding the hardball high above his balding head. The ball had glanced off a man at the end of our row, tipped his son's glove, and landed in Ross's mitt.

If I had been sitting next to him, he would not have made the catch. My reflexive reaction would have been to protect my wife and son or at least help Ross catch it.

People kept coming up and congratulating him on his great catch. They all wanted to touch the ball, saying they had been to hundreds of games and never caught a foul ball. A head usher also came over and examined the ball with an unknown, but official, purpose.

The rain never came, the Giants won an exciting game, and we appreciated a quick exit from the parking lot. During the half-hour drive to our hotel, the ball seemed to glow and hum in the back seat.

The next day, instead of being filled with his normal dread, Ross was excited. He showed the ball to Rolo, our cheerful hospital aide, who had chauffeured us between the intimidating MRI machine, the ultrasound and the bone scan on our frightening first visit.

Ross discussed the catch with his friend Daniel as they played Nintendo while hooked up to their IVs. He proudly displayed it to the supportive hospital staff members and impressed Dr. Link and Dr. Mogul when they came by on their rounds. Later in the day, Stacey used the hardball to rub his sore back near the injection area.

His recovery was quicker than after previous treatments. Perhaps it was the new combination of anti-nausea drugs, but I think part of the credit went to the foul ball. He returned to his second-grade class without missing a day of school. Though most of his hair had fallen out over the weekend, he didn't care; he had a baseball to show off.

After Ross's chemotherapy ended, his weight and energy gradually returned. Soon he was back playing second base on his Little League team as the lump on his neck melted away. His pediatric oncologists said that he should lead a normal life.

Ross is thirty-one now and he's in excellent health.

~Bob Dreizler

22

Miracle Times Three

This isn't just "another day, another dollar."
It's more like "another day, another miracle."
~Victoria Moran

My grandmother was so sick that January. It had been a particularly hard winter already, and my mom and I had just brought Gram to the emergency room. She'd had several bouts of bronchitis in recent months, and this latest round had escalated into pneumonia. When the ER doctor admitted her, I stayed with Gram at the hospital. I hated the idea of losing her, yet I feared that it might be her time.

Other people thought so too. She'd lived a long, happy life, everyone said—a platitude I didn't want to hear. True, Gram was ninety-three years old, but I loved her with all my heart. She had suffered with Alzheimer's for nearly a decade, and even though, over time, the disease had taken her little by little, she'd never come to a point where she didn't know me—until that night. Her eyes looked wild and glassy; she babbled words that didn't make sense. At one point, she reached out and smacked my face, something my cherished Gram would never do. As she struggled to breathe in her hospital bed, I tried to conceal my pain. Letting go a sob, I called a nurse to help, then left Gram's room and wept in the hallway. The shock of it all cut deep.

Moments later, a gentle priest was by my side. "It's okay to cry," he said. "That's why God made tears."

As morning dawned, tears indeed seemed the theme of things.

Gram's doctor came in and kissed her cheek. "Goodbye, Marie," she said, eyes watery. "You've been a good patient."

The charge nurse was similarly emotional. "Her kidneys are shutting down, bless her heart. It won't be long now. Godspeed, Marie."

By noon, my mom and dad, as well as my aunt, uncle, and cousin had joined me in our vigil. Gram had lapsed into semi-consciousness sometime in the middle of the night. She didn't seem to see us, just stared into the distance, mumbling incoherently. Late in the day, Dad called Ellen, a hospice chaplain we'd met when my grandfather fell ill. Now a family friend, Ellen hurried over to Gram, who continued gazing up, as if seeing someone there. Her words still didn't make sense, and all we could decipher was an occasional "yes" or "I will."

Ellen explained that Gram was actually present in both worlds; bodily, she was still here with us, but spiritually she was straddling a chasm. In her tender manner, Ellen coaxed Gram to "Take the Lord's hand. It's okay to cross over, Marie."

I prepared myself right then to accept the inevitable, but Gram hung on through the night. By the next morning, however, it was clear that something truly amazing had occurred. I couldn't believe my eyes. Far from "crossing over," Gram now sat up in bed, fully coherent. She patted a spot beside her, and, in shock, I sat down. Then, in a serene voice, she called me by a name I loved but hadn't heard in a very long time: not "Theres-A," my formal given name, but "Trees-IE," her silly nickname for me.

I didn't know whether to laugh or cry.

As the morning advanced, Gram's miraculous recovery astounded everyone. Eventually, she was well enough to leave the hospital, and after a couple of days, while still frail, she settled into a new routine at a skilled nursing facility. I went home to St. Louis, four hours away, hating to go, but knowing I had to get back to my family. The doctor had warned that Gram could leave us at any time, and for weeks after arriving home I worried.

The dreaded phone call came on an unseasonably cold day in May, and it unfolded in a way I never would have expected. I picked up the receiver to hear Mom's tortured voice. "I have to tell you," she choked out. "I need to say… your dad has died."

At first, I couldn't process her words. "What?" I gasped.

Mom tried to speak again, but then a social worker took over the phone. I listened in disbelief. All along, I'd expected news of Gram, so how could this be about Dad? My mind caught on the memory of him at the hospital, so distraught over Gram's situation, yet knowing just what to do. Solid as a rock, my father. How could he be gone? I couldn't think, couldn't breathe.

Somehow, my husband, Jeff, and I made the four-hour drive to our hometown in record time. We went straight to Mom's house, and while Jeff fetched take-out dinner that none of us ate, I sat with Mom at the kitchen table, watching the setting sun. Dad had gone out to garden early that morning, suffered a massive heart attack, and died right there in his back yard. I stared out at the fledgling tomato plants he'd never get to tend. It all seemed unreal. How could this be?

The next day, Jeff and I took on the very hard task of telling Gram the news—and that's when a second astonishing event transpired. Still in the throes of Alzheimer's, Gram had continued to fade away, with fewer moments of lucidity, but as the words about Dad tumbled out, she nodded. "I know," was all she said, quite articulately. "I came back to help, Treesie. Your mom is going to need me, and I'm supposed to be here."

My mouth fell open in surprise.

Suddenly, it all made miraculous sense.

And two years later, on the night after my beloved grandmother finally did pass, a third little astonishing thing occurred. Staying once more at Mom's, I was awakened from sleep by a wispy touch on my shoulder. Call it a trick of light, call it a shadow, but I could see Gram's presence.

She remained there for the merest of moments, then seemed to float out into the living room, where she hovered beside Dad's chair, and I swear heard her say, "I helped."

I believe Gram knew full well on her hospital deathbed that Dad was going to die. I believe that, far from the nonsensical words we'd all thought she'd uttered, she was actually conversing with someone on the other side, learning about her one final task. I believe she accepted that task willingly, returning to us with a renewed spiritual purpose. She and Mom had always been close, and her presence and required care would give Mom a renewed purpose too.

I've come to think of these events surrounding Gram's death as her trinity of miracles, her Miracle Times Three. They've strengthened my faith and helped me to see that our deceased loved ones don't ever really leave us at all. No, far from gone, they become celestial collaborators with God, our own personal connections in Heaven. They journey from this world on into the next, and sometimes, if we're blessed, they journey back again, to give us hope, to give us counsel, and to give us love.

~Theresa Sanders

23

Tears of Joy

Faith is like radar that sees through the fog.
~Corrie ten Boom

When I looked in the mirror, I didn't recognize myself. My hair was thinning, I had dark circles under my eyes, I was chronically fatigued, and everything hurt from my nose to my toes. I had constant painful and limited blurry vision. I was losing my sense of taste and smell, my voice was hoarse and raspy, my ears were constantly ringing, and I developed a dry cough. My mouth was constantly dry, and swallowing was difficult, I lost my appetite and I choked when I did eat. My mouth always hurt with throbbing ulcers on my gums and I was losing teeth. My diagnosis was an autoimmune disease called Sjögren's syndrome.

Each day my vision worsened and my pain increased. My eyes were so dry that the corneas split open. Those tiny ulcers made my eyes burn constantly and I feared going blind. I used as many as twenty prescription drops each day, but nothing worked. I wore moisture chamber goggles but they didn't do much good and I looked utterly ridiculous in them. In fact, they reduced my peripheral vision so much that I couldn't see people who stood beside me. I was constantly falling because I couldn't see things right in front of me. I had to stop driving and I spent most days on the sofa unable to see anything. I desperately needed my body to produce tears, but the fact is that my lacrimal glands dried up and no longer worked.

I traveled roughly 300 miles to Johns Hopkins because they have a clinic especially for Sjögren's patients. At the Wilmer Eye Institute, my sympathetic doctor worked with hands like a magician. But the news was discouraging: my eyes were as good as they were ever going to be. I made four trips a year to Johns Hopkins, where I received excellent care for my other Sjögren's symptoms, but my eyes continued to deteriorate. My vision was still poor, my eyes hurt constantly, and I still couldn't produce tears.

To complicate matters, I was trying to write my second book with limited and blurry vision. I prayed to St. Lucy, the patron of eye disorders, and while my eyesight never improved and my eyes were still dry and painful, somehow each day I made progress with the book.

When a group of parishioners from our church made plans to travel to Lourdes, France, the idea of asking for a miracle became appealing. In 1858, the Blessed Mother appeared to St. Bernadette in a grotto in Lourdes, where people were being miraculously cured after bathing in the spring water. "Why would Mary grant me a miracle?" I asked my husband Pat.

"Why not give you a miracle? You deserve one! You are doing God's work by writing religious books and prayers."

I thought about the truth in his words for a few minutes. "Can we afford to go to France?"

Pat furrowed his brow. "We'll find the money!" he said. "I'm calling Father Chuck to reserve two seats for us." When he hung up the phone, he said, "We just got the last two seats!" Pat took my hands in his. "We're going to France!" he said. "There's an informational meeting scheduled next week. Father Chuck asked us to attend."

As Pat drove to the meeting, we noticed that puffy white clouds had formed a perfect white cross in the sky directly over the church. Maybe it was a sign.

Father Chuck met us inside with a welcoming grin. He knew about my declining health and poor vision. "Not everyone who goes to Lourdes receives a miracle," he said quietly.

I nodded and sighed deeply. "I know."

"And some people receive a miracle later, after they have returned home." He raised his eyebrows and smiled. "You just never know, but have faith and trust in God."

"I will," I said. "I do."

Pat and I had no idea what to expect at Lourdes, but we both felt Mary's presence there. When I was submerged in the icy spring water, I felt warm with Mary's love. I felt like I was standing before her baring my soul when I asked her to bless me with tears. I figured I could live with my other Sjögren's symptoms, but I couldn't live without sight. I needed to see in order to continue writing. So, I humbly asked for tears.

When I got out of the water, I felt like Mary was telling me I had to change my attitude. I needed to think and act like her.

Changing my attitude wasn't easy, but I tried very hard to be more like Mary. When I got home, I put statues of Mary in every room of my house so they would remind me to be more like her. Each day that I was successful, I felt my heart grow.

On November 1, there was a special mass to celebrate the feast of All Saints' Day. Pat and I made plans to attend, but I woke up with a miserable cold and started to cry when I realized I was sick. Pat looked at me as if he had just seen a ghost.

"What is it?" I asked. Pat couldn't speak.

"Tell me what's wrong," I begged.

"You have tears," he stammered. "In all the years I've known you, over thirty-five years, I've never seen you cry with tears." He wrapped his arms around me and he shed a few tears of his own, tears of joy.

~Barbara S. Canale

24

Silent Night No More

Faith and joy are the ascensive forces of song.
~Edmund Clarence Stedman

stared at our antique player piano, too afraid to touch the keys. Those keys were now foreign, glaring back at me like eighty-eight black and white teeth, one scale away from taking a bite out of my calm. Three years before this moment I had been enduring ENT and gastroenterology visits, endoscopies and laryngoscopies, speech therapy, and a vague diagnosis of "muscle tension dysphonia" that forced me to walk away from the stage and the college classroom. After twenty-five years of performing and teaching, I was no longer able to sing. I thought my life was over.

Yet after reinventing my career with the use of the written word as my voice, I found myself taking a call from a producer for The Young Americans international performance company. She was assisting with *The Magic of Christmas*, a five-show run in Southern California, and informed me, "Our lead singer has laryngitis. She's trying steam treatments right now but if Jessica can't sing, can you go on for her tonight?" My first instinct was to run. All I could think of was my current Sunday morning attempts to sing from the church congregation, voice cracking frequently and throat sore for the rest of the day. Mondays found me without a voice at all. How could I get through a public performance?

More profoundly, beyond the physical performance, however, I took into account my continuing grief. Only a month earlier, I had a conversation with my husband about how heartbroken I'd been away from the stage these years, not able to share my heart with an audience. I told him, "Being onstage was a precious place for me. I felt beloved there. I don't feel beloved anymore." What if something went wrong and I had to spend even more years coping with my loss?

As I contemplated my answer, the lesson from those painful years hit me. It had taught me that when I want to run from what is scaring me, I should lean into the fear and embrace it. So I took a deep breath and said, "I'm available but can you send me the audio file to see if I can even handle it?" The "Ave Maria," Schubert's reverent interpretation of the enduring prayer to the blessed Virgin Mary, was a beast. There would be no faking my way through it.

Now faced with the piano and the alarming task of a simple warm-up, I tentatively depressed the first key, then another and another. Soon I was vocalizing, triad after triad, arpeggio after arpeggio, head voice connecting to mixed and mixed voice to chest until I felt ready. I opened my mouth to try the classical piece and what came forth was decent. It was certainly safer than a singer with laryngitis. I called Tara and told her I could do it if necessary, simultaneously praying for Jessica's total healing before the show. At 2 p.m. I got a text: "You're on."

I drove to the theater, my pulse racing and my palms sweating. I got a brief walk-through and sound check, then went to my dressing room to get ready for an 8 p.m. show. The stage manager gave me a five-minute call, and I slowly walked to the stage right wing. One hundred and fifty choral voices were already onstage performing an excerpt from Handel's breathtaking "Messiah."

I appealed to the Holy Spirit to blow His breath in me, giving a clear voice to Schubert's musical prayer. Then I walked on. What came forth surprised me. There was a clarity of tone and richness of resonance I had not been able to achieve in three years. I did it! At the close, however, I thought, "Whew, that was nerve-wracking. Now I can't wait to hear Jessica in the next four shows," having faith she would be in good voice the next day.

God had other plans.

Jessica texted me the next morning that, though she had regained her voice before going to bed the previous night, she couldn't talk at all when she woke up. I received the same text the third day. So I went on again… and again… and again… and again. Five shows total. That glorious Sunday morning driving to the theater, I realized I had been experiencing a miracle. I had been so focused on evaluating my vocal performance and praying that Jessica heal that I hadn't been focused on the gift I was receiving and giving to others with each performance. Many audience members knew of my vocal journey, of my inability to speak or sing for some time. I began to realize, as people approached, hugging me and crying after the show, that they craved a miracle as much as I did. There were overwhelming embraces, comments and tears as people told me they needed the prayer of the "Ave Maria" just as I sang it. I was blown away.

It dawned on me that God had orchestrated an event that I never could have imagined, even down to the song selection. I reflected that I had been praying the "Hail Mary" my whole life, first on my knees each night with my sisters as children, then many times in the rosary at my lowest. I couldn't have been more intimately acquainted with it. I recalled that my beautiful daddy taught Latin in school, and I was graced to be speaking it in song. It had even been my final goodbye to my grandmother at her funeral years earlier. Oh, so many connections and gifts had rained upon me. Most of all, I realized this miracle was giving me the very gift I had so desired. I felt beloved again, and more than anyone, loved by my Beloved. He was letting me know he heard my prayers, heard my needs, heard my sorrows. He gave me a gift that will last me forever.

The following day my throat was sore and my voice hoarse again. I could barely speak. I had not done one thing to prepare for Christmas. Not one gift bought or wrapped. Not one Christmas card addressed or mailed. But none of that mattered. I had been given the gift of singing a tender prayer for my children, my husband, and hundreds more. I had been blessed to sing for so many who needed His presence, many of whom had lifted me up in my years of loss or who had suffered losses of their own. Most importantly, though I had unwittingly forgotten the meaning of Christmas in years past, I realized the wonder I had experienced is exactly what that sacred season has always been about. We are His beloved, and there are miracles all around us every moment of the season and beyond into the New Year. All we have to do is look for them.

~Cynthia McGonagle McGarity

Chapter 3

Hope & Miracles

Touched by an Angel

25

The Visitor

Hope is being able to see that there is light despite all of the darkness.
~Desmond Tutu

Since the day of the accident, everyone has asked me the same question: "Cheryl, how do you get out of bed every morning?" To tell you the truth, I don't always know how. But sometimes, on my worst mornings, I think of my mysterious visitor.

She came to call three days after my two daughters' combined funeral, as I was sitting in the brown leather chair at home in Wildwood, Missouri, staring into space.

People had been moving in and out of the house all day with flowers, food, love, and tears. My special stranger came to the door to give me a story of hope.

A week earlier, on August 15, 2013, my life and that of my family changed forever in 1.6 seconds. I know the exact time it took to rip our lives apart because I read it on the police report. It took 1.6 seconds for the convertible in which my daughters, Kathleen, seventeen, and Lauren, eighteen, were passengers, to veer off the road and go airborne before smashing into a neighbor's back deck, blocks from home. My girls died instantly.

Hours before the accident they'd been at a friend's wedding shower, laughing and eating frosted cupcakes, wearing party dresses. The day after, I went to the accident site with my husband, Sam, and our youngest daughter, Anna. We found long, lone strands of their hair — one golden and one chestnut—caught in the deck's jagged wood. I took them home and saved them in a plastic bag.

I was no stranger to trauma, loss, and grief.

When I was six years old, my father went to a motel room and put a gun in his mouth and shot himself. When I was seventeen, my mother went to a motel room and overdosed on alcohol and sleeping pills. It took me years of therapy, prayer, and love of friends and family to heal, but I did. And I went on to build a beautiful, happy family of my own.

I often wondered, though, about the level of despair my parents must have felt in order to take their lives. Somewhere along the way, they must have lost hope. And now, I understood the feeling. Just how much pain can one human heart take? Surely, this time I was beyond my limit.

After the girls died, our doorbell rang non-stop with condolences from friends, acquaintances, and even strangers who'd read about the accident. Our home looked like a florist's shop, packed wall-to-wall with carnations, daisies, and hydrangea arrangements. I let my Aunt Carol and mother-in-law, Marti, deal with it because I could barely lift a finger. Doing one load of laundry felt like running a marathon.

I didn't want to bathe, I didn't brush my teeth or hair, and I wore the same shorts and T-shirt for days. I didn't put my contact lenses in—maybe I didn't want to see too clearly the reality in front of me. And I couldn't eat.

"It's not that I'm not hungry," I tried to explain, when friends urged me to eat at the funeral reception, "it's that I can't swallow."

It was difficult for me to describe.

When the doorbell rang three days later, it was during a rare moment of quiet. I was slumped in my chair—surrounded by beautiful roses, staring at nothing. Our Lab, Maggie, barked and lunged for the door so I dragged myself off the chair to see who it was. Standing on our front porch was a tiny old lady, wrinkled and hunched over, with a cane in one hand and a basket of tea and cookies in the other. It was hot outside and she looked like she'd walked a long way.

"You don't know me," she said, "but I heard what happened…"

"Oh, I'm so sorry," I said to her, as I nudged a rambunctious Maggie inside the house and shut the door, stepping out to the woman. "I'd invite you in, but I'm afraid the dog will jump on you and knock you down."

"Oh, no, don't you worry," she said, with a sweet smile, putting her basket down. "I'll only be a moment, then I'll be on my way. I came for two reasons. First, I came to pray with you."

"Oh," I said, a little surprised, "Okay…"

The woman took my hands in hers and we closed our eyes and bowed our heads.

"Dear God," she prayed out loud, "I pray for this family to have strength and not to be angry at You. And I pray that this family holds onto their faith."

She opened her eyes and gave my hands a squeeze.

"And now, the second reason. I want to share a story of hope with you. Would that be all right?"

"Sure," I nodded. I was a bit in a daze. She was still holding my hands and now looked deeply into my eyes.

"My first memory as a child was when I was five years old," she began, "I was sitting outside on my Mama's lap on a hot summer afternoon just like today, when my Daddy came outside from the house and shot my Mama in the side of the head."

"What? No…"

"I was covered in blood. My Daddy picked me up, took me inside, and handed me over to my sister, who was eight years old. Then in front of us, he put the gun to his own head and shot himself. After that, my sister and I were separated into different foster homes…"

Her sad story prompted me to tell her about my own parents. Our eyes locked and in that moment, I knew she understood exactly how I felt that afternoon.

"I tell you my story," she said, "because… I stand here in front of you today a survivor of tragedy. And I know that you will survive, too. But you must hold onto your hope. Don't give up hope. *Ever.*"

She searched my eyes for a moment and then nodded, satisfied with what she saw there.

"You are going to get through this," she repeated, with certainty. "And I hope to see you again one day to have a cup of tea with you."

At that, the old lady hugged me and left.

"Thank you!" I called out to her, as she slowly disappeared down the street. I stood on the porch for a minute, astonished to have had such an intimate moment with a complete stranger, then went inside to tell Marti and Carol about it.

"That," said my mother-in-law, "was an angel."

I barely remember anything about those first few days or weeks after the girls died, it's all a blur to me. I have no recollection of who else came over to the house that day, or that week. But I will always remember my visitor who brought tea and empathy, and a story.

On mornings when I wake up and feel I can't face the day, I think of her. This stranger's belief in me helps me get out of bed, and keeps me away from the despair-filled motel rooms of my family's past.

Never give up hope, she said. Despite family tragedy, my dear visitor went on to become a smiling, sweet old granny.

I hope to do the same one day.

~Cheryl Bland Oliver with Natasha Stoynoff

When Hope Found Me at the Beach

Dogs are miracles with paws.
~Attributed to Susan Ariel Rainbow Kennedy

The clouds were as murky and gray as my thoughts. Brooding about life and deeply preoccupied, I collected some things and pointed my car toward the ocean. I trusted the beach to make everything clearer for me, and I wanted a dramatic, solitary view. On a dismal weekday like this I hoped to find everything I needed at the jetty at Fort Stevens.

I drove for miles without seeing a car before I finally pulled into the parking lot. I was the only person there. Note that I said the only "person." I was, however, not alone. A ragged dog looked hopeful as I parked. Ears up, eyes searching, he looked expectant, wanting to recognize me.

Hoping.

A stiff, steady wind whipped the beach grass, and the rail thin dog hunched against the cold. There wasn't enough meat on his bones to block the chill. He limped slowly toward me. I stepped out of my old Cadillac, and he picked up his pace to greet me. A battle waged in his soft brown eyes, a war between despair and optimism.

A battle was going on inside me, too. My drive had been full of murky thoughts and dark emotions. But I wasn't going to share my darkness, and it looked like too many people had already snubbed this wayfarer—I reached out to the dog, and he came to me.

I looked closer; his feet were swollen and the insides of his thighs were chapped and pink from salt water and wind. His elbow was scraped and covered with fresh blood.

I walked toward the lookout, my destination, to watch the waves break against the great rocks. He followed. There were three short flights of stairs. I took them slowly; he climbed beside me haltingly, limping.

I searched the horizon beyond the violent waves for answers. He stood quietly at my side. The harsh wind whipped the surf into froth. My long hair blew wraithlike; his fur tossed wildly.

I slowly descended the stairs, and he kept pace. I headed for the shelter of my car, and he followed, stopping only to sniff at a trashcan, but he found no food. I turned and saw him trying to eat the sharp-edged beach grass.

I looked at him and called out "Hope!"

It was my grandfather's name.

The dog came. I opened my passenger door, pushed the seat forward, and invited him in. He hesitated, wagged his tail, and stepped in gingerly. Then he stepped back out. He kept looking around, like there was someone still expected, like my car was the wrong car.

But there was no other car.

He stepped in and out half a dozen times, each time staying longer. When a white-haired man walked by my car on the way to the lookout, Hope growled a warning. "Good protective dog, ma'am," the retiree said.

"He's not my dog," I answered.

We chatted and he said coyotes lived in the park, and the fresh blood on Hope's elbow would be like a magnet. I had to do something, so I invited Hope into the car, and shut the door. I rested my hand against the back of the passenger seat to keep it from flopping back and scaring him. The kindly man followed me in his truck. I made it about twenty feet before Hope decided to claw his way out of the car.

I stopped and opened the door and he hopped out. But how could I leave him?

I couldn't.

We coaxed Hope back into the car. More determined, I drove off and just let him claw the door. I opened the window, and drove faster. Hey, my car was old anyway. Hope relaxed enough to curl up on the floor and rest.

Going through Astoria, he sat up. He faced me, and I spoke gently. He studied me, and I rested my hand against the back of the passenger seat. Then he quietly lowered his chin into the crook of my elbow, sighed, and closed his eyes. In moments he was asleep.

All that remains to be said is that I found Hope at the beach one day.

More accurately, Hope found me.

The truth is, he rescued me as much as I rescued him. I can't say what would have happened that day if Hope hadn't been there to meet me, but I can tell you my beach bag didn't have a towel and a sand bucket in it.

I believe God sends us what we need. If a person had tried to talk to me on that dark day, there's no way I would've listened or turned aside from my self-destructive path. But to suddenly be presented with an innocent dog in dire straits? That was a call I could never turn away from.

I've heard people discuss whether angels have wings or not. I think it's a matter of dressing for the occasion. I'm of the opinion they appear from time to time on stone bruised feet—with doggy breath. And I promise you, one angel rested his chin in the crook of a deeply depressed person's arm—at just the right time.

~Christy A. Caballero

My Lucky Day

Angels are never too distant to hear you.
~Author Unknown

After work one day I stopped at the gas station down the street from where I lived to fill up. It was an unusually cold day for March, with a breeze blowing and a thin layer of frozen snow on the ground.

After filling my tank I went inside to pay the cashier. She was a very cordial woman who struck up a conversation about the weather. We talked about how cold it seemed for that time of year while she took my money and gave me change.

I mentioned to her that I needed to wash my car when the weather got better. She excitedly told me, "This is your lucky day! We have a car wash special with a gas fill up and you can get the full wash package, regularly $8, for only a buck."

"That's a great deal," I replied. "But my luck hasn't been so hot lately so I probably should wait for it to get warmer."

The clerk kept pushing the wash until I finally paid her the dollar and said, "Okay, you sold me!"

The car wash was located behind the station, not attached to the main building. I got in my car and drove around to the entrance, punched in the code the cashier had given me and waited for the big metal door to open.

At first it seemed stuck, like it was frozen, but then a large metal chain attached to the bottom of the door slowly moved and pulled up the door. How spooky. It reminded me of a haunted house I'd visited as a kid.

Once I was inside the wash, the water swished and swirled around the car while pink and blue soap bubbles slid down the hood of my car and slipped away into the drain.

I felt more at ease and turned on the radio while I waited for the wash to end. Because I had the full package with seven cycles—tires and wheels, underbelly, wash, wax, rinse, spot-free rinse and blow dry—it seemed to be taking an awfully long time.

Eventually the wash reached the dry cycle and shut off when it finished. However, my sense of relief slipped away as I waited and waited and nothing happened. The metal door remained closed and, like a tomb, I was sealed inside.

This couldn't be happening.

After a few more minutes of silence, the lights dimmed, making the wash seem even creepier than before. I still had my car engine running, but something told me I'd better shut it off before carbon monoxide started to build up and suffocate me.

With my hand shaking, I turned off the ignition and fought back my panic. I couldn't just sit there and do nothing; I had to do something. So I turned on the headlights to get a better look at my situation.

I got out of the car and searched for an exit door or a panic button that would manually open the door, or a phone on the wall to call someone for help since I didn't have a cell phone with me.

My search turned up nothing and I began to lose hope. I could see the headlines in the newspaper the next morning (or when they found my body): "Woman Found Dead in a Car Wash."

Images of my funeral popped into my head and I could imagine the grief-stricken faces of my family and friends at my funeral.

"This is not my lucky day!" I screamed out, hoping someone would hear me.

I got back inside my car and did the only thing I knew how to do; I prayed. I grew up believing in miracles and if ever I needed one it was now. A strange sense of peace came over me. Then suddenly I saw a bright light at the back of the wash. Glancing in my rear view mirror, I saw a man standing in the light.

In a matter of seconds the door lifted and I was free! I jumped into action, turned on the car, hit the gas pedal and sped out of the wash. I didn't slow down or look back to see if the man was still standing there because I was so happy to be going home.

More than a week passed before it dawned on me that I should go back to the gas station and thank the employee who had saved my life. When I did stop at the station, the same clerk who had sold me the car wash ticket was working.

She recognized me and said, "I owe you a dollar. I feel really bad for selling you that bum ticket because I didn't know that old bucket of bolts was broken down until my manager told me about it the next day."

When I told her I'd gotten stuck in there she said, "Honey, that isn't possible. The manager told me that old chain finally snapped a few weeks ago and there's no way it could have opened."

"Yes, I was trapped inside," I insisted. "What about the man who works here that saved me? Is he around so I can thank him?" I also hoped this guy could back up my story.

"Sweetie," she said looking a bit sorry for me. "We haven't had any male employees here for months. I don't know what to tell you."

None of it made any sense! I walked out of the station in a daze with only one answer: God had answered my prayer and sent an angel to rescue me. It must have been my lucky day after all.

~Leona Campbell

Angel at the Wheel

We cannot pass our guardian angel's bounds, resigned or sullen,
he will hear our sighs.
~Saint Augustine

First, I have to mention that I am not a "seer of spirits." While I do believe that anything is quite possible in this world, I have never had an angelic, ghostly or otherwise unworldly experience. I have heard things from other people, but have always taken them with the proverbial grain of salt—neither believing nor not believing. As I said, without proof I can touch, it is all wishful thinking as far as I'm concerned. Until last Thursday.

Taking a few steps back into the history of this tale, Joelese (Jo) Cornhall and I have been best friends since the day we met in 1968. Her talented fingers sewed dresses for my little ones and she has listened for hours as I regaled her with ideas for my writing and painting.

Over the years, divorces happened, people moved away, remarried—life went on and we tended to lose contact. I met Jo's second husband Cliff, twice. Once right after they married and once when their son was about three months old. Her son is now in his forties. What used to be visiting every day turned into a call on a birthday and a Christmas card once a year.

But technology also moved on, and when Cliff retired, he became an avid e-mail friend. We connected on an almost daily basis through e-mail, sending updates on things going on in our lives or just passing on a good joke. He was repairing things for Jo, taking their dog to the local dog park, and having a very happy retirement.

Then the messages suddenly stopped. Jo contacted me to let me know that Cliff had passed away. A sudden heart attack. She invited me to a memorial his friends were holding at the dog park, where a bench and a tree were being dedicated to him. I begged off because of deadlines, but sent my condolences. I am so awkward with things like that.

But, time heals and soon Jo was back driving all over the country visiting friends and staying busy. We got together several times each year for just a "day out for the girls."

This year I wanted to do something special. So, early in the year I bought all-season passes to the Laguna Art Festival and also two front row seats to the Pageant of the Masters.

The week of the Pageant, I had been knocked out by food poisoning, but thought my symptoms would be gone by that Wednesday. I drove the hour and a half to Jo's house in Huntington Beach, and felt tired, but okay.

Jo took me to the park to see Cliff's bench and tree. It is a beautiful little oasis set up as a butterfly reserve. Then we drove to Laguna. I could feel it coming on the minute Jo parked the car: chills, nausea, weak knees. But I tried to push on. I made it to the first bench at the first art exhibit and collapsed.

Long story short, I spent the rest of the day and night on Jo's pullout daybed, in agony, sucking on ice and begging for death to release me. The only words I could utter were, "I'm sorry. I ruined the whole day—and evening. I'm so, so, sorry."

In the morning, I washed up and changed, but was determined to drive home to take care of my cats. I'd left multiple bowls of water and dry kibble, and had fed them wet food the morning before. The AC was on—but even with several cat boxes lining the hall, it had to be an insane mess.

Jo wanted to drive me home in my car, with a neighbor following. But I insisted I was well enough to tackle the long freeway home. So, she allowed me to follow her onto the 405 and then I waved her off with my best smile, and started the hour-and-a-half drive home on what has to be the worst freeway in Southern California.

As I write this, I can't remember everything about the drive. The chills started again, the headache, and the nausea. I was disoriented. I focused on hanging onto the steering wheel and just keeping in my own lane. But it was getting more difficult by the minute. Rather than kill myself and probably take a few other cars with me, I decided that I should get off the freeway. I tried to change lanes but couldn't manage it. I started to cry.

Suddenly, a feeling of calm and peace came over me. I felt two strong arms take the wheel and hold my hands tight. Something enveloped me from the back of the driver's seat and surrounded my shaking body.

A voice as clear as if it came from the radio said, "Don't worry, Joyce. I have the wheel. I'll get you home safely." I never saw anything, but I felt the strength as the car whipped back into total control. I felt the presence, but never heard another word. I knew from the voice I'd heard so many times on Jo's answering machine that it was Cliff.

We drove in silence through all the cities and suburbs until finally we came to the off-ramp that would take me to the city street that led home. Like a puff, the control of the car went back to me. The voice said, "You'll be okay now." All was quiet. I was alone in my car, heading for home. About a mile later, I pulled into my drive, shaking and weak once again. My neighbor came out and asked me if I was okay.

I waved her off, saying I was too sick to talk and just wanted to park the car and get into bed.

Later that day, I called Jo as promised to make sure she knew I arrived home intact. I told her of the experience and said I racked it up to the raging fever I had. But she wasn't surprised at all. She said there had been other incidents where Cliff had interceded to help. "That's my Cliffy. I know he was there to help you. That's the kind of person he was and still is."

All I know is that I am still recovering, and that I am sitting here, safe in my office, writing this all because eight days ago an angel took my steering wheel and saved my life.

~Joyce Laird

The Touch of Love

Love is something eternal; the aspect may change,
but not the essence.
~Vincent van Gogh

M y beloved husband, who I called by his Cherokee name, Yonah Usdi, John Little Bear, used his nickname for me, calling from his hospital bed to where I stood by the door. "Magdalena?"

I turned to look at him. His beautiful face was so tired, the liver failure yellowing his cocoa-colored skin, his dark eyes surrounded by shadows. The pain on his face cut right through me.

My John was dying. And soon. We knew it. We had known for a while. He was in the final stages of a long battle. His liver, heart, and lungs were all in various stages of shutting down, but I still clung to hope that some kind of miracle would happen. Maybe at Emory. He was scheduled to be transferred to Atlanta the next day, and maybe, I thought, looking at his sweet face, our miracle would happen there.

"Magdalena?" he said again. He held out his hand, and I moved to the side of the bed, taking his hand, his guitar player fingers folding around my own. My heart skipped. Even with his body swollen and devastated by disease, he was, as I told him often, still the most beautiful thing I had ever seen.

He smiled wearily, but kissed the back of my hand, looking at me, his dark eyes glittering. "You know, don't you, that I will never leave you?"

I immediately went to tears, my throat thick, my chest aching. I opened my mouth to answer, but he shook his head and reached up to touch my lips, shushing me. I kissed his fingertips. And he spoke again, a soft-spoken determined statement. "Magdalena, you hear me? I will never leave you."

But he did. Less than two weeks later, John died.

And I was broken in half. I didn't even know how to be in my own body anymore. I bumped into walls, stumbled down steps. I'd find myself in rooms, in the yard, without remembering how I got there. I'd feel like I was being lifted off my feet and thrown to one side. My poor loving sons, sixteen and twenty-two, did their best to love and help me, but they didn't know what to do. I cried all the time. I stared off into space. I lost time. I lost track of my keys, my shoes, my bag. I lost track of thoughts. I lost, for hours, the ability, the will, to move, to speak. I lost thought, simply sitting in a silent mind, searching. For him.

I lost track of me.

I learned what it meant to despair. I said words out loud that I had never even thought before: I don't want to be here anymore. Taking my own life had never been an option for me. But I had never known sorrow so deep, so profound. And I simply didn't know how to be anymore. Not without John.

I curled up on the couch a few nights after John died, the bed just feeling too big and too empty. The TV flickered blue light across the room, but I wasn't watching. I was crying, heart breaking so deeply that it felt like my body would break too.

That's when I heard him. Clearly, distinctly, there in the middle of my living room, I heard my sweet John say, "I'm here, Magdalena. Now turn off that TV. You'll rest better."

I stopped crying and sat half up, looking around the flickering room. His voice was so clear, I expected to see him standing there, leaning in the door, wagging a finger at me, or winking, a smile playing at the corner of his lips. But I didn't see anything. I thought, "You miss him so much you're imagining things."

But then I heard him again, that Georgia drawl gentle but insistent. "Missy, hear me? Turn the TV off. You need to rest."

Slowly I reached over, picked up the remote, and clicked the television off, throwing the living room into darkness. I twisted myself up in the coral-colored blanket he gave me in our Cherokee exchange of wedding vows—protection, comfort, sustenance—and rolled over tightly on my left side, pressing my tear-covered face into the blanket, and even deeper, into the back of the couch. I held back the weeping that seemed to be what I was made of now, and held my breath. I felt him so strongly, so closely, and I waited to see if he would speak again. Then I felt it.

A touch.

His hand.

Stroking my leg. A soft caress just above my knee. Again, and again, his touch so familiar, he continued to rub my leg. The same loving gesture he'd made each night when we spooned together, my back to his belly, his face in my hair. He'd rest his hand on the curve of my leg, as he settled in behind me. Always for a moment before sleep, he playfully teased me—bad coffee I'd made, or some something I'd said that he found particularly Carolina country, or he'd croon a few lines, that sweet tenor voice—"See the dog and the butterfly, up in the air she wants to fly"—all while his hand softly stroked my knee until we both fell asleep.

And there in the dark, in the wake of his death, four days after he left his body, left me behind, when I felt most lost in my breaking heart, he touched me again.

The touch continued, and I thought back to the promise he'd made in the hospital room, the last words he'd said to me before he was put on the ventilator, the last words he'd said to me before he left his body for good: You know I will never leave you.

He was keeping his promise.

I had prayed for a miracle.

There in the dark on my couch, I knew John had given me just that, not the miracle I'd asked for that day in his hospital room, but a miracle nonetheless, one that proved that while bodies may end, love does not. I closed my eyes, feeling the soft touch of love, and for the first time in a long, long time, I slept.

~Mary Carroll-Hackett

It Was Not Our Time

We all have a guardian angel, sent down from above.
To keep us safe from harm and surround us with their love.
~Author Unknown

I t was a dark, snowy and icy Saturday evening in December a number of years ago when my husband Richard and I were driving our SUV along Highway 53 in Ancaster, Ontario. We were on our way to his brother David's house for the evening. Our three children were with their friends and we were on our own for the night.

The traffic moved slowly due to the slippery conditions, hampered by blowing snow. A good amount of icy snow was on the ground and it kept coming. It was a terrible stretch of road that was often a tricky drive in bad weather.

Suddenly a large transport truck left its lane and headed straight toward us. It was going to hit us head-on. The only thing we could do was drive off the road, so we veered to our right to avoid the truck. We were out of control and travelled into and out of a large gulley right toward a very large and old tree. It had a huge trunk. I was looking right at it and yelled, "Oh God, help us!" Something would have to happen or we were going to smash our car right into that enormous tree trunk. I could see it all coming at my face. Richard was trying to control the car and turn it away from the tree trunk, but it was coming way too fast. To make matters worse, we also needed to avoid a big red fire hydrant just to our left.

I am not sure what happened next, but I felt us climbing the tree trunk with our front wheels and then jerking to the left very hard. So much was going through my mind. Were we going to roll the car or land on our roof? Would we survive? It was all very crazy and it happened in seconds, but it appeared to be happening in slow motion.

Richard grabbed me and I grabbed onto him, so we were both leaning into the middle of the front seat together. Just as we were leaning in, the windows broke on either side of us. We then violently and miraculously landed on all four wheels. The front window then shattered all over us from the force. Fortunately, we had on winter coats, hats and gloves, but our faces were still exposed. After checking ourselves quickly, we didn't find a single scratch, although we were both shaken and traumatized from our very close call.

We just sat for a couple of minutes to collect ourselves. We were shaking and I was in shock. I guess someone must have called the police, as they soon arrived. The officers looked around at our car and wondered how we survived being in a car with that much damage. They noticed the fire hydrant on the left and the huge old oak tree on the right and commented that it was impossible for a car to pass through the small space between them. We said we knew that and that is why we huddled in the middle of the car in case both sides of the car were sheered off. Our side windows certainly did shatter to pieces and our doors were smashed in on both sides.

The police officers saw bark missing from the tree trunk and also noticed a red paint streak along our roof from the front to the back. One officer pointed out that it matched the colour of the fire hydrant. Our roof must have scratched up against the hydrant when our vehicle was shooting by on its side, with two wheels in the air. We were so lucky that we landed upright on all four wheels instead of on the roof or side of the car.

Since we were only a few blocks from David's house, we limped our car over there (amazingly it still drove slowly) on that snowy cold night, with all of the cold air coming through our broken windows. We just wanted to get to the closest home and pretty much collapse.

We were immediately so thankful to God that we were alive and not hurt in any obvious way.

David and Francine opened their front door to find us getting out of a very battered vehicle. They were shocked at the sight of our car and could not believe we survived.

I tried to explain to them what happened, and could not really explain why we were not hurt given what we had just been through. I had seen that tree coming right at us, and for a moment I thought our lives were over. Sharing the story made me realize how lucky we were to survive and I thanked God over and over for taking care of us.

On the Monday after that awful Saturday night, Richard, a family physician, went to work at his medical office. One of his patients who made crafts of all kinds and had a beautiful store in a neighbouring town came in that day. She said that she did not know why, but a strong feeling had prompted her to bring Richard two white guardian angels to place on our Christmas tree for the upcoming holidays.

When Richard came through the front door of our house that evening, he pulled out those two guardian angels from inside some white tissue. He told me what his patient said and I cried tears of joy, thankfulness and gratitude. We did not say a word at that special moment, because we both knew! We had been saved by our guardian angels because it was not our time. And this gift of two beautiful angels from a patient who knew nothing of our accident was a sign that we are never alone in this world. I had screamed "Oh God, help us!" and He had. It was not our time.

~Karen Vincent Zizzo

31

The Green Signal

The magnitude of life is overwhelming.
Angels are here to help us take it peace by peace.
~Levende Waters

t was an uphill walk as I pushed the pram along in a daze. I blinked with sheer exhaustion. I couldn't remember when I had last enjoyed a whole night's sleep. It was so strange that it was deemed normal for new mums of small babies to have sleepless nights. I had lost count of the number of times I had been told by well-meaning people that these were the golden days of my life and I should be grateful for them. Feeling tired all the time didn't leave any space for feeling grateful. What was wrong with me?

My baby was asleep in the pram and I glanced down to see if the bags of vegetables and sundry groceries were secure. I hoped I hadn't forgotten anything. I couldn't go through this uphill climb again, twice in the same day.

It was getting windy again and I could feel sharp droplets of rain as I pushed my hair off my face impatiently. I struggled to pull the rain cover back on the pram, as the gusts of wind were making it tougher. I knelt down to secure the flap of the rain cover. I peered through the hazy plastic of the shield and saw that he was still asleep, his fists tightly closed. I felt an aching tenderness for him and tears stung my eyes. I brushed them away, feeling angry with myself. A flap pulled off as a sharp wind picked up again. I grabbed the hook of the flap and fastened it quickly. It would never do to let the rain go into the pram.

He was just recovering from a nasty cold and cough; it wouldn't do at all if he caught it again.

Satisfied that the rain cover stayed, I straightened up and resumed pushing the pram along the uphill footpath. There was a couple walking ahead who stopped at the pedestrian signal. I stopped and rubbed my eyes in confusion. I definitely needed a cup of hot tea when I reached home. I didn't think I would clear up the mess in the living room today. If he continued sleeping, maybe I could try to catch a quick nap. I wished I could just sleep for a whole day, maybe two days, maybe forever… I felt a tap on my shoulder.

"You can cross now, dear. The signal has turned green."

I blinked and turned to see an elderly lady smiling at me. Yes, the signal had turned green and was now turning red again. I had been lost in thought and missed it. I could see the couple ahead in the distance, they had crossed on time. I felt close to tears. This was definitely an overreaction. What was wrong with me? Was I losing my mind slowly?

I felt the lady's gaze on me as I turned back to her, feeling weary and lost. She was clad in a warm lime green duffel coat, a woollen hat covering her grey hair, her kind eyes crinkling at the corners as she stared at me, questioningly. She gazed intently at me and then looked at the pram.

"Lovely baby you have there," she said, smiling. Her voice was cool and calm like a softly flowing river. I grinned back faintly. Just as I was about to thank her and start walking again, she nodded her head and said very gently, "It will all get better. I know how tough it can be. I have been there. Believe me, it all gets better. Just hang in there, love."

And with that, she smiled at me once again and walked off. I stood still, staring after her. The wind lessened. A kind of calm stillness took its place.

It was like a great weight had just been lifted from my shoulders. I felt something like… dare I call it hope? I began to cross the road with my pram as the signal turned green. "You can cross now. The signal has turned green." Her words echoed in my mind. I realised their significance now.

It was like she knew. She had read my mind and knew my despair. It was like an angel stepping in and holding my hand. Just in time.

Sometimes that is all it really takes. In life's daily paths, we suddenly come across a kind word from someone who understands. I believe angels connect to us through real people, right on this earth, who are different from others in the most important way… they possess kindness and empathy. They see beyond themselves and care enough to stop and help.

My angel turned out to be right. It did get better. I had postnatal depression, which slowly wore off. Life returned to normal. I began to live again, cherishing the joy of being a mum to two such lovely kids. I never forgot my angel. She created the turning point. She helped me find the ray of hope at a time when all I could see was the endless dark tunnel. When all else fails, when we feel we are at the rock bottom level of anguish, I believe our lives can get touched by angels. A miracle can happen. The signal can turn green after all.

~Roopa Banerjee

32

Reflections of Hope in the Snowstorm

It only takes a thought and your angels will be there...
for although you may not see them, you're always in their care.
~Author Unknown

was homesick. My husband, Keith, was attending Utah State University in Logan, Utah. We lived eight hundred miles away from my parents and family back home in Northern California. We couldn't afford to go home for Christmas. We would just stay home in Hyrum, and have a simple Christmas with our baby, Ann.

Then a most unexpected gift arrived in a Christmas card: enough money for gas for the eight-hundred-mile drive home. We were so excited. Keith took time off from his part-time job and we packed the car. We had family prayer, asking humbly for safety and good traveling conditions.

We drove all day through Nevada, over the Sierras, to the west coast of California. Everything went well and we finally drove up the familiar driveway, honking the horn to signal our arrival. My family rushed out to greet us, welcoming us with love and Christmas cheer.

We celebrated Christmas in my childhood home, all of us together again for the first time in three years. My family rejoiced when we announced that we were expecting our second child in the spring.

All too soon, the time came for us to return to Utah. My parents gave us some money for gas. With tears and hugs, we started on our way. Hoping to make good time, we drove steadily through the day.

Toward evening, we arrived in Wendover, on the border between Nevada and Utah. Snow flurries swirled around the car. We stopped just long enough to fuel up the car. With no credit card and very little cash, we did not even consider staying overnight in a motel.

If the road and weather conditions were good, we had about two hours of driving to get to Salt Lake City. We thought if we could just make it to Keith's parents' home in nearby Bountiful that night, we could rest. Then we could go on to Hyrum in the morning, and he would make it to work on time.

We drove into the darkening night. Frantic flurries of snow swirled wildly about the car. Keith was having trouble seeing the road, as the headlights seemed dim. He pulled over, and got out to brush the snow away from them.

Then he climbed back into the driver's seat and told me the bad news. "We have only one headlight." A simple statement, but loaded with dread.

With another heartfelt prayer for safety and protection, we felt we had no choice but to head slowly out onto the nearly deserted freeway. Our car bravely slogged through the snowy darkness. We desperately tried to keep our eyes on the white line in the road, but it was vanishing quickly in the accumulating snow. We seemed to be all alone on that dark stretch of freeway. There was no traffic in either direction, and the visibility was near zero.

We knew that our parents were praying us safely through the night. We prayed too, for traction and safety.

Suddenly, out of nowhere, a semi-truck appeared, gaining quickly upon us. It splattered a spray of snow onto our windshield as it passed. Then it pulled into our lane, directly in front of our car. Our meager headlight reflected off the shiny silver doors on the back of the truck.

The driver could have sped ahead. Instead, he stayed right with us, lighting our way. The steady flurry of relentless snowflakes dashed against our windshield. The wipers could barely keep them brushed away. The white line of the road was no longer visible. We cautiously crept along, following the truck.

In those anxiety-filled moments, I felt our unborn baby kick for the first time! The miracle of new life growing within me filled us with wonder. We felt that there were angels protecting us that night, and there was a curious peace in our hearts.

Hours later, we reached the welcome streetlights and plowed roads of Salt Lake City. To signal our gratitude, Keith blinked our one headlight at the semi-truck driver in front of us. This man had stayed with us for more than 120 miles on that drive between Wendover and Salt Lake City. Our one headlight had reflected off the back of his truck as he had lighted our way in the dark night.

It turned out that this storm deposited eighteen inches of snow in twenty-four hours, closing the Salt Lake City airport for twenty hours. But we had traveled safely through the massive storm. We offered a heartfelt prayer of thanksgiving for this miracle.

As I gratefully closed my eyes at last that night, the images of the steadily blowing snow drifted before them. More importantly, though, my mind's eye fixed upon the reflection of the unseen angels and the semi-truck driver who had stayed with us, giving us hope through the darkest hours of that snow-filled night.

~Valaree Terribilini Brough

Angel with a Silver Belt Buckle

The wings of angels are often found on the backs of the least likely people.
~Eric Honeycutt

was riding in a car full of giggling, gossiping girls. It was a scorching hot July morning, the kind where the air sits on you like a heavy blanket. My friend's Oldsmobile was wheezing down the highway as usual, but the oppressive heat made "Gurtie the car" struggle. We had just crossed the border from Illinois into Wisconsin. Gurtie was giving the "take me out Coach" signal, but we were distracted by all the signs for cheese. Gurtie did not want to go on our annual canoe trip this year. She didn't care that we had been planning it since January. She decided to give up the fight.

We first lost control of the ability to accelerate and knew we had to pull over. It was one of those moments when time seemed to slow.

Nicole was able to pull the car over to the right shoulder before it totally died. All five girls piled out of the car to take a look under the hood. It was laughable, almost like it was scripted. You couldn't get a better scene of people pretending to know what they were doing. Nicole, familiar with Gurtie's temperament, grabbed a gallon of water from the trunk—she seemed to think the car was just overheating. It was at that moment that I suddenly felt compelled to bend down and tie my shoe.

Down at that level, I glanced under the car and noticed that Gurtie was actually on fire!

Flames licked upwards from the ground and the car's engine started to catch fire. I yelled to all of my friends, "The car is on fire!!" Nicole ran and attempted to get inside the car and move it. She thought that if she moved the car it would no longer be on fire. Kathryn grabbed Nicole's arm, trying to persuade her that the car was in fact on fire. Jenny hadn't moved or said one word—she froze in place watching it all unfold. And I was already way down the highway. I'd seen a lot of action movies—I wasn't waiting for the explosion. I ran far down the highway with my friend Sandy. I actually picked her up and carried her down the highway with me.

Nicole, Kathryn and Jenny were in serious danger at this point. Flames and smoke poured out from both sides of the hood. I remember saying, "Oh my God, Oh my God, someone please help." Not that a teenager saying "Oh my God" is anything new, they tend to say it every other sentence. But this time I was actually saying, "Oh my God, please help."

That was when God sent an angel to take care of us. I watched the orange semi-truck pull over on the southbound shoulder. The driver jumped out of his rig and crossed the road. He jumped the median, bobbing and weaving through the northbound traffic, and delivered a fire extinguisher.

He wasn't dressed in a superhero costume or flecked with gallant bits of gold. He wore a pair of cowboy boots and had a silver belt buckle. But he was definitely our guardian angel. God sent him to run across eight lanes of highway during the morning rush hour, and dive under the car to put out the flames.

After the fire was out, he wiped himself off and simply said. "Okay, be careful ladies." He saw that a car in our caravan had caught up to us and that we had people to help us. He gave us a wave and then ran back across the highway. We yelled thank you to him, but I doubt he heard us.

We would later be told by the insurance company that we were indeed very lucky that the car didn't explode and injure my friends standing next to it. God was there that day. God sent an angel.

~Kristen Margetson

Aunt Jeanne

Don't be dismayed at goodbyes. A farewell is necessary before you can meet
again. And meeting again, after moments or lifetime, is certain
for those who are friends.
~Richard Bach

Sometimes, if you're very lucky, you're blessed with a real-life guardian angel. For me, that angel was my Aunt Jeanne. Only ten years my senior, she was like the perfect big sister. For as long as I can remember, Aunt Jeanne was a vibrant, fun-loving, abiding presence in my life. She was my babysitter when I was a child, the person who helped me navigate the stormy seas of adolescence over tea and angel food cake, and the one who became a treasured friend as I grew into adulthood. She showed me how to put on make-up, shave my legs, and do the Locomotion. A whiz at crossword puzzles, she taught me her secrets. She nursed me through broken romances and fractured friendships, giggled with me over the latest schoolgirl gossip, and shared my frustration when things didn't go my way. She rejoiced in my accomplishments and propped me up when I failed. Aunt Jeanne was someone I could always rely on, as constant as the North Star. And, like a star, she lit up my life with her special light.

When the phone rang one sun-drenched morning in late spring, I had no way of knowing life was about to take an unwelcome turn. I saw Aunt Jeanne's name on the caller ID and realized that I hadn't talked to her in a while.

"Aunt Jeanne! It's so good to hear from you," I said, looking forward to one of our "catching up" chats.

"Darling, I have some news. Is this a good time to talk?" Her voice, usually upbeat and breezy, sounded flat. Something knotted in my stomach.

"Sure. It's always a good time to talk to you." I waited, trying to mask my sudden apprehension.

"I went to the oncologist today," she began, and I wanted to plug my ears so I wouldn't hear what she'd say next.

After a courageous, three-year battle with breast cancer, Aunt Jeanne had developed an inoperable liver tumor. She accepted the diagnosis with grace, assuring me that she'd fight this new battle with her characteristic strength, determination and positive attitude. But she admitted that the prognosis was not good.

A few weeks later, I was on a plane heading for New Jersey.

I spent the next month with Aunt Jeanne. At first, it was like old times as we laughed over the latest family gossip or reminisced about bygone days. Sometimes, I could almost convince myself that she was going to beat this, and everything would go back to normal. But as the insidious disease began to take its toll, our conversations turned to more profound subjects. We talked of the transiency of life and the promise of a better world beyond this one, a world free of sickness and pain. We talked about our children and grandchildren and shared our hopes and dreams for them. During those days, we became more than aunt and niece. We became friends.

Then, unexpectedly, Aunt Jeanne seemed to rally. I decided to fly home to Florida and get my life back in order. My husband, John, had booked us tickets to return to New Jersey in two weeks for our grandson's birthday, and I planned to spend more time with my aunt then.

My first day home was devoted to the mundane tasks I'd put on hold. I was vacuuming the bedroom when John poked his head in.

"Are you almost finished?" he asked. "We've got to get going if you want to make the four o'clock Mass."

I had completely forgotten what day it was. Being a late-riser, I preferred attending church on Saturday afternoons instead of Sunday mornings. I quickly changed clothes, pulled my hair into a ponytail, and jumped into the car. On the way to church, I fixated on all the things I had to do when I returned home.

With those thoughts whirling in my head, I followed John up the church steps. But the minute I walked through the door, my mind was suddenly whisked clean, as if a cosmic broom had swept away all the clutter, and I was overcome by an uncontrollable desire to light a candle for Aunt Jeanne. I found this unnerving, since I hadn't lit a candle in church since I was a child. As much as I tried to ignore it, the feeling grew stronger.

As we took our places in the pew, I glanced at my watch. It was almost four o'clock, and Mass would begin in a few minutes. I nudged John.

"I'm going to light a candle," I whispered, ignoring his raised eyebrows.

Kneeling before the rows of flickering votives, I touched the slim lighting stick to a flame and transferred the flame to an unlit wick. As I watched the ruby glass begin to glow, I was shocked to hear myself whisper, "Lord, please let this light her way home."

Where did that come from? But as I hurried back to the pew, I had the sinking feeling that I knew.

"What was all that about?" John whispered.

I tried to answer but could only shake my head.

When we arrived home, the answering machine was blinking. I hit the "Play Messages" button, steeling myself for what I expected to hear.

"Hi, Jackie." My uncle's voice sounded drained. "I hate to leave this on your machine, but I have a long list of people to call. Jeanne passed away around four o'clock. I was with her, and it was very peaceful. I wanted you to be one of the first to know."

"I was one of the first to know," I thought. "Aunt Jeanne made sure of that."

When I awoke the next morning, my first thought was that this would be the first day I'd spend on the planet without my Aunt Jeanne.

But I soon discovered that wasn't really true. She was with me when I sat down to do a crossword puzzle over my morning tea. She was beside me when I put on the bra she insisted I buy, telling me it was the most comfortable thing she'd ever worn. She was watching over my shoulder as I watered the plant she gave me when I moved to Florida. I heard her laughter in the tinkling of the wind chime she made for me from shells she collected in Sanibel. She was whispering in my ear when I sat down to edit my writing, and I felt her excitement when a summer thunderstorm blew in from the Gulf. When I finally lay down to sleep, I realized that there would never be a day without my Aunt Jeanne. And I know that someday we'll meet again, sit down over tea and angel food cake, and catch up on all that's happened since the day she became an angel.

~Jackie Minniti

Chapter 4

Hope & Miracles

Against All Odds

A Road Less Traveled

*Courage is not the absence of fear, but rather the judgement
that something else is more important than fear.*
~Ambrose Redmoon

When I lifted the flashlight I saw a pair of twinkling, hungry eyes like twin candles in the dark. Behind those eyes were dozens of others—a pack of wild coyotes had surrounded us. My heart stopped. We were dead for sure.

Hours earlier, I'd been rolling across the highway that stretched from Colorado to Oregon with my Labrador, Jack. We were on our way to a family camping trip when I decided to take a detour by an old Indian Reservation in Malheur County—"Malheur," I found out later, was French for "bad fortune."

I happily turned off the highway onto a secluded gravel road. I needed a little distraction. I'd been thinking about my boyfriend and how the romance had to end, but I was afraid to do it. How would I survive? How would I make it on my own?

My fears, I knew, were illogical. I'd survived way worse than a broken romance in my life. And I'd found independence when people told me it was impossible.

Fifteen years earlier, I was a nineteen-year-old engineman in the Navy, newly stationed in San Diego aboard the *USS McKee*. Two months into my duty, police found my broken, beat-up body at the bottom of the nearby cliffs—I'd been raped by a fellow serviceman, thrown off the seventy-five-foot edge, and left for dead. I woke up hours later paralyzed from the neck down—a quadriplegic.

"You'll never be able to feed yourself," doctors predicted. "Walking will be impossible."

But I believed in doing the impossible. So I spent the next fifteen years proving those doctors wrong. I worked hard to regain partial sensation, strength, and use of my arms and legs, enough to live independently. In the last few years, though, I had grown increasingly dependent on this boyfriend of mine, who encouraged it.

I'd lost faith in my own ability to survive on my own.

I was stuck—emotionally and mentally. And then, literally.

I drove fourteen miles along the gravel road, right into a thick pit of mud; my Subaru Outback wagon jolted to a stop.

I honked my horn but there was no one nearby to hear it. The nearest home was fourteen miles away.

I grabbed my wheelchair tires and frame from the passenger side, put my chair together, and set it outside my door. After transferring to the chair, I inspected the damage. The wheels had sunk halfway into the mud.

I slid to the ground and crawled to the tires to see if letting the air out would help. Nope. I put a towel under the wheels to get traction, then hit the gas again. Nope. Jack fetched sticks for me and I lay in the mud trying to dig the wheels out. By this time, the sun was setting and it was getting cold.

"Quad, how far do you think you are going to get with a little stick?" I said out loud. Jack cocked his head, as if to say, *not so far.*

"Jack, it's just you and me, buddy."

There was an outhouse 600 yards away. If we could get there, I figured someone would find us in the morning. I put on all the clothes I had in the car—a pair of pajamas over my shorts and a fleece pullover—and grabbed a can of Red Bull, a can of Ensure, a packet of tuna, a bottle of water, and dog food. With that and my flashlight, we set off toward the outhouse.

For an able-bodied person, it was a ten-minute walk. For me, it was a treacherous obstacle course that took two hours.

First, I had to get out of the mud. I slowly walked while pushing my chair, using it for support, until we got to solid ground. I didn't have function of my triceps, pectorals or hands, but I did have some biceps, traps, deltoids, and leg muscles... so we made it. It was fifty feet and it took us fifteen minutes.

I collapsed into my chair. Then we reached a ramp with a three-inch curb. I stood up and tried to lift my chair over it, but my legs gave way and I fell to the ground with the chair—and our precious stash—on top of me.

Jack looked down at me nervously. He'd been with me for five years and he knew I'd never done the ground-to-chair transfer before.

"I know, I know. But I can do this," I told him.

I inched my way onto the ramp, which gave me just enough height to reach the luggage carriers on my chair. In a complicated series of maneuvers that involved swinging one arm around the backrest, pushing with my feet, and stabilizing myself with my left arm on the luggage carriers, I was able to get myself back into my chair.

I felt ten feet tall! Jack barked in victory.

I found a mound of dirt nearby and used it as a little ramp to get onto the big ramp. We were doing great. Next, I had to get up that steep ramp. It had thick slats every few inches. I pushed myself backwards, uphill, an inch at a time. Every time I reached a slat, I rocked back and forth to get over it. That took another hour.

Finally, the road was clear to the outhouse. The sun had set so I turned on my flashlight. I could see the outhouse twenty-five feet away!

I could also hear the coyotes splashing and howling in the reservoir nearby.

"Don't worry, Jack. They won't bother us."

Ten feet later, Jack suddenly put his head in my lap and stuck to me like glue. He was afraid. I lifted up my flashlight. Dozens of unfriendly eyes stared at us, the closest pair shining a few feet away. *Oh my God.*

"Get away!" I yelled.

They had us and the outhouse surrounded. My first thought: *We're dead meat.*

My second thought: *There is no way they are taking us down!*

I lifted my feet to show the flashing red lights by my front wheels, hoping the coyotes would think it was fire, and we charged. I sped downhill the last fifteen feet with Jack by my side, straight into those glowing eyes. I cursed as loudly, as angrily, and as rudely as I could, and I kept cursing until we were safely inside the outhouse.

We spent the night there, with the coyotes howling outside our door.

At dawn, I gave Jack his food and I ate the tuna, and we ventured outside again. I pushed up a hill; my thumbs were bloody now. At the top, we reached a cattle guard—a grid of metal bars sticking up from the ground. How was I going to tackle that?

As I stared at the grid, a four-wheel-drive appeared in the distance, on the gravel road. I waved my arms wildly and burst into tears when I saw them coming toward us.

My rescuers, Bob and Bud, were out for some early morning bow hunting. They were shocked to see a woman in her muddied pajamas and wheelchair with her dog, in the middle of nowhere. I recounted the story as they bundled us into their truck, and they were amazed we'd survived.

I wasn't. I'd survived worse. And I knew now that I could go home and send that man packing.

~Dana Liesegang with Natasha Stoynoff

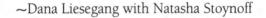

Let's Make a Deal

There's a story behind everything... but behind all your stories is always your mother's story...because hers is where yours begins.
~Mitch Albom, For One More Day

"You know, your aunt was always jealous I was picked that day," my mother would begin. A smile would spread across her face, ever the competitive little sister. "I was no more than twenty-one, and I had on the cutest bunny costume!" Her face would shine even brighter. "I made it myself, you know. I even had a tail. That day I won a year's supply of Reynolds Wrap and Super Glue."

She was speaking of her early 1970s appearance on the ever popular *Let's Make a Deal*. This tale was one of her favorite memories of all time, and I had heard it throughout my childhood far too many times to count. I never minded though; I loved to see her smile so radiantly.

It was now early October, five years and one week since I had last seen my mother smile. As I often did around that time of year, I spent much of my time reminiscing and flipping through family photos. This year in particular though, I desperately missed seeing her face light up and hearing the heartiness of her laughter. For the billionth time, I searched for family videos, but nothing new surfaced. My mother had hated to set foot in front of a still camera, let alone allow herself to be videotaped.

As I was flipping through a scrapbook I had just applied the finishing touches to, it dawned on me. I could search the web for old *Let's Make a Deal* clips. I mean, there are stranger things on YouTube, right? I grabbed my iPad and swiftly typed in "1970s Let's Make a Deal clips." Hundreds of options popped up, mostly boasting 1970s cars (which I knew my mother had definitely not won). But one bold blue line caught my eye.

"Let's Make a Deal Tickets." Tickets? Huh? I didn't know they were still filming. I clicked the link and found information for tapings in the Los Angeles area. I read through, and as the moments ticked by, I grew giddy and excited. Tickets! I entered my information, requesting tickets for a date a few weeks from then. I couldn't wait to tell my husband when he got home!

A few hours later, as Danny and I were sitting down for dinner, I heard my phone ping, alerting me that I had received an e-mail. I would usually disregard the noise during dinnertime, but for some reason I was drawn to the phone. I picked it up, and immediately saw the subject line, "Let's Make a Deal Tickets for Friday!" Friday? Tomorrow? Tomorrow! I checked my Google schedule and lo and behold, I had the day off.

"Babe, *Let's Make a Deal*, tomorrow! Let's make it happen!" I shouted.

"What?" he called from the kitchen. "I wish! I have to work. Are you serious?" I had told him about my previous search and he was as excited as I had been.

I forgot all about dinner and ran upstairs, searching for my newly acquired Halloween costume that would have to work for the next day. I slipped it on and looked in the mirror, finishing off my rather convincing pirate getup with an "Arrrrrg!"

"Verrry nice," Danny said, coming up behind me. He spun me around and hugged me. He held me gingerly for a minute and then said, "Something tells me your mom is responsible for this. I know it in my heart. Just you watch, you're gonna win. I know it."

The next morning found me standing on the back lot of the studio, waiting in line, dressed as a pirate, surrounded by a gorilla and a Greek goddess. There was nowhere else I'd rather have been.

In what felt like no time at all, we were herded into our seats and the cameras were rolling. The music, the people, the lights—it was beyond overwhelming, in the best possible way!

Everyone was encouraged to dance, and that we did. I moved with the music and waited for Wayne Brady to make his debut for the day. Within moments he appeared, and after some more silly moves, he quieted us down and got us into our seats.

"Alright, who's ready for our first game?" he asked after his hilarious introduction. Of course, we all screamed our heads off: "Pick me, pick me!"

"Alright, you," he said, pointing to a brunette woman dressed in bright yellow. "And... you!" he shouted, pointing at me. Me? Me!

I ran down the steps to join the two of them on stage. My ears were ringing, my face was flushed, and my heart felt like it was about to leap out of my chest.

"... Alright, you got it?" Wayne asked. I snapped back to reality. My head may have been nodding up and down, but I sure didn't catch the rules. Everything was going so fast. "Go ahead, which door would you like?" he asked, facing my opponent.

"Door number one!" she replied enthusiastically.

"Alright, Amy, that leaves you with door number two," he explained to me. Thankfully I now had some idea what was going on.

"Now, I'm going to offer you five hundred dollars for your doors, but you both must decide to sell or stay, even though you are ending up with different doors."

Okay, I'm getting it now, I thought. We looked at each other and decided to stay right where we were. "We're not selling!"

He offered us more money, but we weren't interested. Give us our doors!

Wayne revealed my partner's door. Behind it was a... ZONK! A cactus-shaped something or other, who knows? What was important was that was not my door! She took a seat, which left Wayne and me all alone.

"Amy, how are you feeling?" he asked me.

"I'm feeling great, how about yourself?" I quipped.

"I'm wonderful. I'm just hoping to give you something amazing like a brand new car." He smiled.

"I hope so too. I'm going to keep the door. Can I keep the door?"

"Well, you have to," he paused, laughing.

I blushed, but then I saw an opportunity. "You know, my mom was on this show almost forty years ago, and today I know she's with me, watching from up above. Thanks Mom." Tears filled my eyes and the back of my throat. I choked on my words and Wayne continued seamlessly.

"I'm sure she is. Now, do you want to see what's waiting for you behind door number two?"

"Yes!" I exclaimed.

"It's a... brand new car!"

My heart stopped. Or did it speed up? I'm not sure what happened. All I know is that my knees turned to jelly, yet still they helped deliver me into the driver's seat of my brand new Honda Fit. I gripped the steering wheel tightly, thanking the powers that be, and most especially my mother. I may not have seen her smile or heard her laugh that day, but I sure do know she was doing both in the purest and happiest of ways.

~A.B. Chesler

Twenty-Six-Ounce Miracle

We have to pray with our eyes on God, not on the difficulties.
~Oswald Chambers

can still see the hands on the clock: 1:05 a.m. on August 21, 1996. Why was the telephone ringing? I didn't wake up readily but Nancy was already halfway to the kitchen telephone. It was our son-in-law. "Mom, it's Brian. I have to take Elaine to the hospital. Can you come and stay with Jamie?"

Nancy was out the door and across Albuquerque in record time. What was wrong? Elaine's first pregnancy and delivery with Jamie were perfectly normal and this pregnancy had been normal too, until now. Why the emergency call?

With no notice and no preparation, Elaine had an emergency C-section at twenty-five weeks, versus the normal forty weeks. Fortunately, Elaine was in the best neonatal intensive care unit hospital in the region. Naturally she was devastated and depressed by what happened, but she was alive and physically well.

The baby was anything but normal. Survival was unlikely. One pound, ten ounces. 739 grams. Was pulling the plug a possible necessity? If the baby did live, it would face a long list of very likely serious problems common to preemies.

Blindness? Brain? Lungs? Joints? Infections? Heart? Blood? The baby had six of those seven common major problems. And it was so terribly tiny.

After the baby survived twenty-four hours Elaine said, "Brian, we haven't even discussed names. I can't think at all now, but the baby should have a name. Please name her." We could now attach our fervent prayers to her by name — Kimberly Diane.

Was it right or realistic to expect God to intervene in what appeared to be an essentially hopeless cause? We prayed for God's loving presence and support for Kimberly, for her parents and for the extended family. We prayed for God's will to be done.

Five days after her birth, Kimberly had lost twenty-three percent of her birth weight. She wasn't blind, but she had retinopathy and her eyes were fused closed. Both conditions resolved themselves without surgery. She had grade 1 brain hemorrhaging that absorbed itself without treatment. Her lungs were so undeveloped they could not be seen on the first X-ray. With her parents' written permission, Presbyterian Hospital tried a surfactant drug on this youngest and smallest preemie ever to be so treated. It worked.

At six days Kimberly's white count shot up, indicating infection and requiring her return to the ventilator. There was an abnormal hole in her heart, which healed by itself. She received eleven transfusions of her Uncle Marshall's blood, five cc (one teaspoon) each time. The list of her abnormalities and special treatments was seemingly endless.

Kimberly was three weeks old when Elaine was first allowed to hold her. Elaine sat next to the incubator with its "739 grams" label, and fed her. Jamie watched intently and gently touched her little sister's forehead.

Our church family was wonderfully supportive. Our pastor and friend, Leonard Gillingham, faithfully did the required medical scrubbing, donned the mask and gown and visited Kimberly. He was the grandfather of a preemie and keenly understood the situation. It was comforting to know that his granddaughter had survived, but of much concern that she still had serious problems.

Leonard took it upon himself to keep everyone in our church informed about Kimberly. He preached a special sermon on October

27 about Kimberly and her first two months of life. On November 17, Leonard announced in the worship service, "Tomorrow Kimberly Legan will leave the hospital and come home." The entire congregation erupted in clapping and cheering.

She did come home the following day at age ninety days, sixteen days before her original due date. She weighed just under four pounds. All was apparently okay, but it was also scary. Only two days earlier Nancy and I attended a special baby CPR class with Kimberly's parents. The responsibility of what to do in an emergency without the help of trained medical personnel was overwhelming.

Initially an in-home nurse, a physical therapist and an occupational therapist continued to care for Kimberly. She had made amazing progress in the first three months of her life but had a long way to go. And she did!

At age ten and eleven she played Upward Basketball at church better than most of the other girls. In high school, she is on the tennis team. As a junior she is president of her school's State Championship Show Choir and a nearly straight-A student.

Yes, Kimberly survived. She became a healthy child and a vibrant young woman, just as we had prayed seventeen years earlier. It now appears that normal adulthood is just around the corner.

I'm slow to declare miracles, but it appears that I'm watching a miracle continue to develop right under my nose.

~Dale N. Amend

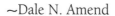

Divine Tapestry

Coincidence is God's way of remaining anonymous.
~Albert Einstein

When the pastoral search committee from the church in the mountains just north of us issued a formal invitation to hire my husband, Bruce and I had some concerns. Don't get me wrong. Everything about the church in Oakhurst, from the friendly people to the surrounding Sierras, seemed perfect. But our youngest daughter had several challenging heart problems. We weren't sure she would thrive at a higher elevation, so we made an appointment to see her doctor.

Dr. Jue had been Ashley's cardiologist for three years and he loved her as much as we loved him. We explained our possible plans as he examined Ashley.

"She seems to be pretty strong right now. We are a few years out from another surgery. You could give it a try and see how she does at that elevation," he mused.

"In other words, we need to rent not buy," I commented.

"Yes," Dr. Jue responded. Then with a thoughtful expression, he remarked, "Wait a minute." Still pensive, he held up his finger and hurried out of the room. He returned quickly, holding an 8x10 glossy of a gorgeous house. Laying it down in front of us he said, "This belongs to a colleague of mine at USC Medical Center. It's in Oakhurst and he's asked me to keep an eye out for possible renters. The house has 2,000 square feet with a trout pond in the front yard and a seventy-five-foot waterfall that pours right into the Fresno River in back."

"That's an amazing place. He probably figured you could find a doctor to rent it. I'm afraid the housing allowance for a pastor wouldn't come close to paying for a place like this," my husband said.

"I wouldn't be so sure," Dr. Jue responded. "I've known your family for three years. I'll put in a good word for you with Dr. Takahashi. He's looking for responsible renters and I think he would be hard pressed to do better than you."

We thanked the good doctor for his kindness and vote of confidence, but inside we both felt like the house was way out of our league, so we pretty much dismissed it as an option—until that evening.

The phone rang about 9:00 and a soft-spoken man introduced himself as Mike Takahashi. He explained how Dr. Jue had highly recommended us as renters, and he and his wife, Marcia, wanted to meet us the following Saturday. We agreed to go to meet this friendly man even though we figured our meager housing allowance wasn't near the amount his fabulous home deserved.

We spent the day with the Takahashis and fell in love with them. They showed us their house. Our kids fed the trout and played in the river. We talked about the church they attended in L.A. and about all the plans we had for the church we had been called to in Oakhurst.

At the end of the day, as we sat on the deck, Marcia stated, "We had a businessman from Sacramento express interest in renting the place. He offered us $1,400 a month, but I really want to rent this house to a family. There's so much for kids to enjoy here. I would like to see your family here. Are you interested?"

"Who wouldn't be?" I replied. "But, Marcia, the housing allowance the church is giving us is only $750. We know you can get much more than that."

"Can we have a minute?" she asked. As we nodded she and Mike disappeared into the house. In a few short minutes they emerged smiling ear to ear. "We'll take $750 with one request. We would like to be able to come and stay here with you on some weekends when we can get away from L.A."

"That would be great for us," I responded. "You get to enjoy your house and we would love to spend time with you!"

That was the beginning of a delightful friendship. We shared many dinners together enjoying the mountains and each other's company.

While we were there, it became clear that Ashley needed another heart surgery. There was a question as to whether the surgeons at our local children's hospital could handle a surgery with all the complexity of her multiple diagnoses. When Bruce called Mike for a listening ear, he got so much more.

"Dr. Jue sent me Ashley's file and her situation is unique and complicated. There are probably only two places in the world that could handle a surgery of this magnitude. One is in Minnesota and the other is UCLA. Both are practically impossible to get into, but you happened to know someone with influence. Hillel Laks at UCLA owes me a favor. He can return that favor by performing Ashley's surgery. Studying under Christiaan Barnard, Laks just happens to be the most prominent heart surgeon in the world right now."

Fighting back tears, Bruce could hardly respond. "How can I ever thank you?" Bruce asked.

"Seeing Ashley thrive will be thanks enough," Mike responded.

After a few stressful weeks of waiting, we had a surgery date with the renowned Dr. Hillel Laks. With the amazing surgeon's skill and a ton of people praying, Ashley sailed through her surgery.

As we visited her in cardiac recovery, an adorable young nurse commented, "This is, like, a miracle and stuff. Ashley is, like, getting better by the minute!"

I'm not sure we truly grasped what a miracle it was until a few days later. As Ashley was recovering, Bruce went down to the medical center bookstore at UCLA. My husband is an avid reader. I marvel that he decided to reduce his stress by reading complicated medical journals.

Bruce picked up a surgeon's journal published several years earlier. He read that the procedure to repair Ashley's set of the congenital heart problems had been performed 347 times and had succeeded zero times. Later Bruce asked Mike if the surgical procedure had been updated. He said no. The only difference between past surgeries and Ashley's was the precision of the surgeon, and she had been blessed with the best in the world.

If I live to be a hundred, I will continue to be awed by the amazing tapestry God put together on our behalf. If the church hadn't called us to pastor we would not have needed to visit Dr. Jue. Then we would not have needed a house to rent in Oakhurst. We would not have met Dr. Mike Takahashi, one of the few men on the planet who could have gotten Ashley a surgery with one of two doctors in the world who could save her life. What a miracle!

~Linda Newton

The Box

Fate laughs at probabilities.
~Edward George Earle Bulwer-Lytton

'm not sure how long I sat there staring at the e-mail. It may have been a minute, it may have been an hour. It was a short message—only three sentences, fewer than fifty words, but I knew it would change everything for me. I was suddenly hearing a voice that had been silent in my life for seventeen years. Until now. Somehow, I had my Amy back.

Even after nearly two decades apart, I could hear her laugh, smell her hair, feel her presence. As the shock and surprise eventually yielded enough to allow rational thinking, the words and wisdom of my late father inexplicably came to mind—sometimes things don't turn out the way you plan.

For the last year my life had been changing at lightning speed. An unexpected phone call on an ordinary Friday led to the abrupt end of my twelve-year marriage. This was merely the opening act of weeks of pain, frustration, and arguments. Children, family, and friends were notified, and I found myself packing for the move that would usher in the rest of my life, whatever it held. That's when I found the box.

It was a square cardboard box, which had apparently been pushed to the back of my now-empty closet. I opened it to discover remnants of my childhood and college days—old awards and certificates, cards, letters, photos, and a small ring.

The ring. I held it in my hand and stared at it for several minutes.

It was familiar, but why? Finally, a long-closed door in my memory opened, and I remembered. I gasped out loud—not an exclamation, but a name—"Amy." Yes, the ring belonged to Amy.

I suppose nearly everyone has a memory of "the one that got away," and Amy was mine. After meeting in junior high, we became best friends in high school, spending our days and nights talking about life and fate. A few years later, we decided to risk the friendship for a chance at love, and we began dating. By college, we were engaged, with a wedding and a lifetime of happiness within reach. But fate had different plans, and we eventually parted ways. As Dad always said, sometimes things just don't turn out the way you plan.

I continued to stare at the ring and reveled in the unexpected trip down memory lane. As I began to repack the contents of the box, I realized I couldn't simply pack the ring away. It belonged to Amy and I needed to return it to her. I had not heard anything about her for years, but the last information I had put her thousands of miles away—and married. Suspecting that the re-emergence of a former fiancé after so many years might be disruptive, I reached out to a mutual friend to ask if I could simply mail her the ring and let her handle getting it back to Amy. So I e-mailed the friend to get her address, and briefly explained my circumstances. She immediately replied, and assured me that I could contact Amy without disrupting her life.

And that's when it happened. In a blink of an eye, I had my best friend back.

A brief e-mail led to another, then another. Within a day, pages of e-mails were exchanged, as we caught up on our seventeen years apart. I learned that Amy was also going through a divorce, having just filed the paperwork a few days before. I learned that we were both in the same line of work. I learned that she was living about 2,000 miles away from me, but ironically, she was minutes away from a town I'd be visiting in a few weeks. I learned about the winding path her life had taken over the years. I learned I was still in love with her.

E-mails gave way to texts, which turned to daily phone calls, leading to a surreal reunion a few weeks later. I don't remember much of the conversation from that night. I remember laughing. I remember trying to keep my heart from bursting out of my chest. I remember feeling at home again.

Over the following weeks and months, we marveled at the miraculous timing of all of it. How could both of us, with zero contact for almost two decades, come back together as we did? How could we be going through simultaneous divorces after we'd each been married for more than a decade? What were the chances of finding the box at that precise moment in time, along with the ring, forgotten dreams, and a mutual friend to connect the final missing piece?

A little while later, I found myself at a secret lunch with Amy's parents. For the second time, I asked for their permission to marry their only daughter. For the second time, they agreed. As I left the lunch, I assured them there would not be a third time. I was being given a second chance that few ever receive, and I wouldn't waste it. Not today, not tomorrow. Not ever.

Several months later I stood in front of family and friends exchanging vows of marriage with the love of my life. She was no longer my ex-fiancée or "the one that got away." She was now simply my wife. My best friend. My soul mate. My Amy.

Life can be a puzzle. At times, it can seem cruel and unyielding. But then there are the moments when the wonder and magic of it are almost too miraculous to fathom. Whether guided by luck, fate, or divine intervention, somehow we find our way to the place we belong.

And as it turns out, Dad was right. Sometimes things don't turn out the way you plan.

Sometimes, they turn out even better.

~Rob L. Berry

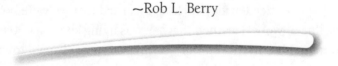

Against All Expectations

A difficult time can be more readily endured if we retain the conviction
that our existence holds a purpose—a cause to pursue,
a person to love, a goal to achieve.
~John Maxwell

n a small Connecticut town, one August morning in 1988, summer ended early for me. I stood over a load of clean laundry piled on my bed. As I started to fold a towel, warm from the dryer, I heard the front door open and the recognizable sound of flip-flops slapping against the soles of my daughter's feet. My chest tightened. I wondered what she wanted from me this time. She climbed the stairs and settled on the corner of my bed.

"Mom," Myra's voice sounded edgy. "Would you take the kids?"

I stopped folding, straightened up and studied my twenty-three-year-old daughter. She wore no make-up. Her T-shirt was stained and ripped. She swiped at her cheek.

"I have a court date and my lawyer said I'll probably go to prison. Will you take the girls?"

My breath caught in my throat. Her addiction to drugs had hurled our family through a vortex of lies, suspicion and fear. She began using drugs at a party in her teens. Somehow her friends who used drugs with her skipped the addiction part. Not Myra. Our family had cycled from crisis to crisis over the past eight years. It had worn me down.

I'd seen the neglect of her children. I suspected she shoplifted. "So multiple larceny charges finally caught up with you," I thought.

"Yes, of course." I didn't need to discuss this with my husband. Ken and I had talked about raising our grandchildren, always circling around to the parental guilt we felt. Where did we go wrong?

I silently asked God to make me brave.

"We'll need legal custody." I emphasized the word "legal."

"Why?"

"Doctor visits, insurance, school admittance…"

There was an icy silence. Finally she nodded and gave into her sorrow, letting tears drip down her face. She let me hug her and then she left.

Three days later, I stared at my daughter and her husband, Ted. They glared back. I told myself they were the parents of my grand-daughters and I should feel some compassion. But I felt nothing.

They dragged their feet through the doorway into the attorney's office. The heavy oak door clicked shut behind them. I stayed in the waiting room with the little girls, afraid that Ted and Myra's anger would cause them to storm out without signing the papers. Had I pushed too hard?

At first, the voices from inside the office sounded soft. I relaxed a little. Then angry protests filtered into the waiting area. Expletives. I glanced nervously at the three-year-old. She sat next to me and ripped pages out of a magazine, turned upside down. The baby slept in my arms.

A strong female voice, one that overrode the invectives, spoke from behind the office door. "You're both going to prison. The state, not your mother, is taking your children away from you. Your children will end up in foster care with no guarantee of staying together." There was a long pause. A strangled sound. Was someone weeping? "That's a fact. You can either deal with the state, or you can deal with your mother. What's it going to be?"

Silence. What was happening? I looked again at the three-year-old, still tearing pages apart. What was taking so long? The baby slept. And I wept.

The door opened and Myra and Ted stumbled out. They'd signed the papers.

A week later Myra began to serve a reduced sentence in a women's correctional facility.

With no time to adjust, Ken and I went from being empty nesters to having a house full of diapers and baby food. Our family room became a playroom. A highchair and booster seat were fixtures at our table. Toys cluttered the floor, locks were affixed to cabinet doors and plastic plugs pushed into electrical outlets.

Three months later, Ted entered a detox program. Myra completed her sentence and wanted the same hospitalization detox program as Ted. But she was denied, then unexpectedly accepted, as though overruled by a higher authority.

After Myra completed detoxification, she and Ted joined an intensive twelve-week outpatient recovery program. During a weekend visit, Myra asked if she and I could talk privately. We headed outside for a walk. The winter chill crept under my jacket. I shuddered and quickened my pace. Myra strode beside me, giving no indication that the temperature had dipped into the mid-twenties.

"I'm going to change, Mom. I mean it. This time I really mean it."

I nodded. I'd lost count of how many times she'd said that. I remained skeptical.

The recovery program was an experiment. Fifteen addicts took the challenge to get clean and sober.

"The counselors in our program warned us that couples don't make it if they stay together." Myra's breath steamed against the cold as she talked. "One always pulls the other down. So I told Ted, if he uses, I'm leaving him. Recovery is the only thing that matters right now."

"I want more than anything for you to stay in recovery and live a purposeful life. Then we'll celebrate your girls going back to you."

Privately, I prayed. I begged. I pleaded with God for Myra and Ted's recoveries from addiction.

Out of the fifteen clients in the intensive recovery program, three made it. Four committed suicide. Most went back to using, chained to their addictions. With only three recoveries, the failed program shut down at the end of twelve weeks. However, against all expectations, two of the three who remained in recovery were Myra and Ted.

Two years later, on Father's Day, our family gathered for a private Reconnection Ceremony at our church. Ken and I stood in the sanctuary, facing the altar and Myra and Ted stood a few feet away, across the aisle. Myra looked straight ahead. The two little girls, wearing pretty dresses with bows clamped in their hair, stood between Ken and me.

After our pastor recited the story of the Prodigal Son and the joy of reunion, he lit a small candle from a lighted taper on the altar. He handed the candle to the older granddaughter. She walked over and passed it to Myra and stood with her parents, stretching her fingers inside her daddy's hand. I bit my lip to control bittersweet tears. Next the pastor removed a bouquet of flowers from the altar, handed them to our younger granddaughter, who joined her parents after she gave them to me. I glanced at Myra. She stood with her head lowered. One hand covered her eyes and her shoulders trembled. My heart went out to her.

The pastor held up his right hand for the benediction.

"The Lord bless you and keep you. The Lord make His face shine upon you and be gracious to you. The Lord look upon you with favor and give you peace. Amen."

Myra blew out the candle and we sobbed in each other's arms. The crying spread like a giant wave, and included the pastor. That day, Myra and Ted drove home with their children, a reunited family. And Ken and I became grandparents again.

Epilogue:
This year, Myra and Ted celebrated twenty-seven years of marriage and twenty-five years of recovery. Against all expectations. For that, I have endless gratitude.

~Judy Buch

Coming Home

Hope is faith holding out its hand in the dark.
~George Iles

Rushing out the door with backpack, kids' bags, and a time clock ticking in my head left me too frazzled to notice another passenger quietly jumping into the back of our Dodge Ram.

Robby faithfully did his duty as the eldest. "Mom, everyone is buckled up. We can go now." And off we went.

With a sigh of relief I crossed Interstate 59, relieved that I wouldn't be late for my classes at USM. Finishing my degree while raising three kids got a little wild some days, but I knew that when I finished and started teaching it would be well worth the effort. I was happy that my husband Glen R. would be home Friday to give me some help.

Smiling contentedly as the kids laughed, I pulled into the babysitter's yard and started to unload the crew.

Melinda let out a squeal. "Mama, Kitty Karen just jumped out of the back of the truck! Quick, go get her!"

"Sweetheart, don't worry, she won't go far! As soon as I get home this evening we'll find her. Kitty Karen will be okay." I comforted the kids, whose frightened big eyes looked to me for assurance.

Glancing at my watch, I quickly kissed my babies goodbye and hurried to pick up my carpoolers on the way to school. Although I enjoyed my classes, I was glad when the time came to scoop up the kids and head home. Little did I realize that the morning's events would come back to haunt me.

"Mom, look at my picture! It's all of us! Look, there is Daddy. See his beard."

"That's great, Robbo. Ryan, what did you make today? Jeri, thanks so much for letting them paint. They really love it. I guess we had better find Kitty Karen and head home. Did you guys see her when you were outside playing? No? Well let's pack up. I'm sure she isn't far."

Melinda sat in the front and helped me scour the neighborhood. As we looked and looked with no sign of Kitty Karen, I got a sinking feeling in my stomach.

Where in the world could she be? I prayed, "Lord, please help us find her. The kids will be sick if she's lost." I was really worried, but I didn't want the kids to know.

We drove around the same streets over and over, but no beautiful fluffy white cat with jeweled eyes of blue and green came running. My heart sank lower and lower as I berated myself for rushing off to class instead of looking for her right when she got away.

I tried to keep everyone's spirits up as the stars twinkled in the evening sky and we gave up looking for the day. "We'll surely find her tomorrow, guys! It's going to be okay. Don't cry now. We'll ask God to take care of her for us tonight."

After dinner and bath time, our bedtime prayers were filled with pleas to keep Karen safe and help us find her the next day. Unfortunately, we said those same prayers the next night, and the next, and the next. Days turned to weeks. We searched and searched, but no Karen.

I started looking less and less. Finally, I faced the realization that our prayers would not be answered. I tried to keep the children busy with activities and distracted them when they wanted to talk about Karen and pray for her return. I didn't want them to have to learn the hard lesson that prayers are not always answered in the way that we would like. They were too young for this harsh reality.

One day flowed into the next. With three kids, a husband, and a dog, it was never boring! Thankfully the kids prayed for Karen less and less. I dodged the bullet of having to explain to them why God didn't hear their prayer and answer.

A year sped by and out of nowhere Melinda said, "Mama, let's pray for Kitty Karen to come home."

What in the world would I tell her after all this time?

"Melinda, let's pray that Kitty Karen has found a good new home. We can pray that God will help us find a different cat that needs a home, too. How about that?"

"No, Mom," Melinda declared with conviction. "I am going to pray that Karen comes home!"

"Okay, sweetie, but you know it has been a long time and Karen may have another home by now."

Melinda looked at me with her big, brown eyes and said, "Mama, you know God can do anything!"

"Yes, honey, He sure can. Let's pray."

The next morning, around ten, I was washing dishes and heard a faint scratch on the front door. Almost afraid to hope, I called Melinda and we opened the door together. There stood our Kitty Karen. Her once beautiful white hair was matted with dirt and her paws were sore and bleeding, but she was home.

~Jan Penton Miller

A Bit of Dad

If I keep a green bough in my heart, then the singing bird will come.
~Chinese Proverb

My dad taught us the magic of bird watching when my brother, sister and I were kids. We would huddle around the window or sit on the patio and watch the birds at one of his many bird feeders. We always had a bird book handy to identify any we didn't recognize. As we grew and had children of our own, Dad continued the tradition with his grandchildren. He would tell them all about the yellow finches, house finches, cardinals, those ornery blue jays, etc.

We continued this tradition with our children. My sister and I both live in areas where we have open spaces, trees, and fields, even though I live in the heartland and she on the East Coast. We both have multiple bird feeders and take delight in feeding the variety of birds they attract. Every time dad would visit he would say to both of us, "I can't believe that you cannot attract Baltimore Orioles."

We would respond with, "Well, it's not because of lack of effort. They just don't seem to want to come." He would shake his head and tell us to try again next year. Try again we did, over and over, never giving up that hope of attracting Dad's favorite, the Baltimore Oriole. After fourteen years, it seemed as though it would never happen.

On Easter weekend of 2011, my dad passed away, and we were all heartbroken. A week after, I was sitting in our office watching the birds at our feeders and thinking of him. Lo and behold, not one, but two Baltimore Orioles appeared in the small tree outside our window. I was so excited that I thought, "I need to call Dad; he will never believe it." Then I was brought back to reality, and realized that phone call would be impossible to make, so I called my sister. Upon sharing my joy, she started to cry and said that her family also spotted their first Baltimore Orioles that very same day.

In the midst of a broken heart, I felt pure joy at this gift God sent to remind us of our dad. He would have had such a smile on his face knowing that we could enjoy his special bird. Every year that has followed his passing, the Baltimore Orioles have returned and given my sister and me a little bit of our dad back. We are truly blessed!

~Beth Huettner Olsen

Can You Hear Me Now?

I may never know when an answer to prayer is going to arrive, but I know that God will never fail me.
~Suzanne Elizabeth Anderson, Waiting with God

The church bulletin advertised a women's retreat in the mountains of Westmoreland County, Pennsylvania. The intent was to take us away from our hectic lives to bask in God's presence for two whole days.

The noise at home had grown so intense that I could no longer hear myself think, let alone hear from God. I needed to get away so I made a beeline for the registration desk.

When the weekend finally arrived and we pulled up to the retreat center, I savored the rolling hills and lush, green trees that filled the horizon. I watched as two swans glided along the pond that sat peacefully nestled at the base of the property. Inside the resort, I found a bed with clean, crisp sheets waiting for me. Even my meals were prepared.

While all these things were a treat, it was not why I went. I had a specific goal in mind: I attended so I could study God's Word and demand some answers. You see, for years, I had felt compelled to write a book. This yearning had begun to intensify in me but it didn't seem to be the right time. I had a home to care for and four children under the age of five. I certainly did not have time to write a book.

Over the course of the two days, I enthusiastically took notes during the sessions, trying to absorb all the lessons. We learned about the Israelites and how they waited forty years to reach the land God had promised them. Was this why I was here, to find out I'd have to wait forty years? I certainly hoped not.

In my alone time, I sneaked off to pray. I begged God to reveal the answers to my questions: Should I write this book? If not today, someday… or was this a selfish yearning to make my mark? I needed some kind of sign.

Several sessions and lots of quiet moments passed. Still nothing. I felt frustrated knowing I would return to the noise and chaos at home with no answers. However, I continued to participate, thankful to be among such lovely women.

Our final assignment for the conference was to find a new prayer partner. We were given a card with half of a picture on it. Our task: to find our card's mate. Once found, we were told to introduce ourselves to the cardholder, share a prayer request, and agree to pray for this person for the upcoming month.

I wandered about the room for a short while, checking first with the ladies I had already met. None of them matched my card. Then finally, I found her. My prayer partner was an older woman with kind and caring eyes. We greeted one another, and I introduced myself: "My name is Darla Grieco. I am married and have four small children. I am a stay-at-home mom, and my husband has his own business. And, that's about it." I smiled nervously.

She nodded, "Okay. How can I pray for you?"

I hesitated, but since I still had no answers to my questions about writing, I thought I'd pass this prayer assignment on to my new partner. For several minutes, she listened intently as I poured out my desire to write a book and all the doubts I had. I ended by telling her, "I think God put this story in my heart, but it just doesn't make sense right now. I want God to give me a clear yes or no if this is something He wants me to do."

Although I didn't know this woman, I saw a reassuring smile spread across her face. Then, she spoke ten words that would change my life forever: "My name is Joyce Hart. I am a literary agent."

Joyce has been my mentor and a constant source of encouragement ever since!

~Darla S. Grieco

Chapter 5

Hope & Miracles

Divine Intervention

Heavenly Voices

Your talent is God's gift to you. What you do with it is your gift back to God.
~Leo Buscaglia

'll never forget the moment Plácido Domingo first kissed me. It was the spring of 1996 at the New York Metropolitan Opera and I was nervous — to be singing Sieglinde in Wagner's *Die Walküre* for the first time and also to be working with the Three Tenors legend.

Plácido was singing the role of Siegmund, Sieglinde's lover and — alas, as fate would cruelly have it — her twin brother. So as you can imagine, my character sang all about love, passion, and heartbreak, and she wasn't demure about it. When is opera ever meek and mild?

In one scene, I had to faint in Plácido's arms as he tenderly stroked my hair and face — that helped my nervousness. And then came The Kiss. Timed to the beat of the music, the orchestra built up, lingered on a chord… and our lips met. I remember how Plácido moved toward me on opening night for The Kiss. In that moment, I wasn't Deborah Voigt the soprano anymore. I was Debbie Voigt from suburban Illinois, thinking: *How did I get here? How did I get so lucky?*

But it wasn't luck that put me on the stage that night, or gave me a career that took me around the world, singing for presidents and princes. It took a tremendous amount of hard work and belief in the natural gift God gave me — a belief I didn't always have and nearly lost, if it hadn't been for a moment of divine intervention.

My parents say I practically came out of the womb singing.

Grandma Voigt owned a vinyl LP of the *My Fair Lady* soundtrack when I was a toddler, and by age three I'd memorized every word the flower girl sang—with a cockney accent, I might add. I'd dress up in Grandma's worn-out apron and her Jackie Kennedy pillbox hat with the netting on front, stand in the center of the living room, and happily belt it out for the family:

"Jusst you 'ait, Enry Iggins, jusst you 'ait!..."

I loved putting on my pretend costumes and performing; it filled me with joy. I couldn't articulate it then, but it had something to do with the power of the music and feelings for both singer and listener. To my little heart, it was a sacred exchange.

My parents applauded politely, but didn't quite know what to make of their pint-sized diva. As strict Southern Baptists, they believed that singing was for, from, and because of God and should only be used to glorify Him. To them, that meant singing church hymns, not Broadway show tunes about star-crossed lovers. That I *enjoyed* doing it so unabashedly was also worrisome to them. I'm sure it came across as very... *prideful*.

"Pride Goeth Before a Fall," our pastor at Prospect Heights Baptist Church used to sermonize, in his booming voice. It was a proverb my parents never tired of quoting.

Sure enough, by age five, my zest for performing was rerouted to the children's choir at church. There, I found ways to channel my love of singing into hymns like "His Eye Is on the Sparrow"—which I liked very much, and sang with all my heart knowing I had a higher, nobler purpose.

But... the contraband music tugged at me as the years went by.

When I was ten years old, my parents gave me a portable record player for Christmas, with the caveat that I could only play "appropriate" music. I wasn't sure what the boundaries of secular/non-secular were, but I managed to sneak some Donny Osmond onto my Philips portable. He was a nice, God-loving boy, I explained to my parents, even if he wasn't Southern Baptist. They allowed it.

In the early Seventies, as I was entering my teen years, I discovered the creamy, dreamy voice of Karen Carpenter. I played and sang her mellow ballads at home on the piano, and my parents didn't protest. She was a good girl, not one of those wild, unwashed, hippie types who had taken over and sang about sex, drugs, and rock and roll.

Then, in seventh grade, the overprotective wall my parents so carefully constructed was blasted to bits. My music teacher in school announced we were to study The Who's rock opera *Tommy* in class. She carefully lowered the turntable needle onto the song "Acid Queen," and my virgin ears and senses exploded. *What was this?*

I decided not to tell my parents about my introduction to Roger Daltrey—I wanted to listen to more. After The Who, there were others. And through my music teacher and my own exploration, I learned there was artistry, beauty and yes—even God, in many types of music. And that a rollicking rock tune or a toe-tapping musical theatre number could be noble in their own way because they expressed and shared the human experience.

One afternoon, around the time of my revelations, I thought I was alone in the house. I went to the piano and dusted off one of my beloved show tunes and began to play. I pounded the keys and sang with gusto, throwing myself into the music with abandon. I hadn't sung at home like that since my *My Fair Lady* gig. I was exhilarated, transported…

…until I heard my father's footsteps coming up the stairs, heading straight for me.

"Who," he asked, "do you think you are?"

I froze. I'm not sure of his exact words or intent, but I remember how I felt: ashamed. For months after that, I was heartsick and didn't play and sing like that again—as if a part of me had died.

Then one morning, I woke up earlier than usual. The dawn was peeking through my bedroom curtains and the house was quiet. That's when I heard a voice, *The* voice—not in my head, but out loud in my room. It was deep, authoritative, and unmistakable: *You are here to sing.*

I sat up in bed and looked around; no one else was in the room. I pinched myself; I wasn't asleep and dreaming. I knew who that voice was, I just *knew*. God spoke to me that day and firmly set me back on my path toward a destiny I knew to be mine since I was a child.

I was meant to sing, He said.

I was meant to sing out loud, unashamed, and sing songs that had meaning to me and brought people together. From that day onward, I never doubted my choice in music again.

God's words and the faith that I had in them led me to the Met stage that night, and into Plácido's arms for his enchanted kiss.

I never heard God's voice again. But forty years later, it's like I heard it only yesterday.

~Deborah Voigt with Natasha Stoynoff

All the Luck I Need

Luck has a peculiar habit of favoring those who don't depend on it.
~Author Unknown

t's not a story I've told before, not even to many members of my family, but I think about it every anniversary of the attack on the World Trade Center. It's a story about good timing and plain dumb luck, and how a single seemingly irrational decision can change your life.

A number of years ago my day job was with a software company. It was a great little company. Nice people, fun work. Everyone worked hard to get us on the map. The technical people were very bright. Not being that bright myself, I looked after sales.

We went to all the trade shows and managed to have more fun than most other people there. And none of it involved booze, flirting or staying out past ten o'clock. We just loved what we were doing.

Then one day a new customer appeared—at the time one of the biggest software companies in the world. They liked what we were doing so much they wanted to buy the company, even though it wasn't for sale. Eventually they made an offer that no one could refuse (this was before the dot-com technology bubble broke, and people were paying stupid amounts of money for software companies), and in the beginning of 2001 they arranged to buy the company.

As luck would have it, since we were such a small company, there were only two of us in sales—the president and me. The president decided early on that he would be leaving his newly sold company with a sack of cash in pursuit of fresh challenges. That left me.

The new owners decided they needed someone to run the new operation, and offered the job to me. To go with the job, they were going to make me their newest vice president. The position came with a bigger salary than I may ever see again, stock options and the works.

The new owners all talked about their private airplanes and personal helicopters, or the multimillion-dollar homes they were building for their very early retirement. There were weeklong seminars in Tuscany and Paris, and bonuses that were bigger than what most people paid for their houses. They even announced before I had said yes that I was their new vice president.

I hemmed and hawed for a while. I wasn't sure I wanted to stay on without my friend, but it isn't every day you walk away from a job as vice president of the fourth largest software company in the world.

Still, that's what I did.

It sounds stupid now, but I wasn't entirely sure why. I vaguely thought the job wouldn't be much fun, and the people I would have been working for seemed a little too sharp for their own good. Eventually I'd likely have to move to California, which is nice but isn't home.

My friend the former president said I was welcome to join him in his new venture. So with a leap of faith, I said so long to the giant golden carrot dangling before me and instead went with my friend to pursue an uncertain future.

About six months later I watched the unimaginable as the World Trade Center crumbled to dust with so many people inside.

When the dead were finally given names, I realized that one of them was the new senior person in the office where I had worked. He had been offered my job after I left. He had been on a company seminar in the restaurant at the top of the World Trade Center, and managed a brief cell phone call to a loved one before he died.

Would that have been me? Who knows? Maybe, maybe not. It's not something I really want to think about too much, especially since he had taken the job that I turned down.

As for me, on 9/11 I know exactly where I was. After watching that horrible morning unfold on TV, my wife and I kept a noon appointment for an ultrasound, where I saw my unborn first son curled up and oblivious to the terrible things that were going on in the outside world.

I'm not a big believer in fate or miracles, but I have never underestimated the power of luck. And if that's the last bit of good luck I ever have in my life, you won't hear me complain.

~Stephen Lautens

The Lucky Strike

It was possible that a miracle was not something that happened to you,
but rather something that didn't.
~Jodi Picoult, The Tenth Circle

Things were looking really good. My father, Jeff, was on a mini-break of sorts, enjoying the back end of his two weeks of freedom between old and new jobs. My mother's lupus had gone into remission the previous year and she had successfully shaken off all of the heavy-duty prescriptions that had kept her groggy but afloat during her years-long flare-up. Now she had tons of newfound energy and was putting it into opening her own business, a gift shop and café, something she had always dreamed of doing.

The business had been open for two weeks, and it was already slowly but surely building up a small, loyal customer base. Even with most things up and running there were always a hundred more little projects to do to get the building fitted out as my mother had planned. Being a handy kind of guy to have around, Dad was always running to The Home Depot down the hill from their house, picking up tools and lumber, bathroom and light fixtures, plumbing and electrical components.... You name a job and he was on top of it, flexing his constructive muscles and getting things done.

On this particular day, he just needed to make one quick stop at the store before heading over to the café. He packed his purchases away in the trunk of his relatively small SUV, buckled up and made his way across the parking lot toward the street. There was a traffic light set up to make sure no one had to take any chances trying to turn out onto Lancaster Avenue, one of the busier streets in an area crisscrossed by busy streets. The light was red when my father pulled up, the first in line to leave the lot.

The thing about my dad is that he has always been a very patient, very cautious driver. He never runs yellow lights or switches lanes on the highway unless there's a really good reason. He always signals his intention to turn and never gets stressed out by heavy traffic. And he certainly never gets mad when some less-conscientious driver cuts him off. Not even a grumble. A wavy, almost cartoonish "whoa!" is just about all you'll get out of him after one of those close shaves. He's just not the type.

Dad was watching for the signal to turn green, not creeping up like so many of us do, myself included, but waiting patiently as ever. When the light changed, he made his way into the intersection to make the left turn that would take him to my mother and his latest café project. But there's this saying, you may know it: "Man plans and God laughs." My dad didn't make it to the café that day.

The woman in the minivan had just about had enough of the three rowdy little boys in her back seat. They had been carrying on the whole ride, and after a while she didn't want to hear any more of their monkey business. The light had been green when she turned around to scold them. She must have just missed it turning yellow in the near distance.

The force of the impact on my father's side of the car was so strong that it flipped the whole vehicle over, rolling it two and a half times before it finally settled on its side. The driver's side.

When the EMTs arrived my dad was already trying to work his way out through the car's shattered sunroof. He had already done a quick assessment of all his limbs, making sure nothing was broken. The EMTs helped him the rest of the way out, marveling over the complete absence of any injuries more significant than the few small scrapes he had gotten from some broken and airborne glass. The air bags hadn't even inflated, making the whole situation that much more impressive, his intactness that much more mind-boggling.

"I didn't want to go to the hospital because I felt fine, but I could just hear your mother's voice in the back of my head yelling at me. 'Don't be stupid; go get checked out. I don't want you taking any chances.'"

The EMTs took my dad to the local hospital. Pretty soon my mother arrived on the scene.

My mother Judy is a lady you don't want to mess with, not when it comes to protecting her family. She also ran a medical clinic for several years, so not only does she know a lot about health and health care, she's also perfectly comfortable questioning doctors on their own turf. And she will question them like nobody's business.

"They said everything was fine, but I told them he needed to get at least a chest X-ray. They didn't think it was necessary, but I told them we weren't leaving until they did it." She also persuaded them to give him a CAT scan to make sure everything in his head looked like it should, which it did.

When the X-ray films came back, my mother knew immediately that something was wrong. She quickly dialed her close friend, a seasoned physician she calls Dr. Bob, and told him what she thought. He was out the door and on his way in mere minutes.

What the X-rays showed—and what we would learn much more about in the coming weeks—was the grapefruit-sized tumor that had been growing unnoticed in my father's chest. After a battery of tests, and appointments with the oncology specialists at the only hospital in the country really familiar with this particular thing, the MD Anderson Cancer Center in Houston, Texas, the doctors explained to us that my father had a fairly rare form of cancer called a thymoma.

The thymus gland sits just under the sternum, nestled between the two hemispheres of the lungs and on top of several major blood vessels that attach to the heart, like the pulmonary artery and the ascending aorta. It's a pretty sensitive and important area.

My father's thymoma had apparently been growing for some time, but he hadn't noticed a thing. He played golf and tennis regularly. He had even played on the company softball team, keeping up with the rest of the group despite being the oldest player by a good couple of decades. By all appearances, he was healthy as could be.

What we learned next was that this tumor was discovered at a particularly critical stage. It had already encroached on his pericardium, the thin membrane that surrounds and protects the heart. A few more months of growth and the tumor probably would have put out tentacles, growing into the cardiac tissue or metastasizing into other organs. A few more months and it would have started pressing on those blood vessels, in all likelihood causing a stroke, if not worse. A few more months and it would have been too late to save him.

But it never got those months.

My father was treated with chemotherapy to shrink the tumor, and when it did shrink enough the surgeons cut the malignant thing out of his chest.

That was five years ago and my dad is still cancer-free. His hair grew back a little grayer and coarser, and he naps a little more often than he used to, but he's back on the golf course, back to walking the dogs around the track at the nearby park until they're ready to drop, back to gardening and fixing things around the house. He and my mother, despite all of the scares they've had, they laugh a lot.

You never know what weird ways opportunity will find to present itself. It isn't always as dramatic as a car accident, but it somehow finds a way to get your attention.

If it weren't for that crash, my father would be gone by now. It was the happiest accident, the luckiest strike I have ever seen.

~Marti Davidson Sichel

One Sunny Afternoon

All God's angels come to us disguised.
~James Russell Lowell

pressed my foot firmly on the gas pedal, wondering how much over the speed limit it would be safe to travel. After months of looking for a full-time position, I'd finally gotten an interview. The job wasn't what I wanted, but as a new college graduate I couldn't afford to be choosy. Perspiration dotted my forehead. With only fifteen minutes until the interview and twenty minutes of driving to go, I said a quick prayer before glancing down to turn up the air conditioner. When I looked up again, I saw him.

A medium-sized brown dog had scampered into the road and stood right in front of my car. I slammed on the brakes. The seatbelt squeezed into my stomach as the momentum threw me forward, but my car screeched to a stop just in time. The dog darted back to the side of the road. His fur looked matted and dirty. A broken chain dragged along behind him. A runaway, I thought, and lifted my foot from the brake to let the car coast. The dog continued to walk near the side of the road with his head down, sniffing at every step.

I sighed and steered my car to the shoulder. Someone in a red car honked and whizzed by, apparently in as much of a hurry as I was. But no matter how much I wanted to keep going, I couldn't bring myself to ignore the dog's plight. His chain could get caught in bushes or he might make another dash into the road. If I didn't help him, who else would? I opened the car door and stepped out on rocks that scratched my new tan pumps.

"Here, boy. Come here," I called out as sweetly as I could.

The dog stopped and looked at me with his ears lifted and his head cocked to one side. I held out my hand, wishing for a tempting treat to offer him as I inched closer. He stood still until I reached out to grab him. Then he cut away from me, past a small scraggly bush toward the expansive acres of an open field. There, he began to scamper in circles as though encouraging me to come after him.

Great. The dog seemed to think my presence meant it was time for a game of chase. I gritted my teeth and tried to keep an eye on him while picking my way over stones scattered helter-skelter on the ground.

The afternoon sun burned my face and sweat trickled down my back. The dog didn't seem to mind the heat and continued what he thought was a game, always staying about ten feet away from me. His tail swished and I could see the sparkle in his eyes. I clenched my jaw and kept moving forward until something caught my leg. A thorny bush had snagged the fabric of my pants and held it tight.

I bent down and carefully pulled the cloth away from the thorns. It left a small, gaping hole. Muttering at my luck, I gritted my teeth and stood. I frowned and scanned the field. The dog had disappeared. I called and whistled. Nothing. The entire area was flat with no trees or large bushes to hide behind. I could see for what seemed like miles. But somehow, chain and all, the dog had vanished like a desert mirage. Finally I shook my head and trudged back to the car.

If I couldn't help a dog, at least I could try to salvage a potential job. I nosed the car back into the road and tried to convince myself the interviewer would understand when I explained what happened. Thoughts of the stray dog shamed me into slowing down as I headed toward a hairpin curve not far from where my improbable pursuit had begun. As soon as my car rounded the curve, I saw brake lights and a line of cars. I hit the brakes and screeched to a stop. There'd been an accident. A car was wedged under the side of a dump truck. It appeared the truck had stopped in the road to empty a load of gravel. The car's hood looked like a crushed aluminum can. My eyes widened when I recognized it as the same red car that roared past me only a short while earlier.

The truck driver and car driver both appeared uninjured. They stood next to each other writing on scraps of paper while the faint sound of sirens grew slowly louder. As my white-knuckled grip on the steering wheel relaxed, I looked around, still half-expecting to see a dog dragging a broken chain. Yet there was no sign of him. It was as though he'd never existed. I looked back at the accident scene and a thought struck me. Were it not for a bedraggled brown dog and the grace of God… Suddenly my spine stiffened and gooseflesh pimpled my arms. Had I stopped to save a stray dog or had a stray dog stopped to save me?

My heart pounded as I recalled how fast I'd been racing down the road, distracted by dozens of thoughts. If I hadn't stopped, it would probably have been my car that rounded the blind turn and hit the truck. I closed my eyes and breathed a prayer of thanks. My disappointment over missing the interview melted away. All that remained in my heart was an overwhelming sense of gratitude and peace.

It's funny how even the most trivial of events may prove to have a purpose beyond human understanding. Though I didn't get the job I'd hoped for that day, a much better opportunity came along later—one that changed my career path forever. I know it wasn't only coincidence that brought a stray dog briefly into my life one sunny afternoon. He'd been sent to protect and guide me, a special four-footed answer to a hastily offered prayer. And for that, I'll always be grateful.

~Pat Wahler

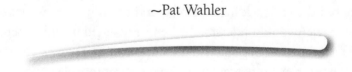

Not Interested

Where your talents and the needs of the world cross, there lies your purpose.
~Aristotle

"No, no. Thank you, but I'm not interested." I hung up the phone, a bit annoyed by the persistence of the telemarketing representative. "I'm not interested," I had said. I wondered why that had not been enough to discourage the telephone barrage.

My thoughts suddenly centered on those words—"not interested." It hadn't been so long ago that I had said that very same phrase in regard to my singing schedule. Many concerts and seminars had occupied my time so completely that I was exhausted. I wanted to take a week off and just stay home.

A phone call was my first hint that God had other plans. The pastor of a church in Crane, Texas called to invite me to come and minister in his church. He wanted me to sing a concert and to share my testimony the very next Sunday night. I did happen to have the date open, but I was really counting on worshiping in my church that Sunday—in the pew, not from the platform.

"I'm just really not interested," I had said. "It would be such a long drive, and I just got back from a weeklong revival. Maybe another time?" The pastor accepted my regrets and we hung up.

An hour later, I answered the phone only to hear that same pastor's voice once again. He had contacted several businessmen in the church and asked them to underwrite my plane ticket. Cheerfully and full of expectation, he offered to send me this plane ticket if I would reconsider coming to his church. "See?" he prodded. "God wants you to come to Crane."

I was not happy. I didn't want to go anywhere. I didn't want to sing. I didn't want to share. I didn't want to minister. Hadn't he heard me say I wasn't interested? But, in my heart, I knew that he was right. I knew that it wasn't coincidence that I was free the Sunday the church wanted me to come. I was sure that the plane ticket was God's confirmation that I was to go to Crane. In fact, I had felt it in my spirit all along, but I was hoping that God would let me slide by.

God doesn't work that way. Never has, never will. It's not his way to let his children slide—not when there's a need to be met—not when there's a miracle just beyond the turn in the road, or in this case, the aisle of the airplane.

The crowd in the Crane church was small that Sunday night, probably less than two hundred. I sang. I shared. I prayed with a little girl at the altar. Then I went home. "What was the point?" I asked myself. "There was no great outpouring, no deluge of souls at the altar." It had been a meaningful but quiet service. Maybe I should have stayed home after all.

A month went by. Two months. Three. On June 5th, I routinely looked through my mail. "Hmmm. A letter from Crane," I mused. "Why won't those people leave me alone? I've never really been interested." I opened the letter and began to read.

Dear Elaine,

When you gave your concert in Crane back in April, our twelve-year-old daughter, Sabrina, went to hear you. I'm sorry to say my husband and I didn't go. When she came back, she told me how beautiful it was and how much it meant to her... On the night of April 27, a tornado struck just as we were trying to leave our trailer home, and it picked our car up, setting it down on her little body. She was killed instantly... Today, I was going through her Bible and near the back of it, she had written, 'Elaine helped me find God.' I wanted to share this with you and tell you how thankful I am for fine people like you who give their testimony in song and other ways and touch the hearts of little girls like our precious daughter.

I bowed my head in shame. Tears began to pour down my face, down my neck, and even to my chest, wetting my shirt. I dropped to my knees and ultimately lay on my face before the Lord, begging his forgiveness. How callous I had been! How selfish!

I was changed after reading that letter—forever unequivocally changed. And I was never again able to so frivolously close the door on an invitation to give of myself, no matter how tired I thought I was. Sometimes, God brings about his miracles through his people.

Not interested? How could I ever have said that? What could ever be more exciting and fulfilling than being part of God's timing? I was a live extension of his hand, offering the answer to a child's question that none of us even knew she had. Later, the discovery of a simple commemoration of that night brought comfort to a mother who laid her child's body in a grave but found solace in the thought that she was really in the arms of God.

I had said I wasn't interested. Fortunately, God was, and always will be.

~Eloise Elaine Ernst Schneider

Voicemail from God

Everything that occurs in your life is part of God's plan to wake you up.
~Leonard Jacobson

The bus was cold. The temperature outside was, in fact, at least ten degrees below average for early November. Being a local TV weatherman, those kinds of statistics were often in my thoughts, but at the moment I was trying to forecast my own personal future. A week earlier, my boss had called me into his office to give me the standard line: "We're going in a different direction." Simply put, I was being replaced, just like that. There was no public announcement, but I had a month to figure out my next move, and I had no idea where I was headed.

It was a short bus ride back to the TV station from downtown. During a break between the morning and midday newscasts, I had visited the office of a former co-worker, wanting to pick his brain about his life since leaving television. I had often thought about changing careers, and though the conversation with him had been informative, I wasn't sure the time was right for me to enter a new line of work. Even more confused than ever about my prospects, I stared out the drizzle-soaked window of the bus (at least I got the forecast right) and remembered that old saying, "When God closes a door, He opens a window." Well, there certainly were no windows opening for me. I half-prayed in my mind — God, help me!

Arriving back at the TV station, I grabbed the latest computer printouts from the National Weather Service and sat down at my desk to update my weather maps. The red message light on my phone was blinking. Looking up from the papers, I punched in my voicemail code. "You have one message," the electronic voice told me, "sent today at 10:14 a.m."

I listened as a female voice I had never heard before timidly spoke over traffic noise in the background. She sounded like she was at a payphone. "You don't know me," the voice said. "We've never met."

I sighed. Another weather fan, I guessed. I listened as the woman cleared her throat and continued. "I was on the bus a little while ago and saw you."

Get to the point, I thought. She did. "I don't know if you'll understand this or not." She hesitated. Then, apparently gathering courage, she blurted out, "God told me to tell you that He holds your future."

The caller suddenly had my undivided attention.

She went on. "He says everything's going to be okay. So... that's it, I guess. I just wanted you to know. Bye." And then she hung up.

I stared at the phone for a few seconds, dumbfounded. Impossible! How could this woman know? Did God really speak to her? Was this some kind of sick joke?

Even as I asked the questions, I sensed that I already knew the answers. It certainly didn't seem like a joke. And why couldn't God speak through others? After all, I had asked God for His help. (It may have been a half-hearted prayer, but here was a whole-hearted answer.) Besides, I knew that what this mystery woman said was true. For most of my life I had believed in a God Who knows us intimately, loves us unconditionally, and cares about us individually. I was ashamed to admit that over the past few days fear and worry had caused me to forget how much He cares. I had needed a reminder.

And what a reminder it was. As her words sank in, shock began to give way to peace. Over the next few days, a mountain of fear began to melt away and an ocean of thankfulness took its place. Yes, it was going to be okay. God had told her, and she had told me.

The woman never called again. I would never learn her identity. But now nearly twenty years later, reporting the weather on television in a different city, I often think of the woman's astounding voicemail message. And I remind myself to never stop trusting the voice of the One Who spoke through her that day.

~Nick Walker

Riding Shotgun

Dad, your guiding hand on my shoulder will remain with me forever.
~Author Unknown

I was a miracle child. Well, that is what my parents always told me. My mother's doctor said that she would likely never have children. But after many prayers for a baby and sixteen years of marriage, I arrived. And how my parents loved me! I was the focus of their lives. My mother was my confidante and counselor. We talked about everything. My father was my teacher and protector. I never felt afraid when he was near. Dad kept me safe.

Excitement and anxiety were high in our home when I hit seventeen and got my learner's permit. My parents celebrated my burgeoning independence, yet they were also concerned for my wellbeing. I begged my mother to teach me to drive. She reluctantly gathered the keys and glanced around her in the vague hope that someone else would take her place. She started my lesson in the empty gravel parking lot of our community swim club. There, I drove our boat of a Buick around and around a center island of trees. I successfully avoided hitting the maples, so Mom let me drive the few back streets home. At each stop sign and with every oncoming car, she stomped on an imaginary brake and fingered her rosary. "I have survived," she told my dad when we returned home. "Now, it's your turn."

And Dad took over permanently. He had the right stuff for the job. My father was a B-17 pilot during World War II. He flew his bomber, the Lady Lylian, wingtip to wingtip with his squadron. He navigated through thunderstorms using only the plane's instruments. On one occasion, the airplane's compass froze, and he used a thirty-cent novelty store compass to find his way back to base. After forty missions, Dad brought his entire crew home safely.

His flying expertise translated to his driving. My father drove our family on vacations across the United States—from North Dakota to Florida and everywhere in between. As a young child, I would stretch out on the back seat and fall asleep, lulled by his steady driving and the warm sun streaming through the window. I felt secure. In his sixty years of driving, Dad never had an accident.

I remember one snowy afternoon when Dad came to pick me up from grammar school. He noticed a group of my friends walking through the blowing snow and offered them a ride. They piled into the back. Dad was nearly to the top of Tank Hill when the car started to slide backwards. He pumped the brakes, but the car continued to slip. The kids screamed. Dad simply turned around, looked out the rear window, and steered the car safely to the bottom of the hill. He would be the perfect driving teacher for me—experienced and unshakable.

On our first time out, Dad tossed me the keys to his prized Mercedes. He settled comfortably in the passenger's seat. "Where to?" he asked me.

Over the next months, we wended through little towns, braved hair-raising Route 17, and traveled the New Jersey Turnpike—boxed in by eighteen-wheelers. My father kept his cool through it all. Every once in a while, he directed me in even tones. "Remember you can always use the brake," he told me. "Check your blind spot and ease over." Dad taught me the trick of accelerating out of a curve to make the driving smoother and that slowing in a downpour improves visibility.

One afternoon, I drove him to his friend Nino's house. "How is your dad as a driving instructor?" Nino asked me.

"He's really relaxed," I said. "Today, he even fell asleep."

"I wasn't sleeping. I fainted from fear," said Dad, laughing.

After many miles of practice, I got my driver's license. I was a bit nervous about my first solo drive. "You'll be fine," my father told me. And I knew I would be.

Years later, I was driving to pick up my fiancé from the United States Military Academy at West Point. I entered onto the Palisades Parkway, which parallels the Hudson River, and my car was engulfed in thick fog. I couldn't see much in front of me. As soon as possible, I turned around and went home. The trip had left me rattled, but my dad offered to sit beside me if I wanted to try again.

We traveled slowly through the fog. "Don't use the bright lights because they reflect off the fog," he said. "Now, use the white line to your right as a guide." We made it to West Point and back intact.

My cadet and I married. After our third child was born, I decided to enroll in graduate school. I was worried about the lengthy drive to campus. "It's a long commute," I told my father.

"What an adventure!" he encouraged.

I lost my beloved father to liver cancer a week before my first semester. Late one autumn night, I was driving home from class on a lonely stretch of dark highway. Suddenly, my father's baritone voice filled the car. "Look out for deer," he said. I wasn't startled or frightened to hear his voice. It was like old times with him riding shotgun and keeping me safe. A few miles later, a massive buck was standing, unmoving, in the middle of my lane. I was ready. I hit the brakes and eased into the next lane, just as Dad had taught me.

~Marie-Therese Miller

Is Anyone Listening?

Evening, morning and noon I will pray and cry aloud
and He shall hear my voice.
~Psalm 55:17

"'m done with you, God. I don't think you're listening anyway, but if you are, I'm done." It was no spur-of-the-moment decision. It was the end of a long struggle with depression and an overwhelming sense of failure.

I was pastor of a small church, and my income was inadequate for a family of four. To provide the things I wanted for my two daughters, I worked extra jobs. I kept those jobs private as much as possible. Working extra jobs would have made me look like a failure, I thought. I was trying to maintain an image of success.

I drove a nice car, but it was a gift from my father-in-law. Unable to afford medical insurance, my daughters' births had been paid for with cash from my pocket. My wife had a major car wreck when she was pregnant, and the bills had piled up.

In reality, I had nothing to complain about. Everyone in my family was healthy. My daughters filled our house with laughter and love. We had a decent home to live in. To the rest of the world, we looked successful. But I felt that I had nothing, and that was the whole point of my depression: how I felt.

I felt no joy in marriage. How could a wife respect a husband who had no respect for himself? My daughters respected me only because they were not old enough to know what a loser I was. That's the way I felt. Now they were coming to an age where they would know.

My church had no idea that I battled depression. I preached hope and inspiration on Sundays, then went home to wonder why I couldn't have done it better, why I wasn't effective, why I wasn't loved, why my income was so small.

For months I had stayed up late, long after my wife and girls had gone to bed. I would sit up and read until my eyes finally closed, until my head finally nodded, and only then I would trudge to my bed and try to find some relief in sleep.

So it was on that fateful night when the stress of bills and relationships finally took its toll. It was well past midnight when my head finally nodded. In my fatigue, I closed a book and laid it on the coffee table. Before I could rise from the sofa, something in me snapped and said, "Enough!"

I slid off the couch and onto the floor, froze on my knees for a moment, and then slid forward until I lay pitifully with my face buried in the fibers of the carpet, my arms outstretched. In this prostrate position I finally divorced myself from hope that God was going to help me. That's when I uttered, "I'm done with you, God. I don't think you're listening anyway, but if you are, I'm done."

I rose, resolute now that I had decided it was time to move on. I went quickly to bed. Almost angrily I undressed in the dark, throwing my shirt on the floor. My wife's soft snoring irritated me. If I was leaving God, maybe I would leave her too. I didn't know. I just knew I had done something big, something final.

Sleep came at some point, but it didn't last long. Around two o'clock, the stillness was pierced by the ringing of the phone. When a pastor's phone rings at 2 a.m., it usually means tragedy has struck. I fumbled in the dark until my hand hit the phone, and answered with my best pastoral voice.

"Hello."

"I'm sorry to be calling so late at night, you don't know me, and, uh, we've never met," he stuttered. Then he started asking me if I was the same person who wrote a column in a certain magazine (I was), and the same person who had written a particular short story in a religious magazine (I was), and after those clarifying questions, he was content that I was the person he was intending to call.

Then he started apologizing again, and I wearied of it and cut him off: "Is there something I can help you with?"

"No, I'm not calling for help. I'm calling because a few nights ago I was praying and I felt like I was supposed to call you and tell you something. I mean, I'm not a super spiritual guy, but I was praying, and it was like God just spoke to me and told me to call you and give you a message, and I was like... oh, man, I don't know him, and he'll think I'm crazy...."

I yawned in the dark, and realized I had answered a psycho's call. My wife shuffled on the other side of the bed, and keeping my voice low, I said, "Well, you've got me, why don't you just cut to the chase and tell me whatever it is you think you're supposed to tell me?"

He spit it out rapidly. "I'm so embarrassed now that I've actually called you. But I'm telling you, I have been unable to sleep for the past two nights, tossing and turning and thinking that God is telling me to call you, and I lay down tonight, four hours ago, and I couldn't sleep until I called you, and now that I have... oh, my, I can't apologize enough...."

"Stop with the apologizing!" I grunted.

He didn't stop. "It's only two words," he exclaimed, "and I really feel foolish that I've wakened you...."

"Just stop," I said. "Just get it off your mind, and let's go back to bed."

"Okay. It's just two words: God hears."

I didn't respond.

The silence rattled him. "I'm sorry, that's it. Does that mean anything to you?"

I still didn't respond, and he starting apologizing again.

I stopped him. "Trust me, it means something. You go back to bed now, and I'm sure you'll be able to sleep."

I hung up on the stranger, slipped out of bed, and tiptoed back down the hallway and into the living room. I slipped between the sofa and the coffee table and lay down, my face buried in the fibers of the carpet, arms spread. It was important to me to try to duplicate the exact place and position where I had been only an hour earlier. When I was sure I was in the same spot where I had told God I did not think He was listening, I began apologizing.

"How could I think that You were not listening?" I cried.

I woke in the morning feeling fresh and energized. Two words became and remain my mantra for every prayer: God hears.

~Danny Carpenter

Divinely Choreographed

All the seeming "coincidences" ...were actually God catching me in his arms.
~Shirley Corder

don't know what made me go into the doctor's office one afternoon when I noticed a dent and a bruise on my left breast. After all, I had just been to see him three weeks earlier and left with a clean bill of health. He had told me my mammograms were normal, he felt nothing suspicious, and he would see me again next year. I thanked him and went back to a temporary teaching assignment I had accepted just a few days earlier—an assignment I hesitated to accept at first until something deep down inside me said, "Do it."

And now, here I was sitting on an exam table, facing a young surgeon I had never met before. He said that the bruise looked like the result of a sharp blow, that I must have hit myself very hard on something.

"But I don't remember hitting myself anywhere," I said, bewildered. "Am I to worry about this?"

"As the wall of the breast heals, it will go back to normal," he replied. "However, I do feel a thickness in the breast."

"A thickness?" I repeated, echoing his words. "It wasn't there three weeks ago."

He said he wanted to do a biopsy just to be sure it was nothing more than a bruise.

"Biopsy?" I felt chills run up and down my spine.

"To err on the side of caution," he assured me.

I went home that afternoon confused and a little scared. Where could I have possibly bumped myself? And not remembered?

The next day I went shopping with my daughter. I was sitting outside the fitting room while she was trying on clothes when I suddenly recalled everything. Since this was Saturday, I had to wait until Monday to call my surgeon.

But before I called him I went back to the school I had been teaching at and retraced the route I had taken to the teacher's room that morning. The playground. The gate. The pain.

"Yes!" I said, as soon as I heard his voice. "I did hit myself! I was hurrying onto the playground and hit myself on the steel handle of the entry gate."

"Did you hit yourself in the spot of the bruise?" he asked.

"Yes. In the exact spot."

A sense of relief washed over me, certain that I would not have to have a biopsy now. "So what do you think the thickness was?"

"It was probably the scar tissue that formed from the bruise where you hit yourself. But," he continued, "I would still like to go ahead with the biopsy to be certain there's nothing there."

That following Thursday I had the biopsy. The surgeon found a lump in the scar tissue that had formed from the bruise. As I opened the gate, I had hit myself in the exact spot where a malignant tumor had been growing for about two years.

That night, I sat my children down on the couch and told them I had breast cancer. I'll never forget the looks on their faces. Confusion. Fear. Concern. Their expressions are etched in my soul forever.

My surgery was scheduled for Good Friday, the Friday before Easter Sunday, the only day that the operating room had an opening. And it definitely turned out to be a good Friday. The surgery revealed that all my lymph nodes were clean, as well as the marginal tissue around the tumor. My cancer had not spread.

"What are the chances of that?" I asked myself over and over again, thinking about the gate hitting me in the exact spot of the tumor.

A sharp blow? A bruise? A thickness? These words kept haunting me. I was the only one on the playground that morning. I merely opened a gate. And collided with it—big time.

While all this was taking place, I wasn't aware that I was walking through a miracle—until I reached the other side of it. And then I suddenly realized that God had divinely choreographed everything.

It had been only three weeks since that initial visit to the doctor for my yearly physical when I got that call from an elementary school needing a teacher for a class of thirty lively sixth-graders. I could have gone the entire year before my cancer was uncovered. Perhaps then it would have been too late.

And maybe if I had remembered hitting myself on the gate at the time it actually happened, I would have realized where the bruise had come from and not have gone into the doctor's office at all.

As I write this piece, it has been nineteen years since that malignant tumor was removed from my breast. Looking back, I'm glad I went ahead and accepted that temporary teaching assignment, listening to the voice inside me that said, "Do it."

I take each day and live it as best I can, making each morning a brand-new beginning—a personal promise of new life.

New beginnings. New life. Nineteen years and counting...

God had truly opened a gate to a miracle.

~Lola Di Giulio De Maci

Mother's Day Surprise

Love is not singular except in syllable.
~Marvin Taylor

'm going for a bike ride and I'll be back in about three hours," my husband shouted as he cycled out of the driveway.

"Be careful," I warned, "it's windy!"

Mark — my husband of thirty-two years — was training for a triathlon and it didn't matter what the conditions were; he was going to keep to his schedule.

I remained on the porch until Mark was out of sight and then as soon as I closed the front door, tears formed in my eyes. It was Mother's Day 2008 and my husband didn't remember. There were no surprises: no card, no flowers, no chocolates, and no brunch — just a wave goodbye.

Training took up all of Mark's free time until there was nothing left for us. Triathlons and marathons had replaced all that was left of our failing marriage.

Instead of feeling sorry for myself, I got in the car and drove to Hershey, Pennsylvania — the sweetest place on earth — for some hot chocolate. There was a shopping mall right off Chocolate Avenue with a bakery and coffee shop. It wasn't exactly Mother's Day brunch, but it was better than staying home.

Hershey was only twenty minutes from our house, but it took

much longer than usual because it was so windy. I had to grip the wheel hard or the car would veer off the road. Then it hit me. If I was having a hard time keeping the car on the road, how was Mark managing with his bike? A chill ran up my spine. I couldn't ignore the feeling that something terrible was going to happen. My mind raced as I contemplated all the possibilities and nearly missed the Hershey exit. The parking lot for the bakery was nearly empty—another painful reminder that other families were celebrating Mother's Day.

When I stepped inside the bakery, there were all kinds of surprises waiting on the pastry shelf. I picked out an iced lemon pound cake and ordered a large hot chocolate with whipping cream. The server asked if I wanted peppermint sprinkles on top and I nodded yes.

I sat near the window facing the parking lot and in between bites of pound cake and sips of hot chocolate I had a queasy feeling. I couldn't explain it—just a strange sensation that something wasn't right.

Just when I was about to take another bite of pound cake, my cell phone rang. I fumbled around in my purse and realized it was Mark's number. Relief washed over me.

"Hi honey, where are you?" I prompted.

"Are you Connie Pombo?" asked an unfamiliar voice.

"Yes, and who are you?" I questioned.

"I don't want to upset you, but your husband has been in an accident," he explained with an unnerving calm. "I'm a paramedic and we're on our way to Hershey Medical Center. We should be there in about ten minutes. Your husband had your number pre-programmed into his cell phone in case of any emergency."

"What kind of accident?" I asked. I could hear sirens in the background and some mumbling, but no one was talking to me! And then my cell phone went dead; I had forgotten to recharge it. I scooped up my purse, grabbed my keys and ran to the car—leaving a trail of hot chocolate in my wake.

The next thing I knew I was at the Hershey Medical Center entrance looking for a parking space. I swerved into the first spot I could find and found myself at the reception desk. My heart was pounding hard and I was out of breath, but I forced out the words, "Mark Pombo—he's coming by ambulance…"

I glanced at the receptionist's name badge—Sandy—and tried to be more polite. "Hi Sandy, I got a call from the paramedics and they said they're bringing my husband to the Emergency Room. Can you please help me?"

She gave me a knowing smile and asked me to take a seat in the waiting room while she made some phone calls. A few minutes later, she announced, "A clergy person will be right with you."

"What?" I asked in pure disbelief.

"I'm sorry, but it's hospital protocol whenever someone has been in a serious accident," she said.

I heard the words, but they didn't make sense. I slumped down in my chair and cupped my hands over my face as the tears came. When I looked up, I saw a name badge that said Clergy attached to a young man about the age of my older son.

As soon as he introduced himself, the receptionist announced that I could go back to Trauma Room #3. I followed the clergyman to the trauma room and wasn't prepared for what I saw. Mark was hooked up to monitors and IVs while the nurses explained in medical terms that my husband had shattered his hip and femur. They were prepping him for surgery and I needed to sign some release forms. The surgeon explained that without immediate intervention, my husband would never walk again. After signing the papers, I was ushered to the waiting room while they finished prepping Mark for surgery.

Three hours passed and there was still no word about Mark. I was about to check with the receptionist when I heard my name being called. "The surgeon would like to speak with you," the receptionist said. "Just pick up the phone by the door—where the red light is blinking."

"Hello, this is Mark's wife," I said in quivering voice.

"Your husband is doing well," the surgeon replied. "We had to place a rod in his femur and screws in his hip, but with time and physical therapy he'll be able to walk again."

Click.

That was it?

Later the surgeon came out to speak with me in person and explained that if it weren't for the two trauma nurses who were cycling that morning and found my husband within the "golden hour" that he might not have been so fortunate.

"What two nurses?" I asked.

The surgeon shook his head in disbelief. "You mean you didn't know?" he prompted. "Your husband was found by two off-duty trauma nurses. They treated your husband on the scene where his bike hit a pothole and threw him twenty feet. They stabilized him and called for an ambulance."

Two miracles happened that day. I had no idea my husband was cycling in the Hershey area, yet I was just minutes from Hershey Medical Center when I received the call. And the two nurses who were cycling that morning weren't supposed to be on that route; they took a shortcut!

On May 11, 2014 — six years after my husband's accident — Mark surprised me on Mother's Day with bikes for both of us. The Mother's Day card attached to mine read: "Please forgive me for all the wasted years of leaving you behind. I want to pedal with you for the rest of my life!"

~Connie K. Pombo

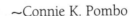

54

From Attitude to Gratitude

Sometimes the strength of motherhood is greater than natural laws.
~Barbara Kingsolver

The day my mother saved me from being killed, or at the very least, from severe injury, I was awakened from a peaceful sleep by the incessant ringing of the phone. I glanced at the clock. It was not yet eight. Who had the audacity to call so early? The phone display said "Unknown Name, Unknown Number."

To be roused abruptly and by a call I did not invite or want always makes me cranky. Then on my nightstand I noticed Larry's note. "Forgot. Have early tee time. Later. Love you, L."

Oh, great! It was Saturday morning and I had planned on a leisurely breakfast with my husband. "But I guess his precious golf was more important," I mused grumpily.

Breakfast? In the kitchen I found his other note: "We need milk. Ours is sour." I don't ask for much in the morning except for my cup of coffee with two sugars and milk—fresh milk.

Grabbing five dollars, I grudgingly threw on my yoga pants and top. There was no need for underwear, I decided. After all, I was only going two blocks away. I drove to the 7-Eleven. I had almost reached the store when a policeman stopped me.

I wasn't wearing a seatbelt and had left my driver's license on the dresser. His professional disinterest added to my foul mood and it was evident he didn't like my attitude either. He gave me a ticket.

At home, I took my coffee, a blanket for my legs and my latest novel out to the back patio.

It had rained overnight. But now it was a perfect spring day. The flowers on the Bradford pear tree created a stunning canopy of snowy white.

The yard was alive with energetic squirrels and the birds provided a sweet symphony of background music. The pleasing sight caused me to question why I was in such bad humor when I was, in fact, so fortunate.

I had good health, a loving husband, a family and friends. Oh, sure, it would have been nice to be ten years younger and have a million dollars, but all things considered, I led a charmed life.

I thought of the officer who had ticketed me. "At least he didn't do a strip search," I spoke out loud, laughing as usual, at my own joke.

I stretched out leisurely on the wooden bench, surrounded by the beauty of nature. My thoughts turned to the bench on which I reclined — my bench. Larry had sanded and stained it a red brick color to match our concrete patio floor.

I smiled as I recalled when we had first discussed marriage. He had good-naturedly warned me that he was not a "honey-do" kind of guy, but his cooperation and eagerness to help over time belied those words.

I must have dozed off. The shrill ringing woke me. Jumping up with a start, I heard my mother shout, "Answer the phone."

I ignored her, until her voice penetrated my ears again, this time with more urgency.

"Eva! Answer it!"

"Can't you pick it up, Mother?" I called out, but she didn't reply.

The phone was on the window counter across the yard. Untangling myself from the blanket, I rushed towards it. A startled little squirrel had been caught up in the blanket and had scampered away in fright.

The phone's display showed those annoying words, "Unknown Name, Unknown Number." My pet peeve struck again.

I'll never know what prompted me to pick up the receiver instead of pressing the "off" key.

The caller seemed hesitant, wanting to talk despite having dialed the wrong number. For some reason it didn't frustrate me like it normally would have. Very politely, I took the time to explain that there was no one in our home by that name. As I was about to hang up there was a deafening thud behind me.

The beautiful Bradford pear tree had uprooted and its enormous trunk had crashed onto the bench where my head had been resting only a minute before. I gazed with horror at the demolished bench, gasping as I realized what had almost happened.

When I had recovered from the shock, I reflected on the miracle that my mother's voice could rouse me from such a deep sleep, sparing me from being injured—or worse—from possible death. What was even more astounding is that it happened on the one-year anniversary of her death!

We later learned that Bradford pears, although exquisite in appearance, are trees that are notorious for uprooting and breaking.

My early morning funk was replaced that day with profound gratitude—gratitude for something even as simple as a wrong number.

~Eva Carter

Chapter 6

Hope & Miracles

Answered Prayers

55

Expect Miracles

Miracles happen to those who believe in them.
~Bernard Berenson

During the Rwandan genocide of 1994 more than a million people were murdered in three months; by the grace of God, I was not one of them. At the time I was a twenty-four-year-old university student visiting home on Easter vacation when the long-brewing tribal hatred in my African homeland erupted into an unspeakable slaughter of innocents. When the killers arrived at our doorstep, my dad sent me running to a neighboring pastor for protection.

For the next ninety-one days I cowered in a hidden, tiny bathroom with seven other terrified women while rapists and murderers relentlessly hunted for us. I opened my heart to God and prayed night and day that He spare my life and also, spare my soul, and not allow the hatred I felt for the killers to turn my heart to stone.

God heard my prayers and answered them.

Whenever the death squads ransacked the pastor's house searching for us, God blinded them from seeing the bathroom door and finding us.

Three months later, the genocide was over and I came out of hiding. I was emaciated, but alive. My heart was sad and I wanted the killers brought to justice, but I wasn't filled with poisonous hatred. On the contrary, to my amazement, I was ready to love and forgive.

With those prayers answered, I thought I'd used up a lifetime allotment of miracles. But I was wrong.

Outside the bathroom, the world I had known was gone. My once breathtakingly beautiful homeland had been transformed into a grotesque landscape of death and destruction. All my neighbors and my immediate family, with the exception of one brother who was living abroad, had been viciously murdered. My childhood home, which my father had built with his own hands as a wedding gift to my mother, had been burned to the ground. All I saw was the smoldering ruins of burnt out houses and a countryside strewn with corpses.

I had gone from being a happily pampered, only daughter to a starving orphaned refugee.

With no money, food or a single friend left alive, I made my way toward the Rwandan capital of Kigali in hopes of finding work, but there was none. No stores or businesses were open, there was virtually no power, no buses were running, there was precious little clean water to drink, the roads were littered with leftover landmines and wild dogs fed on the bodies that still lay in street.

On my way to the city, I met and joined a band of fellow refugees at a temporary camp for displaced persons. One woman in the group owned a house in Kigali, so at least I had a roof over my head—but we had no food and faced starvation. The only remote possibility of employment was secretarial work at the United Nations office that had just reopened. Unfortunately, I didn't speak English, I couldn't type, the only clothes I owned were the rags on my back and I hadn't had a bath in months. On top of that, the United Nations wasn't hiring, and even if it was, it had a long-standing policy of not hiring Rwandans.

Nevertheless, I walked the dangerous footpath to the UN every day to fill out a job application. Every day, they told me not to come back because they had no jobs. But I continued this routine for weeks until my legs buckled beneath me one day, not strong enough to keep walking to a job that didn't exist. I sank to my knees on the charred brick and broken glass of the ruined city in despair, and once again opened my heart to God.

"Lord, you have given me so much already, and I wouldn't ask for your help unless I truly needed it, but I need it Lord! I don't know what else to do. I have no money, my clothes are falling apart, and no one will give me a job. I know you didn't save me from the killers to let me starve to death in the streets. Help me find a way to make these UN people notice me and give me a job! I don't think I can last much longer."

I stood up and brushed myself off, certain God would answer my prayer—and I wanted to be ready when He did. I trusted He would arrange for me to have an interview at the UN, so I would need my high school diploma and some presentable clothes. The only place I could possibly find both would be my university dorm room more than 200 miles away and completely impossible for me get to.

At that very moment a car pulled up beside me and the driver rolled down his window.

"Immaculée, is that you? I hardly recognized you, you are so skinny now. I'm so happy you survived. Can I drive you anywhere?"

I couldn't believe my eyes and ears. It was one of my professors from the university and he just happened to be making the five-hour drive to the campus!

I arrived at the university the next day and the dorm was in shambles; the door of my room had been heaved in with an axe and all my clothes and books had been stolen.

Everything was gone, except for a single envelope on the floor. It must have fallen beneath the bed when the looters pillaged the room. I picked it up and opened it... to find all my school records and $30 from my scholarship award! Suddenly, I was rich! I had enough cash to hire a taxi back to Kigali, with money left over.

When I returned to the city, two shops had reopened near my house while I was gone—a secondhand clothing store where I purchased a new outfit, and a beauty salon where I had my hair done. On the way home I used the last few dollars to buy groceries to feed all my housemates for a week.

A few days later my prayer was answered in full—after an interview, I was picked to start a new job at the United Nations.

I also started a new life, knowing that whenever I opened my heart to God I could expect miracles.

~Immaculée Ilibagiza with Steve Erwin

56

Before the Baby Comes

A baby is God's opinion that the world should go on.
~Carl Sandburg

Donna was the first friend I made after moving from Vermont to Nashville in 1986. Since we both worked in the medical field and enjoyed walking, gardening, and laughing, she quickly became a dear friend. Besides attending a weekly church group together, we hoofed it around the Vanderbilt track on a regular basis in our usual fruitless effort to lose weight.

Donna had always wanted to be a mother but for five frustrating years nothing had happened despite Pergonal shots and endometriosis surgery. We all rejoiced when she finally conceived, but then at three months, the unthinkable happened—she miscarried. I cried with her at the painful loss of her baby and her hope. The painful saga continued into year six: every month starting hopeful but ending with bitter disappointment. Since I knew she and her husband would make ideal parents, I prayed (along with her family and church group), but no further pregnancies occurred.

Unlike Donna, I was ambivalent about motherhood. Did I really want to lose all my free time, money, and sleep? Did I want to deal with nasty diapers and whining? What if I turned into a cranky, inept mother? What if my children turned into selfish brats, drug addicts, or pedophiles? I was afraid to rock the boat, or in this case, the cradle!

My husband, however, wanted children and I knew he'd make a fantastic father. When I turned thirty-one, my husband tossed out the gentle hint: "You're not getting any younger, dear." As a doctor, I already knew birth defect rates increased after age thirty-five, and with Donna's experience, that conceiving could take years. I decided to just let nature take its course. "We're not going to try," I insisted. "We're just not going to prevent it — if it's meant to happen, it will." I figured with our hectic schedules, it would takes months, maybe even years.

Wrong! Try one month! I couldn't believe it when the very first month I got off birth control I conceived. My husband bounced around the room while I retched into the toilet, nauseated and in shock.

Once I was over the morning sickness, I warmed up to the idea of motherhood, except for the overwhelming guilt that consumed me every time I walked the track with Donna. Why me and not her? She had yearned for a baby for years and had tried so hard. I got pregnant the first month. It wasn't fair. It wasn't right, and I dreaded telling her.

In fact, for months I didn't! Instead, I begged God to bless her with a pregnancy before I had to tell her. But by my sixth month, I was showing and couldn't delay anymore. When I told her, she cried. "I didn't even know you wanted a baby." Talk about guilt.

I petitioned God even more on her behalf. I researched promising scripture verses and all the Old Testament stories of infertile women who eventually conceived: Sarah, Rebekah, Rachel, and Leah. As I prayed, I begged God to bless Donna, just as He had blessed these Old Testament matriarchs. I also added a caveat: Please make it happen before my baby is born. I knew it would be difficult for her to watch me with my newborn, and the last thing I wanted to do was hurt her or put a wedge in our friendship. Day and night I uttered the same prayer: "Bless Donna with a baby, and let her conceive before my baby is born." It became my mantra.

Eight months into my pregnancy, my water broke and nine hours later, at 8 a.m. on October 4th, my wonderful son, Steven, made his debut. Instant love and joy flowed through me as I gazed at my adorable little boy, a true blessing from God.

Once Steven was asleep, Nate and I called our friends and family with the news. I dreaded calling Donna. In fact, she was the last phone call I made because I was disappointed with God. Never had I prayed with as much faith, consistency, or fervor as I had prayed for Donna. But I had nothing to show for it. It had all been a waste of time. I made the dreaded call, and she promised to come by later that day.

After oohing and ahhing and agreeing that yes, Steven was the cutest baby on the face of the earth, Donna said, "There's something I'm dying to tell you. I found out at 7:00 this morning that I'm pregnant!"

My mouth dropped. She was pregnant? Tears welled in my eyes and I couldn't stop grinning. God not only answered my prayer, but timed it to the very hour!

Of course, I knew I wasn't the only one praying for Donna. Her husband, family, friends, prayer group, and even a missionary in Japan were all lifting up prayers and petitions daily. Some had fasted. But that God had timed it to the very hour before my son was born was God's special blessing.

Nine months later, Donna delivered a healthy, beautiful baby girl who she named Michelle. Michelle is now a beautiful twenty-two-year-old missionary and will marry this spring.

~Sally Willard Burbank

Faith Happens

Faith is not without worry or care, but faith is fear that has said a prayer.
~Author Unknown

There was no mistaking the lopsided thump my husband, seven-year-old son and I felt as we traveled home from the mall one Saturday afternoon; we had a flat tire. This was the first long outing we had taken since recently acquiring the car from my father. My husband had wanted to stay home that day and watch sports, but I had convinced him that family time at the mall would be more entertaining.

After turning on the hazard lights, my husband guided our car safely to the side of the road. Since we were on the interstate, other vehicles seemed to zoom past us at record speeds, and I worried for my husband's safety since he would be changing the tire so near those speeding vehicles. "What are you looking for?" I finally asked after watching him rifle frantically through the glove box.

"There is a special tool made for this particular car that I have to use for tire changing. I put it in the glove box in case we ever needed to use it," he answered, still deeply engrossed in his search.

Should I tell him I had already seen the "special tool," and had removed it thinking it was something my father had accidentally left behind? Wouldn't it be better to allow him to believe that he had forgotten to place the tool in the glove box? After all, I was the one who had insisted we take this jaunt to the mall in the first place; he had wanted to stay home and watch the game. Finally I mustered enough courage to confess my crime. "Was it a little metal thingy shaped like an L?" I asked, innocently.

"Yeah, that's it. Have you seen it?" he asked. Several alternate explanations raced through my mind as possible means of salvation. I was leaning toward the "mugger snatching it from me as I sat cleaning it in the grocery store parking lot" scenario when I finally blurted, "Oh... I thought Daddy had accidentally left that in the car, and I put it on top of the fridge so we could give it back to him."

There it was. I had confessed my crime and waited for the consequences. I received a look of disgust and disbelief followed by the silent treatment.

With no tool to change the tire, we had only two options: call a wrecker and spend money we didn't really have, or continue at a snail's pace, with the hazard lights flashing, and chance ruining the wheel.

After what seemed to be hours (but was more like several minutes) of slowly thumping down the interstate, my seven-year-old, who had been unusually quiet this entire time, offered some advice. "Mom, Dad... we could pray," he suggested.

The look of frustration and impatience on my husband's face seemed to mirror my own feelings, and I noticed his jaw muscle jump ever so slightly beneath his skin. Of course we could pray, but this wasn't the type of situation to pray about... not when there were far more dire situations in the world that needed God's attention. Besides, how could prayer solve our problem? Would our tire miraculously heal itself and become plump with new air? "Okay, son," I said. I sounded tired. "You sit back and pray."

With each metallic crunch and thud, I felt myself tense against the sound and shift toward the "good side" of the car. Somehow it seemed there would be less weight on the tire if I held my breath. I didn't really believe that, of course, but I found myself involuntarily wincing after each fatal clunk anyway.

A few motorists actually slowed down and offered their help, but none of them had the "special tool" necessary for changing tires on our particular car. It finally got to the point where we wished people would just stop asking. Our luck changed, however, when a large white pickup truck passed us and then stopped on the side of the road. It looked promising, so we eased our car over next to the truck as its doors swung open and five men—all wearing the same sort of T-shirt—bounded out. Our disgruntled attitudes were in stark contrast to their ear-to-ear smiles, and they all seemed overly anxious to help us. The part I found most peculiar was they just so happened to have the specific tool necessary to change a tire on our car. And boy, were they fast! They had the flat tire off and the spare on in a matter of seconds, it seemed. Their smiles never left their faces, even as they loaded our flat tire into our trunk, and told us to have a nice day.

Everything happened so quickly and in such a surreal way that my husband and I just sat dumbfounded watching the men, one by one, pile back into their truck and wave goodbye. Then we heard a small voice from the back seat: "I told you we should pray." I glanced up just in time to see the truck's bumper sticker before it disappeared in the distance. It read, "Faith Happens."

~Cynthia Zayn

Circle of Prayer

Prayer is not eloquence, but earnestness; not the definition of helplessness,
but the feeling of it; not figures of speech, but earnestness of soul.
~Hannah More

Most likely, the doctor found the first birthday card startling. I pictured him pausing, trying to pinpoint my motivation, before tossing the correspondence in the wastebasket, only to lift the card back out and place it on his desk. There, he'd glance at it whenever he passed by, recalling that he nearly took my life, only to save it two days later. He probably thought it odd that I remembered the day he was born. But how could I forget?

At thirty, I needed a tonsillectomy. Years of strep throat and failed antibiotics necessitated their removal. I read the risks and possible complications listed on the surgical consent form. But like most patients, I signed without much thought to the medical warnings and envisioned nothing more than a soothing Popsicle in the recovery room, followed by moderate pain for a couple of weeks. I could not have been more wrong.

After the surgery, I went home feeling as though I'd swallowed shards of glass. My five-month-old son Holden needed my attention, so I rested in between caring for him. The next day, a warm, thick liquid trickled down my throat, followed by the distinctive taste of copper. I called the surgeon's office as instructed for post-operative bleeding.

"Gargle with ice chips," he said.

"Excuse me?" I asked, believing that I'd misheard him.

The doctor explained that a blood clot might be holding a vessel open and, if knocked off, the bleeding would subside. I gargled the ice, and it worked... for a while. The next bout of bleeding—heavier and faster—increased my worry, and I called the office. I gargled with ice chips once again as instructed, and the bleeding stopped. Later in the day, I headed to the hospital without calling the doctor because the bleeding had increased. Shortly after my arrival in the ER, the bleeding eased.

"It looks like the problem has corrected itself," the doctor said as he looked around in my throat. "I'd hate to stir things up. I think we'll let it be and send you home."

The thought of leaving the safety of the hospital frightened me, but I didn't object. The doctor appeared to be a bit rushed. I noted his dress clothes. "Going somewhere fancy?" I asked.

"Oh, it's my birthday today. We were out to dinner. In fact, my wife's still at the restaurant waiting."

I had interrupted his birthday dinner. Probably made him leave before the arrival of his cake adorned with candles. I suddenly felt stupid for rushing to the hospital without calling for his advice. He instructed me to go home and rest and to call the office if a problem arose.

The next day, I actually felt better throughout the day. I went to bed with a sense of relief, but I soon found myself in a dreamlike state. Swallowing. Dreaming. Swallowing. Dreaming. Gulping. I shot up in bed to find my pillow soaked with blood. I shook my husband awake. The next fifteen minutes consisted of a speeding car, the running of stoplights, and my husband's pleas for me to stay upright. Soon, back in the ER, a hose dangling from my mouth transported my life sustaining blood to a nearby canister.

A nurse stood at my bedside, holding my hand and brushing the hair back from my face. "We're waiting for anesthesia to arrive. They're on call this time of night. We've paged them, and they should be here soon."

"How long?" I managed, watching my life travel down the hose.

"Fifteen minutes."

"I don't think I have that long." Her silence confirmed my fear.

The surgeon paced outside the room and glanced at his watch every few seconds, failing to mask his worry. My husband cradled our baby in the corner of the room as the nurse continued to hold my hand amidst the unspoken yet palpable panic. The nurse anesthetist from the Labor and Delivery Unit stood nearby, as a substitute, if the anesthesiologist didn't arrive shortly. The gurney suddenly lurched forward and clipped down the hallway as a strange man in scrubs arrived and placed a mask over my mouth, telling me to breathe deeply.

I awakened to the sounds of distant beeps, hisses, and whispers. Too weak to talk, I could only listen as the surgeon stood at my bedside. This time, he wasn't rushed and looked a tad disheveled.

"We were all praying for you in there," he said. "The surgical team formed a circle around you, holding hands while we prayed. We nearly lost you at one point." I nodded, somehow knowing there'd been a higher intervention.

"I need to tell you something," he said, his voice thinning.

He must've noticed my questioning glance. "During the initial surgery, I nicked your facial artery, and it weakened over time. That's why you've been bleeding on and off."

I knew that he risked repercussions by telling me the truth. Perhaps he told me out of fear that I'd later discover his wrongdoing. Or, perhaps, he did so because it was the right thing to do. Either way, I respected him for admitting his error.

He then explained the harrowing night in the surgical suite: the tricky cauterization of the artery the size of a pencil tip, too short to tie off; the impending need to cut my throat from the outside in order to repair the damage if the cauterization failed—a procedure he had never performed before; the lavage to rid my stomach of the large amount of blood; and the prayers over my body as they painfully watched the clock and waited to see if the cauterization would hold.

"I kept thinking about your baby," he said. "How would I tell your husband that you didn't pull through and that your son had lost his mother?"

With the mention of Holden, the realization struck that I'd been so close to death.

"God listened today, and I'm thankful. I pray that you can forgive me for my mistake." He squeezed my hand before leaving the room.

I drifted off to sleep, low on blood and energy. But I was alive. Over the next six weeks, the risk of bleeding still lurked until I had completely healed, but I knew God would not fail me now.

I forgave the doctor for the near fatal mistake during my tonsillectomy and for rushing me out of the ER the following day to return to his birthday celebration. He had stood before God, asking for His help in saving my life, knowing the burden he'd carry if I didn't survive. Knowing my husband would lose a wife, and that my son would grow up without a mother. If God could see fit to answer the doctor's prayers and grant him mercy, I could grant him his wish of forgiveness.

In the years to follow, my appreciation arrived at his office in the form of a birthday greeting. After all, he had saved my life when given a second chance, and he had asked for God's help that night to ensure my survival. And each day, I'm thankful the medical team believed in the power of prayer.

~Cathi LaMarche

Chicken Soup for the Soul

April Showers

Prayer requires more of the heart than of the tongue.
~Adam Clarke

"Winter storm on the way!" the radio blared. I glanced out the window. Dark clouds were already forming above our small subdivision in rural Illinois. Just then, I heard, "Mom! Mom!" In blew my three bundled-up boys and a crisp October wind.

"Mom!" cried five-year-old Robin. "There's a cat down in the ground!"

"Oh. You mean someone's cat's been buried?"

"No, Mom! Please! Come see! She needs help!"

Six eager hands pulled me outside to the curb. "Can't you hear it?"

Yes, I could—a very faint meow, floating right up from the storm drain!

Chat, almost four, squinted down into the darkness. "Maybe we could drop her a rope."

Two-and-a-half-year-old Jay started calling, "Here, kitty, kitty, kitty!"

By now a crowd of neighborhood children had gathered around. "This storm sewer drains across the street," one of the older boys explained. "If we go down to the opening and call, maybe she'll come out."

At the culvert opening, the children took turns shouting, "Kitty!

Kitty!" Finally, when Jay called, out she came. Muddy, wet, bone-thin, with a woefully deformed tail. But alive.

"Whose cat is she?" I asked.

"No one's," piped up one of the girls. "Her old owners kicked her down there to get rid of her."

"Well, she's ours now," Robin announced. "'Cause Jay's the one she came out for."

Back at the house, we wiped the pathetic creature off the best we could. Then, looking around for something to feed her, I filled a bowl of milk.

She ignored the bowl completely and sat and washed herself all over. Now we could see that she was a longhair with striking black-and-white markings. Only when she was immaculate did she turn to the milk. Even then, instead of gulping it down, she sipped daintily, stopping to clean her whiskers from time to time.

"Look at that!" my husband Don exclaimed. "A real lady!"

And that's how Ladycat came to be with us.

Just in time, too. For all night long we were hit with wave after wave of pounding rain. By morning it had changed to snow.

But inside, our home glowed with the joy of a new playmate. For hours on end, Ladycat would play balls, blocks, and cars with three enchanted boys. She blossomed under this love. But two things about her sad past remained: her deformed tail (perhaps broken in that kick down the storm drain), and her need to go outside and hunt for at least an hour every night.

From then on, frozen days rolled into frozen weeks of 10, 20, and 30 degrees below zero. Then on Valentine's Day all three boys got chickenpox—Chat so severely, he went into a coma and had to be hospitalized. His brothers begged me not to let Ladycat out that night, in case something happened to her as well.

But the air that evening was spring-like, with just a little drizzle. "Don't worry, she'll be right back," I assured them.

Quickly, though, that drizzle turned into a wild rainstorm. And for the very first time, Ladycat did not come back. All night long,

I listened for her. But I only heard the rain. Until it stopped and everything froze.

The next morning, Don's car slid all over the glass-slick road as he headed off on his long commute to work. But I couldn't call him to see if he got there okay. I couldn't even call the hospital fifteen miles away to check on Chat. Or turn on the radio. Or lights. Or heater. For under the weight of that ice, all the power and phone lines had snapped. Our furnace and water heater were inoperable. In fact, nothing worked but our gas stove. Soon it was so cold inside, the boys had to be bundled up in their snowsuits all day long. It was complete misery with those itching pox!

By evening, both boys had bronchitis. But sick as they were, they kept going to the window, looking and calling for their missing pet.

In the middle of the night, Don woke up in excruciating pain and a grossly swollen abdomen. Even though the house was freezing cold (it was 20 below outside and not much warmer inside), his whole body was afire.

"Don!" I gasped. "I think you have appendicitis!"

Normally I would have called the doctor or 911. But with the lines down, I couldn't even call my neighbors next door. Don needed to go to the hospital right away. But Robin and Jay were far too sick to take out into that frigid air. Don would have to go alone.

As quickly as possible, I packed him in ice, covered that with towels, threw a winter coat over his pajamas, and sent him out into the bitter night — praying he'd be able to make it to the hospital without passing out. Or ending up in a wreck.

By the next day, Robin, Jay, and I all had pneumonia. But so did almost everyone else for miles around. Only the most critically ill could be admitted to the local hospital. In fact, Don had to sit in a waiting room all that night — with a ruptured appendix, peritonitis, and double pneumonia — before they could even find a bed for him.

But finally, after a week, the power and phones returned. After two weeks, so did Don. And after three weeks, Chat did, too. But not our missing cat.

February blurred into March, one storm following another. The same with illnesses.

"It's all because Ladycat left," Robin sobbed one day. "Doesn't she love us anymore?"

"God knows where Ladycat is," Chat replied weakly. "I'm going to pray and ask Him to bring her back home to us for Jay's third birthday!"

On April 2nd, just a few days away? What an impossible prayer!

The last day of March was as white, cold, and dreary as ever. But the wind shifted. And on April 1st, the skies opened up.

"Look, children!" I cried. "April showers! It's raining cats and dogs!"

"Cats?" Jay cried. "Is Ladycat here?"

"She will be," Chat assured him. "For your birthday. God will bring her back."

Changing the subject, I asked, "So what do you want for your birthday tomorrow, Jay?"

"Ladycat. Just Ladycat."

That evening the rain finally let up. Then at the dinner table, Robin suddenly asked, "Who's at the front door?"

"Ladycat!" Jay shouted.

All three boys ran to the door, flinging it open. A biting wind roared in—followed by a tiny, mud-covered creature, barely able to move.

Don jumped up. "Quick! Get her some food!"

But as feeble as she was, the cat slowly, painfully cleaned herself all over. Only then would she eat. Ladycat was back.

The next morning we retraced her tiny footsteps in the mud—all the way to the culvert where we had first found her. Ever since the ice storm—that night she had disappeared—the opening had been completely frozen over. She had been down there the entire time, subsisting on mice and snow, until finally freed by the previous day's warm April showers.

Arriving home just in time for Jay's birthday.
Just as three little boys and God knew she would be.

~Bonnie Compton Hanson

Irish Angels in New York

I've seen and met angels wearing the disguise of ordinary people living ordinary lives.
~Tracy Chapman

As my husband, Doug, stood on the curb doing his best to hail a cab, I huddled under the hotel awning with my daughter, trying to angle her stroller away from the cold December rain. When I knelt down to check on her, I wasn't surprised to see her watching the busy New York scene with curiosity. I tucked her pink security blanket tighter against her legs and kissed her cheek where bluish veins crept up the side of her tiny face to her temples.

Frustrated and wet, my husband gave up his attempt to flag down a taxi. Walking back toward me, I saw defeat and complete exhaustion in his expression. I knew the feeling. Just after her first birthday our daughter was diagnosed with a rare brain disorder. Since that moment, Doug and I felt like runners in a marathon race where the finish line kept disappearing.

Doug forced a smile when he saw me looking his way. "It's cab-crazy over there," he said. "I thought I was loud but this Kansas boy can't out-yell these New Yorkers."

We stood for a moment in silence watching people pour out of the hotel, some walking briskly under umbrellas while others joined the cattle call at the curb.

"How's she doing?" Doug asked as he pointed to the stroller. It was a question that was fraught with mine fields, but I knew he was only referring to the chill in the air, not the tangle of arteries and blood vessels that slowly robbed our daughter of the typical toddler experience.

"She's happy as can be. You know Katie, always up for an adventure," I replied. And it was true. Though she had every reason to be willful and fed up with doctor visits, blood draws, echocardiograms and CT scans, she rarely fussed, flinched or expressed her displeasure. Each new doctor meant a different set of toys in the waiting room and the promise of M&Ms on the way home.

A clap of thunder caused my tired, anxiety-ridden body to flinch as the rain intensified. We had been in the Big Apple barely twenty-four hours and spent the previous night trying to pretend we were merely tourists trekking from the Midwest for a fun holiday getaway instead of brain surgery. We ate New York-style pizza for dinner and even stopped at a bakery for black and white cookies, an homage to the famous *Seinfeld* episode. Thirty minutes later, Katie paid her own tribute when she proceeded to vomit the black and white cookie all over my chest.

With only two weeks to go until Christmas, twinkling lights and other decorations were festooned across the city. We marveled at lighted snowflakes hanging from street lamps and animated nutcrackers in shop windows just long enough to forget why we were there. But the enormity of it was always with us, ticking in the background like the countdown clock on a bomb.

Even though Katie wore an ever-present smile, we knew she was running out of time. Despite the gnawing in my stomach telling me something was wrong and my continual pleas for doctors to look at her, really LOOK at her, it had taken months before we received a diagnosis. Finally we had a name for the disorder, vein of Galen malformation, but the prognosis was not good. The surgery to treat her condition was so precise that only a handful of specialists in the world were qualified to perform it.

Now, when it was time to check into the hospital where a brilliant doctor was waiting to save our girl, we were huddled under an awning in a strange city in the rain, waiting to catch a break and trying not to break down.

"Pardon me? May we offer you a ride?"

I turned in the direction of the voice and noticed a middle-aged woman in a long white fur coat looking at Katie and then back at me. Midwestern pride kicked in before I could think and I replied, "No thank you. We're just waiting to grab a taxi."

"It's really no trouble. My husband is bringing the car around now," she countered. It was then I noticed her thick Irish brogue, an accent that warmed me like hot soup.

When a black SUV pulled up moments later, she ushered Katie and me into the back seat before we could protest further and instructed her husband, a tall gentleman with broad shoulders and a full head of snow white hair, to help load our suitcases into the hatch.

Doug and I sat very still trying not to get the expensive leather seats wet with our rain-mottled clothes and checking our feet for mud even though we had been standing on concrete.

As the man pulled away from the curb, the woman asked where we were headed. We knew from our brief time in New York that people preferred short, to-the-point answers so we simply said, "Roosevelt Hospital, please," and settled in for the ride.

I don't know how she knew, maybe it was mother's intuition, or maybe she spied the veins or the dark circles under Katie's eyes, but the wife asked, "Are you going for the baby?"

I nodded my head, choking back a tiny sob as the floodgates opened and we poured out our story. We were only a few blocks away from our destination, but it was a cathartic release and the couple listened intently. Their children were grown and had kids of their own, but the previous evening, the entire family gathered in the city for a holiday dinner and Christmas show at Radio City Music Hall.

At the hospital we thanked them a dozen times for the ride. While

I was strapping Katie back into her stroller, the woman called Doug over and placed a laminated card in his hand. On one side was a picture of Mother Teresa, on the other, a simple prayer. She quickly scratched her name and e-mail address on a piece of paper and asked us to contact them about Katie's recovery.

The woman hugged me one final time. After the embrace I noticed her face was wet with tears and shrouded in worry. She promised to pray for us. Then they were gone.

We would never forget that single moment of kindness. As the double doors of the hospital opened with a "whoosh," we took a deep breath and looked down at our girl. It was time to find her miracle.

After three more visits to New York and two more brain surgeries, Katie is cured. During the frenzy of that first trip we lost the e-mail address of our kind Irish angels, but we still have the laminated Mother Teresa card. It sits prominently on our refrigerator as a constant reminder of a tiny ray of light delivered on one of our darkest days.

~Dani M. Stone

My Two-Second Miracle

Blessed are those who mourn, for they shall be comforted.
~Matthew 5:4

"I saw him! I SAW HIM!"

I excitedly told my husband the news as he asked the obvious question, "You saw WHO?"

"I just saw Donnie!" was my reply, as tears rolled down my cheeks.

I had to sit down. My husband Don looked at me with half a smile but mostly wide-eyed disbelief. We both knew very well that our twenty-eight-year-old son Donnie had died in an auto accident in 1999, and it was now 2007!

As I sat down at our dining room table, I tried to recall what had just happened. Dinner was ready, and Donnie's cat Audrey was on the back of our green easy chair. I had placed the casserole dish on the table and turned to call Don to come and eat when I glanced at Audrey out of the corner of my eye. She was about to jump down from her perch on the back of the chair. She usually joined us in the dining room when it was dinnertime, so it was not unusual of her. What was unusual was the misty form of my son, Donnie, hovering over her with one outstretched arm to pet her! It only lasted a couple of seconds, but he was instantly recognizable with a very big smile on his face! As she leaped down, the vision was gone. Gone in seconds, so that I had to sit and think about this. Did it really happen? YES! I knew it had happened!

Don began eating but I could hardly move my arms to begin my meal. "I was not even thinking about him today," I related. My husband said something like, "Hmm."

"Are you doubting me?" I asked.

"Hon, I have no idea what just occurred, but if you think you saw him…." he began. I wiped my tears and softly said, "It happened. I know it happened. I wish it had not been so brief!"

This was my miracle. After our son died, I prayed that God would bless me with a dream or a vision of him, just to know he was fine and in His care. I had experienced a couple of dreams where I felt my son was there. The dreams left me feeling warm and comforted and truly at peace when I awoke.

This was different. I always had the feeling in the first few years after his death that if I did see him I would probably faint. My faith was not that strong and I was deep in the throes of grieving. I wanted to see a vision of him but at the same time I was afraid.

It happened when I was ready to accept it. God allowed me to see my son, perhaps one last time! I do not believe he is a "ghost" that haunts my home, as some people might surmise. No. He is in a wonderful, peaceful, loving place and his spirit can come and go as God wills. That is what I believe, and I am thankful God allowed me one glimpse of my son in spirit form! He just had to pop in and check on his cat, and showed me by his smile that he is very happy indeed!

It took some time to convince my husband that I'd had a vision of our son, and he still is not sure why it happened for me. He does, however, know that I vehemently believe the miracle occurred.

I thank God daily for the two-second miracle that left me with such peace.

~Beverly F. Walker

The Textbook

Prayer is the medium of miracles; in whatever way works for you,
pray right now.
~Marianne Williamson

"Too much textbook left at the end of the money!" I muttered to myself in the college bookstore. I had bartered for used textbooks for some classes and had purchased as many others as I could afford but there was nothing left for my Urban Sociology textbook. I needed to buy it new because it had been revised, but even if I had been able to use the old version there were no used copies available.

When I got home that evening I shared my dilemma with my grandmother.

"Honey, what are you going to do?" she asked.

"I'll make do the best I can," I told her. "Maybe someone in the class will allow me to borrow a book to read the pages assigned each week. I'll take good notes in class and hopefully I can pass the course without a textbook."

Grandma sighed and said, "You know if I had any extra money, I would give it to you." She paused to kiss the top of my head, and I knew in just a few minutes she'd be down on her knees in the bedroom taking my concern to the Lord.

On Saturday morning Grandma and I went to the grocery store downtown. As we parked across the road from the market, she said, "Honey, let's run into this secondhand clothing store for a minute. You need an extra white blouse to take with you. Maybe we can find one in there that I can fix up for you."

While she browsed through clothing, I wandered to the side of the shop where they kept books, furnishings, and odds and ends. As I searched among the books, I spied a familiar book. Moving closer, I could not believe my eyes. It was a copy of the Urban Sociology book I needed for my class! It was the edition being replaced, the book used the previous year, but it looked the same on the outside. Since I didn't have the $75 for the new edition, perhaps I could learn part of the material from the old edition.

"How much is this book?" I asked the clerk.

"Oh, honey, we can't sell old textbooks around here. Everyone wants novels like mysteries and romances, not educational stuff. I'll let you have it for a quarter and I'm glad to get rid of it!"

About that time, Grandma came over to show me two good white blouses she had found and I showed her the book. She beamed and said, "God works in mysterious ways, His wonders to perform," and we went to the cash register to pay.

There was an additional surprise for me when I went to the first day of my Urban Sociology class. The professor held up a copy of the textbook and said, "Now class, take note of the text we are using. In the bookstore you will find the new edition. In case you have not yet purchased your textbook, my advice to you is to seek out a student from last semester and offer him a fair price for his book. I have examined the new text and I totally disagree with the revisions. I will be teaching this class using last year's edition."

I hugged my twenty-five-cent textbook to my chest and whispered my thanks. "Thank You, Lord! Thank you, Grandma!"

~Helen Wilder

Soda Miracles

A prayer in its simplest definition is merely a wish turned Godward.
~Phillips Brooks

One beautiful day in Northwest Arkansas, while visiting the sixty-seven-foot-tall Christ of the Ozarks statue in Eureka Springs, my then-thirteen-year-old daughter asked for a Sprite. Looking at her with barely veiled surprise, I reminded her that we were deep in the Ozark forest, on top of Magnetic Mountain, and that mountain forests did not provide sodas for teenagers. Besides, I could really use a restroom, which also were not naturally occurring in forests, so soda was not high on my list of priorities.

This explanation was not convincing to my dear daughter, who promptly provided a solution. "I'm going to pray for one."

"Sweetheart, one can not pray for soda," I explained.

"Yes you can," she continued, defiantly. "The Bible says to pray for EVERYTHING."

"While this is certainly true, I don't believe God had soda in mind when He handed down that little tip," I reasoned.

"Well, I'm going to pray for it anyway," was her unwavering response.

I told her to go ahead and do so if it made her feel better, but not to be too disappointed if it didn't happen. I did ask her to pray for a restroom while she was at it, and we headed toward the car to drive home.

As we neared the parking lot, I noticed a small building situated not far behind the car. As we got closer, I realized that it was a restroom! How had I not noticed that before? Well, I guess it wasn't really that bizarre. After all, we were in what was probably a popular local attraction. Regardless of the reason, the sight was welcome!

"Well, ask and you shall receive!" I exclaimed. I asked if my daughter needed to use the restroom before going. She didn't. Tucking her safely in the car, my husband and I headed to the newly discovered restrooms, hopeful that they would be unlocked even though it was the off-season.

"Do you think I handled that okay?" I asked my husband, feeling uncertain about the message I was sending by discouraging prayer, even if it was just for soda.

"It might be confusing for her. After all, you tell her to pray for everything, then when she wants to pray for, literally, everything, you make her feel silly for doing it," he admonished.

"I didn't say it was silly!" I defended. "Just that it wasn't what the verse meant! Doesn't it seem kind of, I don't know... blasphemous I guess? Praying for something as trivial as soda?"

"Not really. The Bible does say 'everything.' Who are we to put limits on that?" was his wise reply.

No sooner did he finish his sentence than we reached the tiny structure that housed the restrooms. And right next to the restroom entrance what should we find but a soda machine? We looked at each other in surprise and moved toward the machine to see if it was even on. It was.

"I don't have any change. Do you?" I questioned.

"All I have is fifty cents," he answered.

"It's a dollar. We don't have enough. That's a shame, since that would have been a mini-miracle to her," I said, disappointed.

"Let's put the fifty cents in anyway," he said.

"What would be the point of that?" I asked.

"She prayed for soda in the middle of the wilderness. Two minutes later we found a soda machine, in the middle of the wilderness. It's worth a try," he explained.

"I guess," I said skeptically.

He plopped in the two quarters, and we instantly heard that reassuring click that signifies the acceptance of full payment.

"You've got to be kidding me. There was already fifty cents in there?" I asked.

And then I did something incredibly selfish. I hit the Coke button even though she wanted Sprite. After all, I reasoned to myself, she'll still be getting soda. Just like she asked for.

When they say that God works in mysterious ways, we all nod our head in agreement. But do we really stop to consider what that means? Not only does He work in mysterious ways, He also manages to use one situation for multiple benefits. The cherry on top is that He can use seemingly inconsequential moments and seemingly minor events to create profound changes within us. This was the day I realized these facts in a new and enduring way. Why such a transformation in foundational thought? Because when I hit the button for Coke, after the machine taking fifty percent payment as full payment, a Sprite dropped into the retrieval tray.

We wordlessly stared at it. I was astounded by the lemon-lime packaging before us, but I think my husband was a bit more astounded by the fact that I had hit the Coke button after what had happened up until that point.

He looked at me. "I think you owe her an apology."

I can't describe the feeling of sorrow and shame I felt in that moment, as humility born of self-realization washed over me. In the midst of my daughter's miracle I had tried to put myself first. What a terrible thing for an otherwise caring mother to do. I was sincerely and completely sorry, and ready to offer my deepest apologies to my faithful little girl. I turned toward the car, prepared to deliver her liquid miracle to her before even heading to the restroom that I increasingly needed to use. Two quarters spit out of the machine.

Tears sprang to my eyes, and I turned to my husband, a sense of awe filling me. He looked at me, retrieved the quarters, and, without another word, put them in the machine. I reached over and hit the very same button I had hit only moments before. A Coke dropped out.

I handed him the Coke and, Sprite in hand, walked to the car, opened the door, kissed my daughter, and handed her the Sprite.

"Pray for everything, and don't ever let anyone convince you otherwise."

~Sandy Novotny

A Precious Mess

Every happening, great and small, is a parable whereby God speaks to us, and the art of life is to get the message.
~Malcolm Muggeridge

When I saw Oliver, my teenage daughter's energetic thirty-something youth group pastor, bound up the seven steps leading to the stage to deliver the Sunday morning message, I did something I'd never done before. Turning to my husband, who sat beside my son and younger daughter, I tersely said, "I'm going. Don't follow me."

Oblivious to the eight hundred people who filled the dimly lit sanctuary, I strode down City Church's outer aisle. Oliver's opening words echoed behind me as I flung open the door that led to the oversized lobby, but I wasn't listening. The glass door that led to the outside banged open after I pounded too hard on its metal bar. I didn't care. I was free.

Heading left, I started walking past row after row of cars until I reached the long concrete drive that led to the main road. I had no idea where I was going. Or why I had left.

Maybe it was because a new wave of grief had crashed over me the night before. Or maybe it was because, during greeting time, the unsuspecting woman in front of me turned around and asked, "How are you?" I should have responded with the customary "Fine, how are you?" Instead, I replied honestly. I had to tell the story I didn't want to share one more time—that six months ago bullying had driven my fourteen-year-old, Jenna, to end her life. Normally I found joy and freedom while worshiping God as I remembered Jenna praising Him beside me and pictured her adoring him now in heaven. Today, however, the tears cascaded down my cheeks.

Whatever the reason, I did know one thing. I wanted to be alone.

Minivans were swerving by me on the busy road as I walked on the narrow shoulder. So, I veered left into the first neighborhood I saw—a subdivision I'd never been in before. On either side of the entrance I noticed a black-and-white oval sign that adorned the towering twenty-foot-high wrought-iron gate anchored by thick brick towers. I was entering Holland Place.

As I walked down the sidewalk of Netherland Lane, my hands stuffed into the back pockets of my thrift-store Abercrombie jeans, I passed landscaped lawns and lofty brick homes. But my mind was engaged in a raw and real conversation with my King.

"I don't understand any of this. I've done every healthy thing I can think of to walk through this grief, and nothing seems to be helping. I don't know what else to do. If I can't see or hear you, you've got to at least show me that you're here. I need to know you care."

I wasn't expecting an answer. Half a mile into the Holland Place subdivision, however, I heard a voice.

"Mrs. Saadati?"

As I rounded the cul-de-sac, a woman dressed in a University of South Carolina Gamecocks navy t-shirt and denim shorts emerged from a grand house.

"Yes?" I answered, wondering who she was and how she knew my name. No one I was acquainted with lived in this neighborhood. "I'm Mrs. Saadati."

"We've never met," she said, "but my son is a seventh grader at the middle school your daughter attended last year. Jenna hasn't been forgotten. The teachers, especially her band director and English teacher, and students still talk about her. Jenna's photos and awards are still displayed. She was so talented and beautiful. Her impact is felt all over the school."

The conversation under the crape myrtle at the end of the driveway was short. I had no words. Shocked, I simply listened.

"I think of you often and I pray for you," she said. "I haven't forgotten."

"Thank you," is all I could manage to mumble. Before continuing on, however, I asked one question.

"How did you know who I was?"

"I was passing my front door when I saw you walk by," she said. "I don't know how I knew who you were. I just did."

Replaying the conversation in my mind, I retraced my steps. After walking for ten minutes, pondering what had just happened, I reached the entrance with the tall iron gate. That's when I spotted it.

Squashed up against the curb beside the storm drain sprawled something fuzzy and flattened. Road kill, I thought. During my half marathon training runs, I switch to the other side of the street to avoid seeing the smashed critters. But that day, for a reason I'll never know, I did something different. I stopped and crouched down to examine it.

What I saw surprised me. Rather than road kill, it was a run-over, rain-soaked teddy bear. It lay on its back, arms flung open as if waiting and wanting to be rescued.

That bear is a mess, I thought, but I'll bet it's precious to someone.

Then, though it wasn't an audible voice, somewhere in my spirit God seemed to whisper, "You're a mess, too, but you're still really precious. To me."

With tears flowing, I picked up the bear, almost afraid to touch it but not wanting to let it go. I didn't have a purse to put it in and didn't want to carry the filthy mat of fur into the service and explain. So, I cut through the parking lot to place it on my car before returning to the sanctuary.

Along the way I looked up twice. Still teary-eyed, I wasn't focused on anything. But my eye caught a decal on a van that read, "Run... like a girl. 13.1." The distance of the half marathon. The second time I raised my head, my eyes saw a different car's magnet. The picture silhouetted four people—a dad, a mom, a boy, and a girl. My family's new normal. Above it were written the words "Blessed Family."

The crowd was filtering out of the sanctuary just as I returned. I found my husband, who looked at me with an expression that said, "You missed all of it."

Little did he know that God had crashed into my world and filled me with hope.

As I shook my head, my lips formed a delicate smile.

"Wait until I tell you," I said. "God showed up. Even when I was AWOL from church."

~Beth Saadati

Chapter 7

Hope & Miracles

Think Positive

The Godfather and His Daughter

A truly rich man is one whose children run into his arms
when his hands are empty.
~Author Unknown

My father and I were both good at pretending to be people we were not. I spent the first nineteen years of my life pretending I wasn't gay, and he spent even longer pretending he wasn't sane. Truth, you see, was a relative concept in our family.

Between the two of us, he was the better actor. After my father died in 2005, psychiatrists marveled at his ability to not break character or waver from his story for so long, saying he could have won Oscars for such a performance.

But my father, Vincent Gigante, was no actor; he was a crime boss.

Known in that world by his nickname, "Chin," he was the head of the Genovese crime family and believed to be the *capo di tutti capi* of all five New York crime families.

Our respective worlds of invention were for our own survival. Growing up in an Italian-Catholic family in the Seventies, to be gay was a worse sin, a bigger crime, than being a murderer. You were hell-bent for sure. I was different than my sisters and friends from a young age and it wasn't going to change. All I could do was hope and pray that God wouldn't punish me for how he made me.

My father spent more than two decades feigning mental illness to stay out of jail. In the West Village neighborhood where he mostly lived, he put on daily street performances. Dressed in pajamas and a worn-out robe, he'd meander the one block from his apartment to "the Café"—a small room with windows painted black, where he'd meet a bunch of men to play cards. Sometimes he'd stop and talk to a parking meter on the way. The New York tabloids dubbed him "The Oddfather."

Once in a while, I'd see glimpses of the father he could have been. He'd put on Elvis and dance around the living room in his boxer shorts. He'd kiss his mother on the cheek and stuff her apron pocket with one-hundred-dollar bills. He'd kneel at his bedside, eyes shut, and pray the rosary.

By age nineteen I couldn't sustain my lie any more. I'd dated boys and worn a frilly prom dress, but living a double life was making me physically and emotionally ill—for *real*. I was plagued with mysterious pains and anxieties, so I decided it was time to come out to my parents. I hoped and prayed they would accept and love me as I was.

"Mom, Dad… I have something important I need to tell you," I said to them one night when Dad was staying over at the family house in Jersey. My throat started closing up, but I pressed on. "I like women, I'm gay."

My father was silent—deadly, scarily so. I expected yelling, but this was worse.

"It's a phase," he said, in a cool and controlled voice that made me shiver. "I don't want you to see any of your girlfriends anymore."

In that moment, I realized he wanted nothing to do with the truth; he wasn't willing to accept the real me. And so, I continued pretending for a while longer. Until three years later, when federal agents broke down my father's apartment door with a battering ram and arrested him, charging him with racketeering and murder, among other crimes. He was put on house arrest to determine if he was mentally fit to stand trial, and he revved up his act as feds watched him 24-7 from across the street in parked sedans.

Seven years later, in 1997, my father was sentenced to twelve years in prison. But even then, on the inside, he stuck to his elaborate ruse in case it would get him out. While he continued his lie, I embarked on a search for truth. I went into therapy to unravel the confusing layers of my childhood and get clarity on our father-daughter relationship. I studied the art of Reiki and other healing techniques to find health for myself, and help others. In the process, I discovered I had an ability to sense spiritual energies around me.

With my new understanding of the power of energy, words, and intent, I wondered if I could mend something between the two of us, even as he sat in a dreary jailhouse 500 miles away.

I wrote him a long letter, and here's a small portion:

Dear Dad,

I am writing today to tell you who your daughter really is...

Before I begin—first and foremost, I forgive you. I forgive you for all the things you couldn't do; for the father you couldn't be; and for anything that was said, done, not said or done. I also forgive myself for all the anger, rage, and resentment—and for anything I said or did that hurt you in any way...

I told you previously that I am a healer. I am committed to helping people find their way.

I see miracles every day, small and large, in my life and in the lives of my clients...

Dad, I know that when you read this, you will understand what I am saying because it will resonate with your soul. I will continue to pray for you and send you good energy. Thank you for being my father and for helping me learn my lessons in this life.

In gratitude and love always,
Rita.

I mailed the letter, and hoped and prayed one last time that my father might accept and love me as I was.

Two weeks later, he called my mother looking for me.

"His voice was shaking," my mother told me, shocked. "He said, 'Tell Rita that I love her very much… tell her *I understand*.'"

My heart raced; I was ecstatic. I could feel something monumental happening within my father.

Not long after that, he was up for parole after serving six years and he desperately wanted to come home. But there was a new problem.

In an effort to keep Dad in jail, federal authorities wanted to charge the family with obstruction of justice, saying we helped him lie all those years. He didn't need to hear any more.

My father made an admission shortly thereafter, shocking both the family and the public.

THE NEW YORK TIMES: April 13th, 2003.

An enduring urban mystery was solved last week when Vincent (The Chin) Gigante, the Mafia leader who spent decades slobbering, muttering and wandering Manhattan in his bedclothes, admitted in a Brooklyn federal court that he had deceived the teams of psychiatrists who had evaluated his mental competency…

My father died in jail two years later. But in that time, he was a freer man than he'd been in decades. He loved me without judgment and he told the truth—those, to me, were miracles both small and large.

When I married the love of my life, Bobbie, in 2013, I know my father was at the wedding in spirit—walking us both down the aisle. After the ceremony, we put on an Elvis tune for him—"Jailhouse Rock"—ha! As Bobbie and I danced, we both could feel my father take our hands and spin us around on the dance floor. It wasn't the traditional father-daughter dance, but then again—we weren't your everyday kind of family.

But prior to this, and shortly following his passing, my father appeared to me in my treatment room. He came with an unlikely offer of love, healing and redemption, communicating to me that he wanted to make a pact with me to assist in my healing work from the other side. To say the least, I was overjoyed and embraced this wholeheartedly.

~Rita Gigante with Natasha Stoynoff

Recovering Together

You've gotta have hope. Without hope life is meaningless.
Without hope life is meaning less and less.
~Author Unknown

We have learned that when life brings tragedy, you must search for that speck of light, that speck of hope within it. It may not always manifest itself right away; you may not be in a place immediately to see that light. Sometimes we need to let ourselves hurt, to grieve. And then sometimes that speck is more like a boulder when you come upon it.

Our story starts on January 3, 2010. Mike was on a routine patrol in Afghanistan. He and his Air Force teammate were assigned to an Army unit to call in air strikes. On this day they were ambushed and shrapnel from an improvised explosive device (IED) hit Mike. Four of his brothers lost their lives and many others suffered injuries. Mike was left completely blind. He faced an unknown future in a pitch-black world.

January 3rd was a hard day for me too. My whole world turned upside down when I was informed that my husband, Sgt. Joshua Lengstorf, would not be coming home. The grief was overwhelming and I prayed I would be strong enough for our fifteen-month-old daughter. I felt so lost and the world felt like such a dark place. I was struggling with my pain, my anger, and trying to understand. I learned that it was okay to just let go and feel all the emotions. It was okay to ask, "Why?" Letting it all out helped me to start healing. And then I learned that I had an inner strength I never knew existed.

I met another young widow at a memorial for our husbands. Her husband had lost his life in the same attack as mine, while helping with the chaos from the first explosion. He had been Senior Airman Mike Malarsie's teammate. And that's when I learned about Mike, whose family was chronicling his journey of recovery on a blog. I began to read it. A few times I felt that I should reach out to him, but quickly squashed those thoughts. He was probably coming to grips with his new life and I was trying to cope with Josh's passing. But one night I couldn't ignore the prompting and I contacted my friend about meeting Mike. A few weeks later my young daughter and I were on a plane.

Mike was in California learning to live his life blind. His dream growing up had been to serve in the military and now he was on a new adventure. Since learning of his four fallen brothers, he had dedicated his life to living with purpose. He had lived and they had not, so he was determined to avoid feeling sorry for himself. Mike pushed himself to get through blind rehabilitation so that he could give back and begin again. He remembers being a little lost. He didn't know what to expect. He didn't know anything about blindness.

Josh's outlook on life had been to just get out there and do it. I realized the best way to honor his memory was to be brave enough to live again. I know it sounds clichéd, but something happened when Mike Malarsie and I met. It was like soul recognized soul. We both felt it but were confused by it and a bit afraid. Eventually we had to discuss it. The timing wasn't the best, but we put our trust in Heavenly Father and took a leap of faith.

Fast-forward four years, and we are married and that young daughter is a big sister. We have moved several times, and most importantly, we have learned amazing lessons about life and ourselves. We have had ups and downs but we are strong. We have learned not to take life for granted and to live life to the fullest.

Mike has attracted a lot of media attention and has been interviewed on TV shows all around the country, spreading our message of hope and faith. He even became part of the Chicken Soup for the

Soul family when his guide dog, Xxon, won the seeing and hearing guide dog category on the American Humane Association's Hero Dog Awards nationally broadcast TV show. Chicken Soup for the Soul's pet food business was one of the sponsors of the Hero Dog Awards and as a result Mike and Xxon have appeared at Chicken Soup for the Soul events and our family has expanded again to include those new friends.

Now Mike has a wife, children, a guide dog who has given him back his freedom of movement, a new career motivating other people, and friends all over the country. As a couple and as individuals, we have learned that there is always hope. Our whole story is about hope — hope that each of our futures could be good again, hope that we could continue to grow as people. We each had our dark moments, but we saw that speck of light. Hope is right around the corner for all of us. We sometimes have to put in some effort to get there, but there is always a light. Just keep looking for it!

~Jesse Malarsie

Much More than Hope

'd driven the route to the old church the night before to be sure I wouldn't lose my way. On the actual meeting day, I had invented a migraine and left work a half hour earlier than necessary.

It seemed foolish to care so much about punctuality—surely being late wouldn't exclude me from the meeting, I told myself—but we are what we are, and I was determined to be on time. I pulled into the church parking lot with thirty-five minutes to spare, more than enough time to change my mind, but not quite enough to chicken out.

It was early October, cool to the point of chilly, well dark by 6:30. The church, sitting high on a hill overlooking the grimy city, was buffeted by wind. It whistled around me, crooning it almost seemed, reminding me of the loons that used to call to each other eerily after sundown when I was a child spending summers on my grandmother's farm. A school-sized milk carton skittered roughly across the pavement, a newspaper page flew directly in front of the windshield. It all felt foreboding and I badly wanted to turn the ignition key and head my old Volvo wagon back to the empty apartment on Dead Horse Hill. I told myself it wasn't a good night to be out—I was hungry and headachy, had forgotten my gloves and was wearing only a light jacket. So I gave the key a hard twist and the engine roared to life. Home and safety were twenty minutes away.

But the door to the church was only a few steps away across the parking lot. I was almost there. "God, give me strength," I said out loud. I turned off the engine and headed into the wind.

The meeting room, as plain vanilla as the church was gingerbread, was tucked away at the end of a long, fluorescent lit, maze-like collection of corridors in the church basement. Hand-lettered signs and arrows were tacked at each intersection and turn of the carefully neutral, non-threatening walls. The threadbare carpet was beige. The ceiling, which needed painting, was beige. Beige bulletin boards hung on beige walls and there were no windows, making the atmosphere even less inviting. Nevertheless, I followed the signs and arrows. And then without warning, I was at the last set of beige double doors.

"Al Anon" the hand-printed sign read. And underneath, "AA" with a smudgy arrow pointing back the way I'd come.

I hated new things, unfamiliar places, first times. I hated doing things I'd never done before or feared I couldn't do well. I had no gift for small talk with friends, let alone strangers. I'd forgotten what a genuine smile even felt like. I was afraid of crowds. All things considered, it was some mild form of insanity to think that some old, sorry, clichéd self-help group would be of any use to me. I had my pride, my privacy, three cats who depended on me, and a husband locked up in a sterile and unfriendly alcoholism treatment center. I wasn't about to admit or advertise my troubles to a bunch of losers or religious do-gooders. I was thinking I'd go home to the little apartment on Dead Horse Hill, forget all this nonsense and crawl into bed when the door suddenly swung inward and open.

"Welcome to Al Anon," a pretty, young, well-dressed blonde carrying a tray full of coffee mugs said to me. "I'm Alma. You can sit anywhere."

And for no good or comprehensible reason, standing there in that lonely, windowless hall with its harsh lights, the smell of coffee, and this sweet-faced stranger, I began to cry.

"Please," she said gently. "You've come this far. It's only a few more steps." She balanced the tray with one hand—it trembled slightly and on sheer reflex I reached out a hand to help her steady it—she took a step back and leaned toward me with a confidential smile. "Besides," she stage whispered, "we have cookies."

"Oh, well," I somehow managed a shaky smile. "If there are cookies…"

The room was as beige as the hall, with a wide circle of what my grandmother would have called card-table chairs lining the walls. A table just inside the double doors offered an array of books, pamphlets, T-shirts. Another was neatly laid out with Styrofoam cups, paper napkins, plastic spoons and a chirping coffee pot. The promised cookies were there too—chocolate chip and oatmeal raisin. Hung above the tables were brightly colored, if tattered, posters held in place with tape, the Serenity Prayer crookedly centered between the Twelve Steps and the Twelve Traditions. Above them, a sheet of poster board proudly proclaimed the name of the group, its meeting times, and in heavy black script an invitation to "take what you like and leave the rest."

"Your first time?" a voice at my elbow asked quietly.

A woman about my age, holding a chocolate chip cookie in one hand and a small blue book in the other, smiled at me. She had kind eyes.

"I'm Denise," she said matter-of-factly. "I know the first time is the hardest. You're welcome to sit next to me."

I hesitated, not at all sure I could handle this much kindness. She smiled again, nodded to the round clock on the wall.

"I'm sitting right under the clock," she told me, then added, "It gets better, hon, it really does."

I don't remember most of what was said or who said it. I do remember that there were very few empty chairs, that there were mostly women, that there were horror stories I'd never imagined a person could live with, and that somewhere along the way, the knots in my belly untangled and I began to chip away at the walls I'd built around myself.

Hope is a funny thing, sometimes elusive and hard to hold onto, sometimes hiding in plain sight, just around the next corner. I'd gone to the meeting hoping to learn how to make my husband stop drinking. Instead I learned about detachment, patience, boundaries, self-esteem and faith.

Hope blindsided me with a lot more than I even knew I needed.

~Barbara Beaird

Our Silver Lining

Let your hopes, not your hurts, shape your future.
~Robert H. Schuller

Life for our family was as close to perfection as I ever imagined. I had four healthy sons, secure jobs for both my husband and myself, a nice home, and good friends. I mean, what else could you ask for?

Jason, our oldest son, was in the Army. He was getting ready for deployment and while my heart was heavy with worry, I had to believe that he would return home safe and sound in a year. I knew I had no control over what was happening in the Middle East and, as he reminded me over and over, this is what he was trained to do. I had to accept his words and believe that my nineteen-year-old "baby" would come back to me as perfect as he left.

On March 2, 2003, just days before he was to leave for Iraq we got a call that would forever change our lives. "There has been an accident...." I will never forget those simple, yet crushing words. Even now, eleven years later, my eyes fill with tears and my heart aches as I recall the moment that our world came tumbling down.

Within hours we were on a plane to Kansas City where Jason had been airlifted to a trauma unit. As we stood vigil at his bedside we listened as the word "paralyzed" echoed in the room. The doctor spoke, we listened. I wanted to scream but I was frozen in place. My perfect "baby boy" was now confined to a life far from what I imagined for him in the delivery room nineteen years before. His neck broken, he was "dead" from mid-chest down. At that moment I was paralyzed with him. My limbs could move, but my heart was broken and I knew I would never recover from this darkness.

They say that information is power, so why was it that the more I read the more powerless I became? The more I learned about spinal cord injuries the more I was consumed with fear, terror, hopelessness. I knew I would never smile again.

I watched Jason work hard to gain as much independence as possible. The people at the VA hospital were amazing. They say when you lose one sense you gain intensity in others. Like how the blind come to "see" with their ears. Well, while his arms and legs lay still, his heart and mind kicked into full gear. I was dumbfounded by his new purpose. Suddenly he liked to read. His bookshelves were bursting at the seams. Academics became his friend. Philanthropy was on his radar. His desire to make the world better was what drove him every day. I found myself staring at him in awe.

It took years for me to learn, to accept what was all around me, to embrace the energy that surrounds us. The power of positive people, the love of true friends, the support of a community. It is truly amazing how strong and resilient we are. It still blows my mind to know that there was laughter and joy hiding behind our tears and despair. Little by little I learned to "weed my garden," to remove the negative forces around me, whether they were things or people. If there was anyone or anything in my reach that would allow me to return to the "darkness" I had to let it go. I had to walk away from people I had known my whole life if they were not good for my healing or the healing of my family. I had to be strong enough to move on, to say farewell.

I gathered only hopeful, positive, loving people. I chose my army carefully. I needed people who would be strong when I was weak. I had three other children and a husband who needed me.

The thing that amazed me the most was that Jason was my strongest soldier. He was the one sitting in that wheelchair, but he was also the one who taught me that there were two choices. The first was to allow his tragedy to swallow us up. The second was to embrace it and figure out the best road to follow so that we could get on with life.

The proverbial "silver linings" were the lessons we learned. We learned the meaning of true friendship. We learned compassion, looking at others and realizing just how lucky we were. We learned patience since normal, everyday things took just a little longer to accomplish.

Most of all we learned the true meaning of unconditional love. My husband and I saw, with wider eyes, just how strong our marriage was. We watched as the bond of brotherhood grew between our four sons, seeing how they meshed together in ways we never knew possible with siblings. We saw that the love of a true friend can help you breathe when you are suffocating in your own sorrow. We learned that having hope when things are hopeless is a lifeline that keeps you afloat even as the waters rise around you.

As Jason's mom my hope transformed many times over. In the early days, weeks, and months it was my hope that he would be "healed." I hoped that a miracle would find its way to his door and make him "whole" again. I hoped that I would turn on the television and hear a report that they had found a cure for spinal cord injuries. I was using these hopes, as far-fetched as they might have seemed, to allow me time to heal and to feed the strength that was buried inside me. Once I was armed with the tools I needed, my hopes changed; and this time they were more attainable and in many ways more favorable to moving forward in the world we were now a part of.

Today my hope, my dream for my son is the same as it is for all the people I care about. I hope that he loves and is loved in return. I hope that he lives his life to the fullest. I hope that he won't allow his disabilities and/or challenges to stop him from being the very best he can be. I hope he keeps positive powers all around him. And more than anything, I hope that no matter what life throws his way, he always finds the laughter and the joy that are hiding behind the tears.

~Trish Bonsall

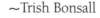

The Missing Key

Trust in the Lord with all your heart
and lean not on your own understanding.
~Proverbs 3:5

I was the oldest never-married person I knew. It wasn't that the opportunity to be a wife had never presented itself. Proposals had come—even been plentiful—but at the age of forty I didn't feel that any of the men had been proper candidates for a lifelong partnership. I had made so many wrong choices, experienced so many dead-end relationships. "Enough," I had said finally. Six years had passed, and life without dating had become comfortable for me. I was enjoying a busy and productive life as a single woman, but I did still dream of the day I might actually meet "Mr. Right."

I had been thinking about switching to a smaller church with a stronger "family" atmosphere. One Sunday my sister attended such a church in her neighborhood and later told me about the man who led music there, a widower with two children whose wife had died of cancer. His name was Jerry Sladkey.

Something inside me rose up. This was someone I should meet.

The following week, I accompanied my sister to the church, and shortly afterward began attending a Bible study led by this man. I was attracted to his faith in God and to his relish for life. Though I struggled with my uncertainty about men and their motives, and Jerry struggled with loyalty to the wife he had lost to cancer nineteen months before, our relationship began to blossom slowly.

As we got to know each other, I felt certain of one thing: I was to let Jerry make all the moves. I was not to "make" this relationship happen. In my prayer times, if I had an issue that needed to be addressed regarding our relationship, I took it to God in prayer—and trusted that He would deal with Jerry.

Jerry still wore his wedding ring from his ten-year marriage. As the months passed and we grew closer, this began to bother me. I suspected that Jerry was growing fond of me, but why did he still feel married? One evening as we sat and talked, he spontaneously held up his left hand and said, "Does it bother you that I still wear my ring?"

My inclination was to shout, "Yes!" But something stopped me. Instead, I responded, "If it does, I'll just talk to God about it."

That night, I went home—and had that promised conversation with God.

A couple of days later, as we talked on the phone, Jerry mentioned offhandedly that the ring finger of his left hand had suddenly broken out in a rash. The inflammation was so irritating that he had to remove his wedding ring. The rash didn't heal for two weeks. By then, Jerry had gotten the message—and so had I. If I would trust God with the little details of my life, He would ultimately work them out in His own way.

And so He did. At the age of forty-one, fourteen months after I met Jerry I said "I do" for the first time.

To those who knew us, our marriage made perfect sense. It has made sense for twenty-three years now. And why shouldn't it? Until age forty-one, my name had been Sandra Slad. God had provided the missing "key."

~Sandra Sladkey

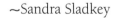

Circle of Compassion

Our task must be to free ourselves by widening our circle of compassion to embrace all living creatures and the whole of nature and its beauty.
~Albert Einstein

After a long hot day, I eagerly welcomed the setting sun. The long shadows falling across the scorching pavement signaled the beginning of the cooling for the night. On my way to meet friends, I pulled into a busy neighborhood gas station to fill the tank of my truck. As I pumped my gas, I watched the people around me. Some looked like they were on their way home from work while others appeared to be heading out for the evening. The click of the pump shutting off brought my attention back to my task. I put the gas nozzle back and closed my gas cap. I headed into the mini-mart to pay for my gas.

As I waited in line, I overheard bits of the conversation between the young woman in front of me and the cashier. The young woman had written a check for the gas she had already pumped. The cashier's face was pinched, her jaw set and her lips pursed as she listened to the young woman's explanation.

"I can't accept this check," the cashier said tersely. "The name you signed doesn't match the name printed on the check. Your ID doesn't match the name printed on the check either."

I didn't clearly hear the young woman's reply, but I heard the pleading tone in her voice. The cashier repeated she could not accept the lady's check as payment. The young woman said she had no cash, no credit card, just the check. As the cashier questioned her about whom the check belonged to, the tension mounted. The cashier told the young woman she was going to call the manager and then turned to wait on me.

The scene I had just witnessed left me feeling uncomfortable. I paid for my gas and started to turn away. A line had now formed behind me. One customer shifted his weight, another fumbled with his purchase. They were becoming a bit annoyed with waiting. But I couldn't help myself.

I turned back to the cashier. "How much does she owe?"

There was silence from the lady behind the counter. It was one of those moments when the stillness screams out loud. The cashier stood with her eyes boring into me. I turned and looked at the young woman's face. I looked into her eyes and I saw something there, maybe fear, maybe desperation. Her need was so strong it was almost tangible. I didn't know if she was a struggling single mother or even if the check was stolen. But I could clearly see she needed help and I couldn't just stand there and do nothing. I said a quick prayer that I was doing the right thing.

I turned to the cashier and again asked the amount of the bill. With disapproval in her voice, she told me how much the young woman owed. I ignored the cashier's tone and dug through my purse collecting my last dollar bills, nickels, dimes, and pennies. My movements felt mechanical as I placed the bills and a pile of coins on the counter. I tried to hide my anxiety under the unfriendly eyes of the cashier. I knew I needed to do this. A man walked in from the back area and approached the counter. Surveying the scene, he gave the cashier a questioning look.

The young woman who had been the center of the controversy stared at me. She said a quick, "Thank you."

I turned and nervously walked out to my truck. As I was buckling my seatbelt, the man from behind the counter ran up to my vehicle and knocked on my window. With a furrowed brow, he held up a handful of dollar bills. I rolled my window down.

"Hi, I'm the manager," he said, his voice catching in his throat. "I want you to take this. It's to pay you back for the woman's gas."

"No," I replied. "I want to pay for her gas."

"Please take it," he said. He paused for a moment, seeming to collect his thoughts. "I didn't know there were still people like you left in the world. Please, take the money." His face was twisted with a half smile and confusion. His troubled expression convinced me to accept the money. It took only a moment to realize that it was not the girl I was meant to help, but the manager. For some reason he needed my random act of kindness more than she did. For some reason he needed his faith restored.

I thanked him and pulled out of the station. Dusk had settled in deeper and I remembered how much I love this time of day, how relaxed it always makes me feel. The last remnants of the sunset were disappearing. It took me a few moments to process my emotions about what had just happened. I was grateful I had listened to my heart, ignoring the cashier's disapproving looks and my own doubts. I was thankful I had been in a position to help the woman pay for her gas, remembering many times when others had reached out over the years to help me. I was glad that I was able, in some small way, to give this man some kind of renewed hope.

A calm came over me as I realized there is more to the circle of life than simply life and death. There is a circle of giving and caring, and passing these things along when the opportunity arises — a different kind of circle — a circle of love, a circle of compassion.

~Nancy Engler

A Divine Letter

Faith is taking the first step even when you don't see the whole staircase.
~Martin Luther King, Jr.

'd moved from my hometown on the Mississippi River to Los Angeles at the age of twenty-six to work in the music business. Initially, it was stimulating and thrilling. But after four years, L.A. lost its allure. The bohemian quality I once loved in my West Hollywood neighborhood began to fade for me, and all I could see were the cracks in the sidewalk on the seedy side of town.

Turning thirty was an awakening. I evaluated the course of my life. I kept thinking if I didn't make a change, I'd wake up one day to find myself with permanent roots in this city where it seemed everyone jockeyed for position in one form or another. I was uninspired. I was tired. I wanted serenity. I needed a plan.

I resigned from my job in the music business and took a position in client services at a thriving post-production facility in Santa Monica, where I was one of twelve assistants to the clients from major movie studios that came to the cluster of recording studios to synchronize audio with film. It was a unique job, something new and different, but I was still living in Los Angeles. A sensitive friend addressed my discontent by asking two simple questions: "If you could live anywhere, where would it be, and what would you be doing?"

Ireland was my answer. I saw myself in a best-case scenario living upon verdant fields partitioned by gray stone walls on the way to the sea, writing poetry and novels. "There's only one way to do this," I said to my friend, "and it starts with a plane ticket."

It seemed once I'd made the decision, the powers that be aligned in support. After I gave my resignation to the managing director, uncanny things transpired: I'd be standing on a Los Angeles street corner just as a stranger approached to exchange pleasantries in an unmistakable Irish accent. I received useful information repeatedly from surprising quarters and it gave me a feeling of being in tune with destiny. I was certain I'd made the right decision by following my bliss.

And there I was a year later: living by the sea on the west coast of Ireland and employed in the music business because everything had fallen into place. I was living the life I had imagined: I had friends, a rented home, a schedule, a purpose, all from a start-up business dedicated to the careers of Irish musicians. My life had certainty and security. I grew accustomed to Ireland and its cultural nuances and truly believed I'd found my place in the world.

But the rhythm of life has an ebb and flow. By the end of that year, the tides started to turn so subtly they were imperceptible, up until the moment there was no recourse. My non-profit place of employment lost its funding, and there I was in a foreign country without a job. I was baffled and bewildered. What had seemed like destiny became ambiguity, and I was indecisive and riddled with doubt over every option I weighed. I was not ready to leave Ireland; I hadn't exhausted her charms but it seemed all was lost, that fate had conspired against me.

I'm the kind of person who possesses an optimistic faith in the goodness of things, that life has meaning and God has a plan. The quandary was I couldn't see anything beyond the roads that appeared blocked. For two weeks I prayed, I meditated, I believed, and I vacil-lated between hope and despair. Then a letter arrived at my door.

One of the things I had to accept about living in rural Ireland was that it took ten days for a letter to arrive from California. I lived way out in the countryside where there were no mailboxes, so the postmaster would leave my mail at my door. One day during my two weeks of quandary, I bent down to inspect a letter at my doorstep, recognizing right away it came from the United States. I tore open the envelope to discover an offer from the post-production facility in Santa Monica. I had to read it twice, I was so surprised. "The woman who hired you in client services is leaving to have a baby," the letter began, and by the time I got to the managing director's signature, I realized he had offered me her job.

My first reaction was complete resistance. No way in the world I'd ever go back to L.A. I put the letter back in its envelope and threw it on the kitchen counter until my disbelief compelled me to read it again. It was then I noticed the letter's postmark, which was only three days before. "What is this," I said out loud, "divine intervention?" I considered and weighed until I arrived at the conclusion I didn't have a choice. Yet all the while, a voice in my head whispered, "Follow this; you don't have to know why."

"Follow this to Los Angeles?" my petulance screamed, but that is exactly what I did. I talked myself into returning to Los Angeles by holding to faith, by deciding this might be a stepping stone along a bigger path, that perhaps someone or something would be waiting where I least expected.

Today, I am married to the man who wrote that letter. This year, the novel I wrote inspired by my year in Ireland will be published. I now have a way of deciphering life's supposed ambiguities, which is to say I now see life's quandaries as full of potential. When in doubt, I don't fall into despair. Instead, I look for a bigger picture, and if I keep my faith and narrow my eyes, I swear I can see divinity.

~Claire Fullerton

The Dance Encounter that Changed My Life

Dancing with the feet is one thing, but dancing with the heart is another.
~Author Unknown

"Oh, Lord, I'm so tired of being lonely!" I deliberated about another depressing singles dance. I was closer to Medicare than college age, yet something in my spirit nudged me to persist, to never give up on finding true love.

I had been divorced for seven years and the empty nest was looming. I dreaded being alone. Girlfriends from church had been praying for a soul mate to arrive in my life for years, yet I didn't expect God to deliver Mr. Wonderful to my doorstep. I needed to take action, so I forced myself out the door.

Even though the dance felt a bit like entering the movie set of *Revenge of the Nerds*, my policy was to accept any dance requests, out of courtesy and kindness, unless they were truly creepy. Soon a clean-cut gentleman with lots of mileage approached.

"Let me give this old chap a thrill," I charitably thought, being a ballroom dance teacher and priding myself on the ability to follow anyone, regardless of how inept their dancing might be.

Within seconds, it was apparent that this geezer could really cut a rug! He moved with grace and fluidity and his dance frame was impeccable. Gliding around the floor with this stranger was sheer delight.

"You're so smooth," I swooned as he twirled me out.

"I used to be a Fred Astaire dance instructor," he modestly confided.

Exuberant and now totally in my element, my hustle moves exploded with a style and grace reminiscent of my Saturday Night Fever disco days growing up in Brooklyn. As I scanned the tables of admirers, I caught the attention of a handsome man with scintillating blue eyes and biceps to die for. Not to mention, he had a gorgeous smile.

Upon capturing his gaze, I accentuated my movements even more, coquettishly tilting my head back and swirling my arm upwards, wrist arched delicately with feminine flair. The flirting continued as I was led seamlessly from one dance move to another.

Apparently, this antiquated ballroom teacher was also a black belt in karate. After swinging me out in a double turn, he assumed a side-by-side position and executed a perfect side kick that would have stunned Bruce Lee. Now, we were really putting on a show, with disco moves and martial arts combined into one! I glanced at the handsome admirer, who could barely contain his laughter. Reveling in the attention, I continued flirting with the hunk for several more minutes.

Finally, our performance was over and I was back at my table. My heart fluttered in anticipation of the potential suitor. Thankfully, the good-looking heartthrob made a beeline in my direction.

"That was quite a performance with 'Miracle on Ice,'" he joked. He introduced himself as Joe.

Just as the humorous banter with Joe hit a high note, I discovered he was a forty-nine-year-old bachelor. My heart sank as I waited to hear that he still lived in his mother's basement. But I was pleasantly surprised that Joe was a school social worker. Also, he was a professional counselor who owned a condo. Could it be that he was as much a people person as I was, finding joy in teaching, inspiring and counseling others? I felt an immediate kinship, and we danced and chatted the night away.

The next day I received a call from a dorky guy named Harvey in desperate need of dance instruction. A few minutes into the conversation, I realized it was Joe, playfully honing his acting skills. Thoroughly amused, I prepared to dazzle him with my culinary skills, using tried-and-true recipes from my grandmother's Italian kitchen. He was smitten, but I was even more flabbergasted when he reciprocated and cooked a scrumptious dinner of roasted chicken and potatoes.

Astounded that he had more cooking apparatus than I did, I perused the shelves of his kitchen to discover every conceivable food processor, blender and other contraptions. Joe demonstrated one unfamiliar gadget, the apple corer, by creating a delicious apple pie. When Mom, the quintessential baker, complimented his pie crust, I knew he was a keeper. Was it possible that this Irish bachelor enjoyed cooking and entertaining as much as I did?

Several months later, an acrostic poem with my named showed up in which Joe captured my very essence. Yes, we completely understood each other.

At last, I found my soul mate! On a beautiful summer day four years after that momentous dance, I married my Prince Charming. The fifty-three-year-old bachelor gave me his heart, and he was definitely worth waiting for. How grateful I was that I never stopped believing and trusting in a second chance at love.

Nestled between my two grown sons as I glided down the aisle, I noticed tears of joy from my praying girlfriends. Our hearts marveled at the goodness and faithfulness of God, providing the perfect man in His perfect timing. It all started with "Miracle on Ice," and now my own fairytale miracle had finally come true.

~Leslie Tierney

The Full Circle Miracle

Faith is not belief without proof, but trust without reservation.
~Elton Trueblood

"But my debit card has to work," I said to the store clerk. "My paycheck was deposited into that account just this morning."

The clerk shrugged. "It's declined your card three times."

"But there's money in my account," I said. I looked at the much-needed groceries and then into the faces of my two young children. "I'm going to my bank to get the money," I said. "I'll be right back."

While driving to the bank, I fought back tears. Why did everything have to be so hard? I was going through a divorce I didn't want. I was struggling financially, emotionally, even spiritually.

Maybe especially spiritually.

The news at the bank wasn't good.

"According to our records, your checking account has been frozen because of unpaid taxes," the teller said.

"But that's not possible," I protested. "I don't owe any back taxes." But even as I said the words, I realized what must have happened. "I'm going through a divorce," I explained, "and my name is still on a lot of my ex-husband's liabilities. I'll bet this is just a mix-up."

The teller shrugged and said, "We can't remove the lien from your account until we get the government's approval, and that can take several weeks."

I could feel tears in my eyes. "So I can't use my account until then?"

"That's right," the teller said and then she looked past me to the next person in line.

When we got home, my three-year-old daughter, Julia, began to cry. "But I wanted chicken for dinner," she whined. "We have to go back to the grocery store."

"We can't," I said. "The card that I use to pay for things doesn't work right now."

She shrugged. "Let's just use regular money."

"I don't have any of that either," I said.

Six-year-old Jordan's eyes grew big. "How are we going to buy stuff?"

The tears I'd been holding back finally spilled over. "I wish I knew, buddy."

That night, we had macaroni and cheese for dinner. It was the last box in my nearly empty pantry. By bedtime, Julia had forgotten about the chicken she'd wanted, but I could tell Jordan was worried.

"We're doing all right, bud," I said, rubbing his back. "Mac and cheese is your favorite anyway."

His blue eyes looked troubled as he said, "Yeah, Mom, but what about tomorrow?"

I pressed my cheek to the top of his head and muttered, "Yeah, Lord, what about tomorrow?"

Although I knew what the Bible said about God hearing our prayers, lately I'd been wondering if those verses applied to me. I would definitely need some divine intervention to get through this one.

The next day was Saturday, but I still woke up early. I was wondering how I was going to tell the kids that there would be no milk for their cereal that morning when the doorbell rang. It was my neighbor, and she was holding a bag of groceries.

"We're going on vacation," she said, "and this food won't be any good when we get back. Can you use it?"

My mouth dropped open. "Oh, yes, thank you so much," I said.

"I've got some milk too, if you want it," she said.

"Yes, please," I said quickly. "We just ran out last night." I felt tears fill my eyes. "You don't realize how much this means right now."

My neighbor waved her hand through the air. "It's no big deal."

"You've become an answer to my prayers," I insisted.

I hugged her and wished her a safe trip. I closed the door and breathed a sigh of relief. My kids would have milk for their cereal that morning, and as an added blessing, chicken for dinner that night.

The food from my neighbor didn't last long, but when it was gone, another unexpected bounty appeared. And then another one after that. A friend lent me some money, my mom sent a pre-paid card for the gas station, another family member invited us over for dinner. Somehow, we were getting by.

Five weeks later, I was finally granted access to my checking account. The first thing I did was head to the grocery store to stock up on non-perishable food. If something like this ever happened again, I wanted to be prepared.

I filled my cart to overflowing. Both of the kids looked at me with wide eyes. "Why are you buying so much food, Mommy?" Julia asked.

"Because the last few weeks have been really hard, and I want to make sure nothing like that ever happens to us again." I smiled. "I have to take care of you and your brother."

Jordan frowned. "Isn't taking care of us God's job?"

His words stopped me short. "Yes, but I'll just feel more secure if I buy this stuff."

"But why, Mom?" Jordan asked. "God answered our prayers. He made sure we had milk for our cereal and gas for the car." He smiled. "God even remembered Julia's chicken."

I looked at the grocery cart and realized its contents would feed my small family for several months. There is nothing wrong with being prepared, but I was going too far. This shopping trip wasn't about stocking up on canned goods; it was an indicator that my heart wasn't in the right place. Despite God's faithfulness during the last few weeks, I still wasn't trusting Him to answer my prayers.

I murmured a quick prayer, asking God to help me trust Him. I felt His peace come over me, and when I opened my eyes, I knew what He wanted us to do.

I smiled at my children and said, "You're right. God did take care of us. And now, we have a chance to care for others."

I purchased every bit of food in that cart, but we took less than half of it home with us. Most of it went to our church's food bank.

Answered prayers are always a miracle, and more often than not, God uses other people in that process. My children and I had been the beneficiaries of answered prayer, and now, the food we were donating could become the answer to someone else's prayer.

And that was a full circle miracle.

~Diane Stark

Teacher in a Wheelchair

A few years of trouble, ten thousand years of bliss.
~Chinese Proverb

Hobbling across the parking lot like a crippled old man, I was feeling mighty sorry for myself. My injured back was not getting any better, and I had begun to wonder if the constant pain would ever go away. The doctors and surgeons, specialists and therapists, chiropractors and acupuncturists, pain pills and cortisone injections, spinal manipulation and electrical stimulation did not seem to help me, and my insurance coverage and savings account were both running out. Therefore, I was being "shown the door" and left to battle the problem alone.

Such was my mindset as I entered the grocery store in Durango, Colorado that afternoon to pick up a few things on my way home. Walking down the aisle, I spotted a young man in a motorized wheelchair. His entire body was twisted and deformed. Something horrible had happened to him, possibly while still in the womb, and as a result his arms and legs and torso and neck were all curled around each other. Everything was completely out of whack.

Well, not quite everything...

For right behind the boy stood his mother, a small blonde woman with a round and gentle face. Blissfully shopping for groceries while simultaneously operating the control stick at the rear of the wheelchair, she seemed to be moving in some sort of sacred synchronicity with her son as if they were one living being rather than two.

I could see the whole story with just that first look. The early signs of trouble, the worry, the diagnosis, the confirmation. The silent agony, the growing darkness, the "Why me, Lord?" questions. The endless doctor appointments, the operations, the ever-ongoing therapy. And yet also plainly apparent was that stubborn, steely, never-say-die attitude.

Because, you see, that child needed help, lots and lots of help, and his mother gave it to him. Simply, freely, unconditionally. In essence, his suffering became hers, and her joy became his. Something was being shared here, exchanged here, transformed here. It reminded me of a scene in the movie *Resurrection* where the healer cures a crippled woman of a similar affliction, but then temporarily exhibits a grotesque contortion of her own limbs, even as the patient stands up for the first time in her life.

This marvelous film from 1980 starring Ellen Burstyn is based on a true story about a woman who almost dies in a car crash, but then somehow returns from Heaven with the ability to lay hands on sick people and heal them. When pressed to reveal exactly which God or entity enables her to perform such miracles, she describes it simply as "the power of love."

As I neared the woman and her son in the wheelchair at the end of the supermarket aisle, he appeared to be trying to say something, but it wasn't easy for him to do. His mother leaned down to listen, and then suddenly both of them burst out laughing! Whatever he said was obviously outrageously funny, and the two of them enjoyed a good long belly laugh together.

Normal, healthy, able-bodied people walking past must have wondered what these poor souls could possibly have to laugh about, and yet laugh they did. Unrestrained, unashamed, unstoppable mirth emanated from them both, as if they had not a single care in the world.

Instead of a hundred of them.

As I passed this tender scene, my mind ran down a list of things that the young man had never done, and probably never would do.

Yet he seemed, at least for a precious minute, to be happy. I suddenly found myself in a totally different frame of mind than the pitiful one I'd known only minutes earlier. For as I walked around the store—on my own two legs—and carried my groceries—with my own two hands—and prepared to leave—all on my own—I stopped moping and feeling sorry for myself. My back problem no longer seemed so serious, so worrisome, so capable of ruining my entire life. In fact—almost miraculously—I could scarcely feel it anymore.

Just before heading out the door, I glanced back and saw the young man in the motorized wheelchair approaching the checkout stand with Mom right behind him. Although no longer laughing out loud, both had serene looks on their faces in spite of the enormous lifelong affliction that they shared. For the two of them, together, had discovered the key to happiness.

While I was still learning.

~Curt Melliger

Music Is His Voice

Music is the universal language of mankind.
~Henry Wadsworth Longfellow

Music is a very important part of our son's life. In fact, at a recent karate lesson, John asked his teacher, "Do you know 'The Reflex'?" His teacher was not familiar with John's new favorite song, "The Reflex" by Duran Duran. In typical John fashion, he was stunned that his teacher did not know about "his music." He promptly asked me to make a karate mix to introduce his teacher to "The Reflex." We have come such a long way, I thought.

It's not easy to go back to that time—the time before the diagnosis. Our precious Johnny was different from the other toddlers in our group of friends. We would go to playgroups and I would feel so isolated and lonely because all of the other moms were talking about the milestones their kids were achieving: potty training, reciting the alphabet, making animal sounds, etc. My son was not achieving these milestones. Heck, he could barely talk! Even at two years old, I had to translate John's special language for everyone because no one could really understand him.

I wished I had the key to unlock my son. Then one day, we turned on the Disney Channel and the most miraculous thing happened to our family—The Wiggles! If you're not in the know, The Wiggles are a children's musical group from Australia. As soon as we turned on The Wiggles for the first time, John began to dance. It was almost like there was an instant connection between John and this brand new type of music. Could The Wiggles be the key?

The Wiggles became John's obsession, although I prefer the term "special interest." We bought their DVDs and CDs, and on the night before he was supposed to start preschool, we attended our first Wiggles concert.

I never thought I would say that a Wiggles concert was amazing, but it was! John was mesmerized by the light show and we sang along to the songs. The look of sheer and utter joy on my son's face was almost too much for me. I teared up throughout the concert and tried to swallow my love and gratitude for this lovely band that brought my son to life.

On the next day, John started preschool. I let him wear his new Wiggles T-shirt and I really thought that the T-shirt was a kind of suit of armor, one that would protect him and give him comfort when I could not be there for him. He jumped into the classroom and started "talking" to everyone about the "Errrgles." No one knew what the heck he was talking about. As usual, everyone looked at me, and I said, "He's talking about The Wiggles." Oh! And there was a connection for the teacher to engage John. Yay!

The year passed, and although John had differences, we thought he was doing quite well at school. We were lulled into a sense of comfort, until the Christmas party during his second year of preschool that changed everything.

I was very happy as I drove to the preschool that day to volunteer at John's Christmas party. John's classroom was decorated beautifully: green and red paper chains were all over the room, and paper snowflakes filled the ceiling and walls of his cheery classroom. Games were set up, and all of the children were excited — all the children except my son. John was extremely detached from the action. He did not even really respond when I walked into the classroom with his sister, Colleen. He sat alone in the corner of the room. My world collapsed. What was going on?

Even though I prodded, John would not participate in any of the games. Rather, he wanted to stare into a seemingly empty fish tank.

The difference between John and the other students was glaring and vast. I felt myself wanting to cry. When I asked the teacher if John participated in school activities, she said, "Well, no. John is very sweet. But John likes to sit in the corner and watch the hermit crabs." I was shattered. What was going on? It seemed that John was becoming more and more detached from the world.

After that revealing day at school, I made an appointment with a developmental pediatrician. After that appointment, we had our answer. John was diagnosed with autism spectrum disorder in March 2010. Although I should have been relieved, I believed it would have been easier to suffer a gunshot wound. I was traumatized because after every other diagnosis — speech delay, sensory processing disorder — I thought, well, at least it's not autism. Autism became somewhat of a death sentence in my mind. It was a scary disorder about which I knew nothing, yet I feared it more than anything.

Months went by, and with the help of his new language stimulation school and The Wiggles, life was getting better. We were able to talk and dance, and his meltdowns occurred a little less frequently. It was at this time I needed to ask for a favor — not from my parents, my husband or my siblings. No, I had to write The Wiggles for a favor. Using some "Mama Bear Magic" as my friend called it, I wrote a letter to The Wiggles. I explained how John was diagnosed with autism and how their music was truly the only way we were able to connect to our sweet little boy for many years. Now he was learning to talk and I just wanted to share my appreciation with them. We had concert tickets for the upcoming Wiggles concert, and I wondered if John would be able to meet them, live and in person.

I received a wonderful letter back from The Wiggles. They said they would love to meet John and gave us backstage passes to meet them. Oh my gosh! I was so excited. Things were coming together!

Well, anyone with a child on the spectrum can attest to this fact: nothing happens like you think it will happen. We went to meet The Wiggles and John was so astounded to meet them that he couldn't speak. In fact, he hardly shook their hands. He seemed to be in a trance, which I mistook for indifference. So, I thought he didn't get anything out of this magical meeting. However, just before The Wiggles exited, John yelled out "Wake up, Jeff" to Jeff Wiggle. Jeff turned around, laughed and gave John a big thumbs up! Yes! Victory! John met his idols and gathered enough courage to speak. I was one proud Mama Bear.

Is everything perfect now that John is older? No. But I have learned that there is hope in the unseen. All you have to do is be open to the unexpected inspirations that surface in everyday life; even if they are a bit "Wiggly."

~Elizabeth Adinolfi West

Dreams and Premonitions

76

Divine Mothers

All that I am or ever hope to be, I owe to my angel Mother.
~Abraham Lincoln

don't know if I chose to be a palmist, or if palmistry chose me—but I do know that if not for a mother's love and guidance, I would never have followed my heart and fulfilled my true destiny.

Deciding to become a palmist may strike some in the West as an odd career choice. But in India, where I grew up, palmistry is a venerable profession whose origins stretch back thousands of years to the teachings of the Vedas, Hinduism's most sacred scriptures.

My earliest memories are of my grandfather practicing palmistry in the courtyard of our home. He was a deeply spiritual man who spent decades studying the Vedic Arts of Ayurvedic healing, astrology and palmistry. When he retired from the construction business, he devoted his life to helping others with his great spiritual knowledge.

I was in awe of his ability to diagnosis the exact cause of a person's physical, emotional, or psychological ailment by studying their palms, help them heal themselves by suggesting specific changes they could make in their diet, attitude, habits or behavior—and never once charging for his services. To Grandfather, palmistry was about growing closer to God and teaching others to do so. When we meditated together he always encouraged me to invite "Mother Divine"—the female essence of God and embodiment of compassion and love—to guide me along my path in life because "a mother's love will never steer you wrong."

He taught me about the geography of the hand, how the delicate lines crisscrossing our palms form a roadmap of our lives that can reveal great truths about ourselves and lead us toward happiness. His passion for palmistry took root in my own young heart and I began reading the palms of both my schoolmates and strangers on the street. I kept sketchbooks filled with pictures of the hands I had studied; I was drawn to an open palm like an explorer to an uncharted continent.

But my enthusiasm soured when I discovered that Grandfather's approach to palmistry was unique. Because most Indians believe their destiny is determined more by fate than freewill, palmistry was used as a tool for fortunetelling, not for personal and spiritual growth. And I had no interest in becoming a fortune-teller.

Thankfully, Mother Divine stepped in.

She arrived in the form of our white-haired family astrologer, who was summoned on my twelfth birthday to read my astrological chart. The entire family gathered for the event and were astounded at the great sage's pronouncement:

"This boy will revolutionize palmistry. One day he will travel far and wide teaching thousands about the spiritual benefits of Vedic Palmistry the way a minister teaches the Gospels."

My grandfather was overjoyed, but my father, a no-nonsense military man who expected me to follow in his footsteps, was quiet. Dad had tolerated my palmistry preoccupation as a childish dalliance but now he worried his eldest son could end up as a mad monk reading palms on a New Delhi street for a pittance. So he made an announcement of his own—I was being shipped off to a militaristic boarding school.

However, Mother Divine must have chosen the school because it had an enormous collection of Vedic texts in its library, which I spent the next three years devouring. To keep peace in the family, I promised my father I would get a university degree before setting out to become a professional palmist, which I did.

Several years later, I had a fulltime government job teaching physical education at a college and was married with two small children. I had also realized my dream of opening up a Palmistry Center in New Delhi and had a busy private palmistry practice. By all accounts life was very, very good. But the fatalist Indian mindset had not changed—people still came to palmists to have their future predicted, not to seek ways to improve their lives and change their destiny. I feared I would never be free to fully practice the spiritual palmistry I had learned from my grandfather.

Then, in early 1970, I saw a newspaper ad placed by a Montreal restaurateur looking for "the best palmist in all of India" to work in his Indian restaurant in Canada. I knew nothing about Montreal except that it was in the West, where freewill was valued over fatalism. The realization hit me: Montreal was where I needed to be! More than 600 palmists applied for the job, but it was offered to me—provided I could be packed and ready to go in four days.

But everyone was against the idea. My friends predicted I'd starve in a snow bank, my wife accused me of abandoning her, my father wouldn't lend me the money to buy a winter coat, and my boss refused to accept my resignation. The general consensus was that I was crazy.

I didn't eat or sleep for three days, wracked with guilt and indecision, as my extended family set up camp inside my house, hoping to dissuade me. The night before my flight, I was praying for guidance when suddenly, my anxieties calmed. I saw a shimmering pool of light in front of me and the beautiful face of Mother Divine.

"Mother?" I asked, completely flabbergasted.

"You are going," she answered, in a voice as soft as sweet music. "Don't worry about what others think, they will accept your decision later. But now, you must follow your heart and go."

A moment later, she vanished. I left for Montreal the next day—my own saintly mother was the only one to see me off. We rode to the train station together in a rickshaw before dawn.

"You are doing the right thing," she told me, in tears. "Your grandfather told us long ago that your destiny would take you away from us."

A few days later, I was in the Montreal restaurant excitedly preparing to give my first reading when I noticed something odd—the restaurant patrons were all English-speaking white people.

"Where are the Indian customers?" I asked the owner, in Hindi.

"We don't have any," he said.

"But… how will we understand each other during the reading?"

He looked shocked: "You mean… *you don't speak English?*"

I shook my head.

"I've got sixty clients waiting for readings. I'm ruined!" he cried out, throwing his arms up in despair. "I guess I'll have to make you a bartender."

I politely excused myself and retreated to the men's room, where I promptly burst into tears.

"Oh, Mother Divine! Did you take me far away from my home and family only to embarrass me and turn me into bartender?"

Suddenly, I felt Mother Divine's calming presence again, and heard her sweet, soothing voice.

"Dry your tears and go out there with a smile. You can do it. I will be with you."

I went back to the dining room and told the owner I was ready. While I'd been weeping in the bathroom, his wife had volunteered to translate for me until I learned English. Moments later my first client was ushered in—a glowing young woman who was nine months pregnant. I smiled: Mother Divine!

I can't for the life of me remember what I said to that first client, but it must have been good because she approached the proprietor afterward.

"This is the best palmist you've ever had," she told him. "Don't lose him, he'll be great for business!"

That was more than forty years ago. I've been in Montreal practicing my beloved Vedic Palmistry ever since. I've even been able to open my own lakeside Palmistry and Wellness center on a beautiful 500-acre forest reserve north of the city where I am happily teaching college-level courses in palmistry to students from all over the world.

I owe my good fortune to all my Mothers Divine, whom I will always heed. I know from experience that Mother knows best.

~Ghanshyam Singh Birla with Steve Erwin

77

Small Voice, Big Message

Never be a victim of inner conflict.
Listen to your inner voice and fight your way bravely.
~Anil Kumar Sinha

F red was a seasoned electrician; he had worked at the paper mill for over fifteen years. I, on the other hand, was a newbie, with only two weeks of experience. It was still a bit of a puzzle for me to find my way around the maze of old buildings and noisy machinery. I had to rely a great deal on others when it came to knowing where to go and what to do in the course of the day. Fred was the outgoing sort; he socialised at every opportunity and seemed to be friends with just about everyone in the mill. He never seemed to have a strongly held opinion on any subject, at least until the person he was talking to was out of earshot.

It was a maintenance day in the mill. We had an eight-hour window to shut down equipment, which normally ran twenty-four hours a day, seven days a week, inspect its condition and make any necessary improvements. This particular shutdown day, our task was to clean and inspect a bank of 2200-volt electrical controllers. The work itself was fairly straightforward and much of the time we would be waiting to have the power turned off.

The safety procedure was that the powerhouse operator was informed of the identity of the electrical feeder. He would then isolate it and lock it out. A station guarantee would then be issued to the supervisor who had made the request when the lockout was complete. This was to be my first shutdown in the mill and I was eager to show myself as a conscientious and capable worker. Fred and I gathered our tools and other equipment together in the damp, dripping basement and waited for the all clear to be given.

After a short time, the electrical foreman arrived to give us the okay to start the work. He was very keen on getting us started, as the time allotted to do the job was a bit on the tight side. I had no practical reason to question the lockout process; after all, it had been successfully used in the mill for many years. In spite of this, I suddenly, and to my own surprise, heard a small voice in my head demanding that I confirm the power was off before we started our work. Not wanting to be seen as a difficult employee so early in my new job, I asked the foreman if we could do a voltage test on the system.

This request seemed to irritate both Fred and the foreman, and both made the observation that we already had a station guarantee from the powerhouse operator. In any case, he continued, the only tester available was located in another mill some two kilometres away. In spite of his reassurance and steadily rising impatience, my little voice wouldn't give up. I said I was prepared to take a stand on the issue and not allow us to remove protective covers from the equipment until the proper tester was brought on site.

The foreman contacted the Chief Engineer. Soon a harried and stressed-out individual rushed onto the job site. The Chief was a large man who dressed in a blue lightweight suit with a cravat at the neck of his shirt. It was certainly not the recommended wear for a paper mill basement. He gave every indication of having been hauled out of an important meeting and not being happy about it. In spite of the lightweight suit, he was sweating profusely and the cravat, coupled with a rapidly reddening face, gave the impression that he was about to choke.

He didn't speak directly to me at first, but through the foreman, as if he needed an interpreter to underline the severity of the situation. When he did finally address me, it was only to point out that he would now have to travel to another mill and fetch the tester, and that it was entirely my fault that the work was being senselessly delayed. Muttering loudly under his breath about new employees who knew nothing about how things worked in the real world, he headed off to pick up the tester.

I thought it was odd that there was only one high-voltage tester available to service three mills, likely an indication of how seldom it was used. As time dragged by, I grew uneasy that this stand of mine would not exactly help to advance my career prospects. I had the sense that the Chief was likely the kind of person who could hold a grudge. Perhaps I had overstepped my authority.

The little voice, although convincing, was after all still just a little voice. I am sure that very few people have ever come forward to credit a little voice in their head with sound career advice, but it was too late to start doubting it now. While we waited for the tester to arrive, the foreman confirmed that I had not made a very impressive start in my new job. I was beginning to feel a little foolish at having made such a fuss, especially one motivated by the little voice in my head.

When he finally arrived with the thousand-volt tester in his hot and sweaty palms, the Chief was out of breath and looking more than a little put out. I took the unit from him, wiped it down, and touched it to the high-voltage bars; it lit up like a Christmas tree. There was still full voltage on the system. Everyone was speechless.

I turned toward the three men and saw them stare open-mouthed at one another. Without a word, the Chief walked over to me, his red face quickly turning white, and bear-hugged me, all the while muttering, "Oh God, oh God." With thoughts of recrimination now a thing of the past, the foreman approached me, shook my hand and in a voice full of emotion said that he had never been so happy to have one of his orders disobeyed. Fred, who seemed to have been hedging his bets up to that point, took over the situation from the two stunned supervisors and demanded that we all pay a visit to the powerhouse and get to the bottom of the lockout failure. It transpired that the operator who was responsible for the station guarantee was also relatively inexperienced and had been left on his own to muddle through as best he could.

I was never able to identify where the little voice came from, but both Fred and I certainly owe our lives to it. I never did explain to anyone why I had taken the stand I did, as many people do not believe in little voices. Since that day in the mill I have never heard the little voice, but rest assured that if it ever does pipe up, it will have my full attention.

~James A. Gemmell

78

The White Owl

Lovely are the curves of the white owl sweeping
Wavy in the dusk lit by one large star.
~George Meredith, "Love in the Valley"

t was a steamy, hot morning during the August monsoon season in Tucson, Arizona and I was in my bathing suit, headed to the pool. At 6:45 a.m. there was no one else outside. I arrived, peeled off my towel and dove into the pool. What a relief it was to swim in the desert summer. Being from Maine, here in Tucson on a sabbatical leave for one year, the searing desert heat never felt familiar or comfortable to me.

When I surfaced, I sensed that I was being watched—but as I scanned the pool deck and bathhouse, I saw no one in sight. I began to swim my laps, but I still felt like I was being watched. I kept looking but I didn't see anyone.

About forty-five minutes later, I completed my laps and stood up in the shallow end, stretching and scrutinizing my surroundings. It appeared that I was alone… but I really didn't feel alone. I shrugged off the concern and decided to relax, floating on my back. Within thirty seconds I was startled by a whoosh above my body. Still floating on my back, I opened my eyes and saw a little white Pygmy owl hovering over my head!

"Now where did you come from?" I asked out loud. The tiny owl couldn't have been more than seven or eight inches tall, and it hovered patiently, seeming to have no fear of me or my voice. "What do you want?" I asked. The owl's penetrating gaze was the only answer. I felt like it was trying to convey a message of some kind. What could this owl want?

"Well," I thought, "now I know why I felt that I was being watched." The tiny owl, now perched in a nearby saguaro cactus at the edge of the pool, was still looking at me intently. Thinking that this was odd, I continued my morning exercise routine, said goodbye to the owl and headed over to the University of Arizona campus.

The next two mornings the owl returned to visit me at the pool. It continued its penetrating gaze and watchfulness. Every time I glanced at it, the owl was watching me.

I know when something unusual happens three times I need to pay attention. I wondered if this had something to do with the owl being known as a spiritual messenger. Recently I had been "putting in a request" to the universe. I had been divorced a decade already and I had finished raising my two children. Now that they were both off to college, I wanted to end my ten-year relationship drought. I was very serious about wanting to meet someone special, and had made a list of the seven characteristics I wanted in a new partner. One of the items on my list was that he have an affinity for spiritual experiences! Was this tiny little white owl a messenger?

Ten months went by and I did not meet anyone special but I continued to pray for a miracle. The little owl gave me a spark of hope.

In January I received a phone call from a church camp in Maine, asking me to teach for a week in July. I agreed and looked forward to the experience with great anticipation. In March, I had a dream in which I heard a voice say, "You will meet someone at the camp." I trusted that dream, so on my fourth day at the camp, when a man walked into the kitchen to get himself a cup of coffee, I trembled all over. I heard the words: "That is him."

Ken joined me at the big table in the dining room where I was working on my computer. It turned out he was there as a volunteer to do some work on the chapel foundation. After introducing himself and finishing his coffee, he asked if I would like to go for a walk down to the ocean shore, just a few hundred feet away.

"Sure!" I replied, and jumped to my feet.

Walking down the hill beside him, trying to think of how to start an interesting conversation, I thought of the little white Pygmy owl back in Tucson and asked if he knew anything about birds. He replied that he had studied birds quite a bit.

My story about the little white Pygmy owl at the pool in Tucson tumbled out of my mouth. Ken became very quiet. We had arrived at the gravel beach and I looked at his face and felt really uncomfortable. He looked pale. I asked him if he was all right and he told me his own white owl story.

"About three days before my maternal grandmother, who raised me, passed away, she called and wanted my father and me to come and sit with her. She was one-quarter Micmac Indian, so when she explained that she was ready to go Home soon, we knew that meant that she was close to death. She said, 'I am going Home soon, but I will return and give you a sign that I am okay. I will return as a white owl and you will know it is me.'

"Two days later she died, and a few days later was her funeral. My father, who was 6'8" and close to 400 pounds, and I were still in our suits (we were pallbearers) on that hot August day. It was over 90 degrees and we were hot. After the funeral, Dad and I walked out into one of our 5,000-acre farm fields to sit on a log, where we kept coconut shells to drink water from a spring that poured out of the hill. We sat and drank the cool water in silence. Suddenly there was a silence so powerful that the hair stood up all over our bodies. Looking up, we saw a huge white snowy owl flying silently toward us, landing on a nearby tree branch where its yellow eyes looked first at me, then at Dad. It sat in silence for a few minutes, never breaking its gaze. Then it gently lifted off and flew away.

"'Did you see that?' I asked my father. 'Yep,' he replied softly. 'She came back to let us know. I wonder how she did that, since snowy owls are never here in the summer. They live way up north in the Arctic at this time of year.'"

Three days later Ken and I knew that his grandmother had brought us together, even though we were 3,000 miles apart just a short time before. Honoring Ken's paternal grandmother, his Native American heritage and my own Maliseet ancestry through my great-great grandmother was a wonderful way to begin our life together. We have now been married almost twenty years.

~Laura Lee Perkins

79

The Voice

The guardian angels of life fly so high as to be beyond our sight,
but they are always looking down upon us.
~Jean Paul Richter

My alarm rang at 8 a.m. I was tired. I had been up all night at the hospital delivering a baby. I got back to my student apartment at 5 a.m., exhausted. I was in my third year of medical school at the University of Washington, and I chose to do my six-week Obstetrics and Gynecology rotation in Boise, Idaho. At this smaller away-from-Seattle site, I would get lots of great experience. This was supposed to be a really exciting and fulfilling time, but it seemed most days I was just too tired to appreciate it.

As I fell into bed at 5 a.m., I thought about shutting off the alarm so that I might get more than a few hours of uninterrupted sleep. But if I did that, I would miss my karate class. The karate group was the other main reason I chose to do obstetrics in Boise. I had the opportunity to train with Renshi Rick Boyes, one of my favorite karate teachers. So I reluctantly dragged myself out of bed.

I pulled on a pair of jeans and a T-shirt and grabbed my gi (the standard karate uniform). I jammed a piece of toast and a banana into my mouth and jumped in my little yellow Volkswagen Super Beetle. It was less than a ten-minute drive from the apartment by St. Luke's Hospital to the dojo, which was on 13th Street.

As I drove down Idaho Street, the heaviness of exhaustion coursed through my whole body and I wondered why I was doing this. Wouldn't it be more beneficial to get a few more hours of sleep? I pushed these thoughts out of my mind. Just stop that negative thinking right now, I told myself. The discipline and exercise is good for you. And you always feel better after a good workout.

My little pep talk behind me, I focused on driving. I was going 25 mph. Every light turned green as I approached. I would make it to class on time and not have to endure the "look" from my karate teacher.

A quiet voice in my head said, "Slow down."

Huh? Why? I checked my speed: 25 mph, the perfect speed for hitting each light just as it turned green. As I approached 8th Street the light turned green! I sailed through the intersection.

The voice said again, "JOLENE, slow down." Huh? I checked my speed again. "JOLENE, SLOW DOWN, SLOW DOWN!!!" The urgency and loudness in the voice really startled me this time, and I almost involuntarily stepped on the brake. I didn't stop, but I slowed enough so that the light at 9th Street turned green several seconds before I got there. I was not yet to the crosswalk when a large green pickup barreled into the intersection from the right, traveling at least 50 mph.

OMG! Disbelief and shock flowed through me. I pulled over to the side of the road, my whole body shaking. I sat there for a few minutes breathing as the realization sank in.

That pickup ran a red light! I would have been smack in the middle of that intersection! My little Volkswagen Bug and I would have been smashed if I had not listened to that voice. If I had not slowed down. I had narrowly escaped death!

While I waited for my heart to stop pounding before I proceeded to karate class, I thought about the voice that had warned me to slow down. Until that day, I had never thought much about guardian angels. Now, I was convinced that I had one.

~Jolene Starr

80

Conduit
for a Dragonfly

The union of heaven and earth is the origin of the whole of nature.
~I Ching

M y job advising medical providers gave me the opportunity to drive through twenty-three sleepy, cozy, friendly counties in southeast Georgia for over ten years. My territory included towns with everything from blueberry festivals to rattlesnake roundups. Over time, many of the people I called on for business became friends.

One day, I found the office manager at one office having a quiet day because the doctor was on vacation. Leslie and I sat on two soft leather chairs in the doctor's inner office in front of a grunting antique fax machine. She asked me if I would do my presentation while she worked on a fax. As she fed the paper in one sheet at a time, we talked.

After my presentation, we had time to talk about our families, and I shared with Leslie how my married daughter had suffered an injury that resulted in a rare nerve condition that left her in constant pain. Leslie listened patiently. She was sympathetic and understanding, as no person had ever been to me before. When she spoke, I was surprised when she revealed that her own daughter also had a terrible disease, and it was my turn to listen, understanding better the reason for our connection. We were bound by our despair and our helplessness to do anything about our daughters' medical problems.

I was preparing to say soothing things to Leslie about how we needed to have hope and the courage to endure, when I heard the end of her last sentence, "…and we lost her four years ago." All I could do was blurt out, "Oh no!"

I had no soothing words for her. I felt the painful distinction between our common ground; my daughter was alive, still able to wait for someone to find a cure… Leslie's daughter didn't have that chance. I remember very little about the rest of the visit, except that for the first time at the end of a visit, we hugged.

Several months later, my route took me once again to the office that Leslie managed. This day, I found a gaggle of medical students in the vestibule, student nurses at the window, a waiting room full of patients, and the inner office lined with people on chairs in various stages of having their vitals taken. Today would be the short and sweet version of my visit. I hit my target without preamble, gave Leslie the handout, and turned to leave.

The office was very busy. I wished I could reach out to Leslie and acknowledge that I remembered our previous meeting but I knew clearly wasn't the time or the place. Still, I couldn't dispel the feeling that I needed to do something more. I thought, "Give her a pin." My mother had given me some leftover dragonfly pins she made for a local craft fair and I still had them in my car. My mom had said to me, "Just give them away to anyone as you see fit." In addition to the pins, she had fashioned out of gift paper tiny shopping bags to hold the sparkly creations. She placed each dragonfly made of crystal beads and silver wire in the center and covered it with a tuft of tissue paper.

I continued to feel what could only be called a compulsion to give a dragonfly pin to Leslie. I didn't want to, because I planned to give the pins to people in my immediate circle who would relate more to something made by my mother. Even so, I couldn't ignore the nagging thought, "Give her a pin. Give her a pin."

I thanked Leslie for her time and walked out to the parking lot. As I got into my car, the idea became a command: "GIVE HER A DRAGONFLY PIN!" I looked over at the perky points of tissue paper and picked one bag at random, relocked the car, and feeling silly, walked back into the office. I hit the buzzer at the window, and they let me in again. Leslie turned her head and looked at me inquisitively. I handed her the tiny bag. Almost apologetically, I explained that it was just a little homemade craft my mom had made and I wanted her to have one.

Leslie looked at the little bag made from wrapping paper and looked at me. I could see that she didn't want or need this in the middle of the swirling action that was the office that day. Yet, she unwrapped the pin and held up the dragonfly. The staff around her suddenly stopped what they were doing. I felt the energy in the room change as everyone stared at Leslie. For a brief moment, I noticed her eyes had opened wider when she saw the pin. Then her face seemed to show no emotion at all. She seemed to look at the pin for an extra moment, then fastened it to her starched white collar.

The staff was still frozen in place. I started to feel I had made a bad decision. Everyone was staring at her and now at me! I couldn't understand what was happening. Leslie saw my confusion, turned to me and said, "I never told you this, but my daughter loved dragonflies. She studied them. She photographed them. She documented all she observed. Before she died, she told me that she would communicate to me through the dragonflies; that whenever I would receive one unbidden, it would be her signaling me that she was nearby. Thank you."

~Kathleen Pellicano

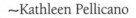

An Angel for Becki

81

Pay attention to your dreams—
God's angels often speak directly to our hearts when we are asleep.
~The Angels' Little Instruction Book
by Eileen Elias Freeman

The darkness was oppressive as she wobbled in heels along the side of the highway. The car had choked to an unexpected halt, and like a normal teenager she did the only thing she could think of... get out and walk.

It was cold and late, and the young girl shivered as the reality of her situation became clear. Home was far away. This could be a long night. If only someone would stop and offer her a ride—anyone—and preferably soon. She offered up a prayer for help and plodded on.

The lights of a truck shone from behind her as it approached. "Maybe he will stop," she hoped. The brake lights flashed on as it halted. "He's stopping!" Her words were lost in the night.

The transport ground to a screeching halt and the cab door opened. A wordless invitation was extended and she understood. Without hesitation the girl climbed up into the seat and closed the door. Slowly the truck pulled back onto the road and disappeared into the night, never to be seen again.

I bolted upright in my bed, lathered in sweat. Was that a dream or was it a vision? It was unbelievably real, and the girl was my daughter! I jumped from my bed and ran to her room, positive I would see her sleeping soundly under the covers.

Her bed was empty. I stood in horror trying to think why she had not come home. As the mental fog began to lift, I remembered she was visiting with friends that evening. Perhaps she stayed there for the night. It was 1:30 a.m. but I raced to the phone and dialed a number.

"Hello?" The voice was heavy with sleep.

"Hey. Sorry to wake you. Becki didn't come home tonight and I was wondering if she stayed at your place?"

"No, she left here a few hours ago. She should have been home at least by midnight!" The voice on the other end began to reflect my own panic.

I told her about the vision that woke me. She promised to pray, and we hung up.

Instantly I felt a force upon me, a spiritual presence driving me to prayer. Over the next forty-five minutes I alternated between lying prostrate in petition and pacing the floor in praise.

At 2:15 a.m. lights appeared as a car turned up our long driveway. I could tell immediately that it was not my daughter's. Was it a patrol car?

My face pressed against the window. I could not breathe.

A small vehicle pulled in front of the house, and tears stung as I watched my precious daughter emerge from the car and make her way up the steps.

Throwing open the door, I pulled her inside, hugging her tightly while plying her with questions.

"My car stopped on the highway and I decided to walk home." She began to explain. "I knew I was never going to make it in my dress shoes so I prayed that someone would give me a ride. A truck slowed down and was about to stop, then suddenly picked up speed again and carried on. Right after he drove away, a car with a mother and daughter stopped and offered me a ride. They saw the truck begin to stop as they passed me and were concerned, so they turned around and came back."

There were no words to describe the emotions that screamed through me. Her story was an exact parallel to the vision that woke me from deep sleep. God had provided an intercessor for His child in an hour of grave danger.

I don't know why that truck driver decided not to stop, but something tells me it was because of an angel walking beside Becki. All I know is that I am eternally grateful to the mother who stopped to save her, and for the dream that caused me to pray for her.

~Heather Rae Rodin

82

Hold Fast
to Your Dreams

Dreams are today's answers to tomorrow's questions.
~Edgar Cayce

I should have known I was having a dream, but somehow you never do when you're in the middle of it. You never just stop in the middle of a dream and say, "Wait. Really? Circus clowns in my classroom, and I'm walking on a tightrope? This must be a dream!"

So I didn't jolt myself awake that night in May of 2003 when I found myself standing at the doorway of an old mountain cabin, asking the wizened caretaker if it was safe for me to venture out to my car, since I'd heard there were bobcats in the woods.

"Oh, go ahead, you'll be fine," he assured me. "There aren't any bobcats around here." But immediately a terrifying bobcat lunged out of the woods and began furiously circling around me. I opened the door to the cabin and let him in, but soon he was pushing out of the door I was struggling to keep closed. I braced against the door with all my weight, but he was too strong for me, and he pushed the door open, dragging out a large, whimpering dog in his jaws.

End of dream.

The next night, the bobcat appeared in the doorway of my husband's parents' house, circling around me. On the third night, it clawed on the outside of the tent I was sleeping in with a little baby. It burst in and dragged the baby away. I awoke and knew that something was very wrong. But what?

I knew to be attentive to dreams like this—dreams that come in twos or threes, or dreams that have a recurring theme—because, decades ago, my friend Gloria had had a troubling dream about riding on a horse that, in the middle of a jump, lay down and died. Get to the doctor today, advised her friend, the Jungian dream analyst. And sure enough, she had a large ovarian mass.

My own mother died of ovarian cancer, and I had been faithful about my own surveillance for the disease. For over a decade I'd had the CA-125 blood test and an ultrasound every six months. Even though they are notoriously unreliable, they are still the only tests available for this deadly disease, and I was not going to be caught off-guard. So I knew that if I ever had a dream about horses stopping a jump mid-air and lying down and dying, I should get in to see the gynecologist.

But what could my dream mean? For several weeks I tried to pay attention. I had two friends who had studied dreams, and both Jeannie and Patty said that cats are often an indication of female energy. I couldn't relate to that. For my money, the dream was more about the dog that was being dragged out of the cabin, or the baby dragged out of the tent. I was going through a hard time that spring, and wondered if the dream was about my fears of being dragged away from the work I love. "Most dreams don't work that way," they told me. "Pay attention to the cat."

And then, as so often happens with heavenly messages, the dream began to lose its power. I was busy teaching Scripture, busy teaching people to pray, busy teaching people how to hear God. Busy, as it turned out, dying.

The following January I was giving a retreat at the beautiful Trappist monastery in Snowmass, Colorado. The Trappists invite the retreatants to pray the liturgy of the hours with them in true monastic fashion. And so at 4 a.m., we all walked in frigid silence down the mountain dirt road to the chapel, lit by a single bulb in the dark night.

After Lauds, I foolishly left my flashlight with some in our group who wanted to stay to pray so that they could go up the mountain later. I walked out into the pitch-black night, took a wrong turn and was immediately, dangerously lost. I walked in the freezing winter night, walked until the light from that solitary lantern was lost, walked until, desperate, I turned off the road and made my way to a cabin in the distance.

While standing on the porch of the old cabin, I heard some stirring in the bushes. I caught my breath as I remembered that we had just sung Psalm 104 — "You give the lions their food in due season" — and then, standing at the doorway of the old mountain cabin, my dream of eight months earlier came back to me. I had walked right into my dream.

Is this what it was all about? Is that how dreams work? Had I been given a preview of my own horrible "death by bobcat"? And if so, what possible good was that? Why have prophetic dreams if we don't have the tools to unlock them in time?

I stood absolutely still, and the rustling stopped. Soon the sun came up over the valley, and I could see the retreat center, way off in the distance. I made my way back just in time to join the group as they were once again going down the mountain for Morning Prayer.

I returned to Denver pondering all of this, astonished that I had once again been visited by the dream, only this time while very much awake! But almost immediately I was tired — too tired to work, too tired to move, too tired to investigate strange, recurring dreams. And when the quarterly newsletter from NOCC (the National Ovarian Cancer Coalition) arrived in the mail, I noticed that extreme fatigue was listed as one of the symptoms of the disease. I called my gynecologist and said, "It's happened. I have ovarian cancer."

From that moment, the moment I finally recognized it and named it, the dream stopped chasing me, circling me, signaling to me that my "female energy" was being eaten alive by a ten-centimeter tumor. Many months later, after the emergency hysterectomy and months of chemotherapy, I asked my oncologist how long he thought that tumor had been growing. "Probably about ten months," he said. The very same time that the dreams appeared.

On March 24, 2014, I reached a milestone too few women with this cancer ever reach—the victorious ten-year mark. I am the longest living survivor of ovarian cancer at the Rocky Mountain Cancer at Rose Medical Center in Denver.

I will always wonder about this dream, and the dream that preceded it, the one my friend Gloria had years earlier, the one about the horse lying down to die. She couldn't have realized that sometimes the dream sent to one finds its fuller meaning in the telling to another. And with that same sense of wonder I tell it now to you.

~Kathy McGovern

83

The Song and the Dance

Music is what feelings sound like.
~Author Unknown

When our son deployed to Afghanistan, God gave me a song. At the time, it was a popular song, played often on the radio, but I purchased my favorite version of it on CD. Listening to the song was one way of releasing all the pent-up emotions of fear, anxiety, and longing. A soldier in the U.S. Army, Phil had been through Basic and AIT here in the States, but once he was deployed halfway around the world in the midst of a war-torn country it was hard to bear.

On my normal route to work, I had what became a daily ritual. After some minutes of whispered prayer, I would pop in the CD and sing along until my tears overpowered the lyrics. Then I would sob quietly and pray until the song was over. Before reaching work I would pull myself together.

When I slipped into the office, the first thing I did was check my e-mail to see if I had one from our soldier. Two or three times a week, there would be a short note; those hastily written e-mails were the greatest treasure imaginable. Often I would print the contents and carry them to the staff prayer meetings. Most of the people I worked with had known our son since he was a baby, and they joined with me as we offered up fervent prayers for his safety. Over and over, day in and day out, week after week, month after month, we prayed. Our voices raised together in prayer were sweet times. I needed the comfort because deep in my heart, I knew he was in a real life-and-death struggle.

Then, one day while still overseas in the war zone, Phil had a dream. I firmly believe it was our prayers that caused this to happen. To this day, he does not know whether he was actually asleep or awake—only that the dream was more real than his physical location. Nevertheless, when it was over, he knew two things with certainty. He knew that he would not die in Afghanistan, but would return to the States alive and well. And he also knew that when he returned he would marry the most beautiful woman he had ever seen. When he woke up, he wrote everything he could remember about the dream and sent it to me via e-mail.

Since Phil believed the Lord gave him the dream, he embraced every part of it. An astonishing faith carried him through every possible fear. Armed with heavenly protection, he volunteered for highly dangerous missions, then would write home about them—at least the ones that weren't classified. I would e-mail back and remind him that he was the one who had the dream, not me, so would he please be a little more careful? I had never seen a physical manifestation of the peace that passes all understanding, but when he received some R&R time and came home for two weeks, it was evident on his face. No one could pretend to be at peace like that; it's not humanly possible. He simply had no fear at all concerning battle missions.

Eventually the deployment ended, and he came home for good, safe and sound notwithstanding some bouts with PTSD. That was the stuff of nightmares. He experienced acute anxiety around crowds—even people he had known and loved all his life—and a distinct disassociation from our present-day culture. His dad and I continued to pray. It wasn't over yet.

Meanwhile, his father and I moved to a different city. After several months of miserably existing on his own, Phil visited and decided to move to our new location. Still figuring out what he wanted to do, he hired on with a company in the oil field industry, but his main focus proved to be the church we attended. He began to attend regularly, got involved and made good friends, then started back to college with a fresh vision. And, yes, he finally met that beautiful woman from his dream.

They dated while he finished his degree, then married. At their wedding, when it was our turn to dance, he and I gingerly stepped out onto the floor. Since neither of us cared much for wedding dances, we hesitantly shuffled around the dance floor. Suddenly I was mesmerized by the music playing. When I asked him what the song was, he responded, "Mom, I have no idea. Jasmine chose all the music."

By that time, though, I knew.

It was the same song the Lord gave me all those mornings I drove to work, crying my eyes out, pleading with God for our son's safety and wellbeing. It was the song not one person in the world knew about but my heavenly Father and me. Same one, same version, now playing in honor of the mother-son dance at my son's wedding. Only this time, he was not a million miles away in a war zone, but safe and marvelously happy in his role as groom.

Admittedly, my eyes watered and the room blurred, but only for a moment. I was just too happy to stay choked up this time around. As the song played, I snuggled into his strong arms one more time as we laughed, dancing our way into his bright future. He got the girl—I got the song and the dance.

It was more than enough.

~Mary Pat Johns

84

Rainy Day Rescue

Your mind knows only some things. Your inner voice, your instinct,
knows everything. If you listen to what you know instinctively,
it will always lead you down the right path.
~Henry Winkler

cannot remember the first time I had a strong intuitive feeling I needed to act on. But I do remember the day that feeling saved an old woman's life. It was the day after Easter. I was fourteen.

A couple of friends and I were helping the minister at our church with a collating project, assembling books for a meeting to be held that day. Suddenly I heard a voice inside my head: "Go for a walk in the cemetery. Go now!" I looked up. "Did you hear that?" I asked my friends.

"Hear what?" my friends said.

"Never mind," I said.

"Go for a walk in the cemetery. GO NOW!" Afraid of looking foolish in front of my friends, I did not mention the voice that apparently only I could hear. The voice was so compelling, so loving, and I felt so safe, that there was nothing I wanted more than to take a break from our task in the church library and go for a walk.

"I m going for a walk in the cemetery. I'll be back in soon."

"It's a little gray and drizzly," one friend said.

"I know." Out I went.

The large, rambling cemetery that bordered the huge church on three sides was deserted. Wreaths and vases of flowers decorated many headstones, but not a person besides me was out. I wandered among the graves, enjoying the damp quiet of early spring. From a young age, I could feel the presence of God anytime I was in nature, and even in the chilly drizzly overcast, this day was no exception.

A lone car drove into the cemetery, stopping down the gravel road from where I walked. An old woman got out. As she walked away from her car I saw it begin to move, rolling backwards. The old woman reacted, racing toward the car door, and as the car's back wheels slid down over a small bank, she disappeared from view.

I ran toward the car and saw a terrible sight — the old frail woman, her leg pinned under the wheel of the car sunk in the mud!

"Ma'am!" I yelled, running toward her. "I will get help! I will be right back! I will help you!"

Running blindly around the outside of the church, I stumbled inside, and found the meeting room full of clergy. "There is a lady in the cemetery! Pinned under her car! She needs help! Someone call an ambulance, please!"

There were blank looks around the boardroom table, until the light dawned and finally my own pastor asked, "Where?" as he and two other men got up to follow me.

We raced to the cemetery and I knelt down by the old woman, who was shaking and incoherent but still conscious. "It will be okay," I said. "An ambulance is on its way. These men are here to help you." The three men had jacked up the car and had pulled the woman out by the time the ambulance came. My next-door neighbor, a volunteer firefighter, was driving. They loaded her up and drove her to the hospital.

I sank to the ground, shaking and crying. I thought about what might have happened if I had not been there. She could have died afraid and alone in a deserted, rainy cemetery.

I found out later, from my neighbor, that the old woman survived, although bruised and battered, and she was able to go home in a few days. I never learned her name and never saw her again.

~Deborah J. Kinsinger

A Green and White Dixie Cup

Earth has no sorrow that Heaven cannot heal.
~Author Unknown

It happened on a Wednesday evening. I stood before the stove preparing supper for my husband and two-year-old son. One minute I was stirring buttered corn, and in the next, I felt the life of our ten-week-old embryo escape my body. My husband called the doctor, and as directed, he scooped up what was to be our second child in a paper cup and headed to the hospital.

Only an hour before, I had cradled this baby within me, and now he or she was being transported in a green and white Dixie cup. I held the cup tightly as I stared at this warm tiny life. Tears fell as I wondered what his or her face would have looked like and what his or her future might have held. After arriving at the hospital, I went through the normal procedures that follow a miscarriage. Soon afterwards, they sent me home to recuperate for the rest of the workweek. As much as I enjoyed my job as a secretary for the head nurses at a local hospital, I was relieved to get a break, both emotionally and physically.

On the Friday following my miscarriage I found myself alone at home, being pestered by one particular question, "Where is my baby?" I couldn't help but wonder if the embryo was old enough to go to heaven or if he or she had simply vanished, never to be seen again. I believed in God but I didn't know much about him then, and I knew nothing about the future of the baby we'd just lost. Questions about this baby's whereabouts consumed my entire day.

When I returned to work the following Monday morning, Steve, my second cousin and chaplain-in-training, tapped on my window and asked, "When you have a minute, can you come down to my office?" He wasn't wearing the happy-go-lucky smile I was used to seeing so I quickly made my way down the hallway to his office.

He shut the door and sat directly across from me. He shared how he was sorry to hear of our loss, but it was obvious there was more going on than just sympathy.

"Can I ask you something, Cathy?"

"Sure."

"What was on your mind last Friday? I mean, were there any specific concerns you had that day?"

"Steve, I thought about only one thing on Friday. I wondered where my baby was."

I'd barely finished my sentence before he began sobbing. I quietly sat on the red leather chair, confused by his tears.

"Here's why I ask. I was on call last Friday night. It was a busy day in the ER so I decided to take a nap on one of the cots in the back room. At some point, I was startled. When I opened my eyes, I saw what appeared to be God standing in front of me. He was so real I felt like I could reach out and touch Him. He pointed and told me, 'Go put Cathy's mind at ease. Tell her the child is with me and she will see him one day.' With that, I sat straight up on the cot. My clothes were soaked and dripping with sweat. My wife could tell you that I'm not a dreamer, and this was no dream. I'm still shaken from the experience."

I'd barely opened my mouth to speak when Steve interrupted me.

"There's one more thing, Cathy. God was holding a baby in his arms when he spoke to me."

Tears streamed down my cheeks as I made my way back down the hall to my office that Monday morning. I recalled how I'd felt just minutes earlier—broken, sad, and full of misgivings. Although still sad, my questions and doubts began melting into peace and confidence. Because of the miraculous appearance that Friday night I now live with hopeful confidence.

I know now, without a doubt, that one day I will see the face of the tiny baby who once inhabited a green and white Dixie cup.

~Cathy S. Baker

Hope and Reality

There is a fine line between dreams and reality, it's up to you to draw it.
~B. Quilliam

Disney World? We're going to Disney World! Both my kids were beyond ecstatic while I sat there in shock. My brother had just given us our Christmas present: a trip to Disney World. I was a single mom, always broke. I didn't even have a reliable car to make the long drive from Conyers, Georgia to Orlando, Florida. Before I could thank him, he stated, "There's only one condition, I get to drive y'all there."

Both my kids, then six and twelve, adored their uncle. He was still single, so we did a lot of fun stuff together. He was one of my best friends during some very tough years.

Four months later, the four of us piled into my brother's new, red Ford Escort hatchback and off we went on our magical Disney vacation.

I was extremely tired and worn down. Working, taking care of the kids, constantly being broke, and still healing from a terrible divorce left me feeling hopeless most days. I felt like I was living in a dark tunnel with no end in sight. My lack of education kept me from getting a better paying job. I was thankful for the job I had, but it barely supported three people.

I'd already been through foreclosure and bankruptcy. I lived one paycheck away from eviction all the time. I longed for a break from everything.

Sometimes I'd wish there was a place where single moms like me could go live temporarily while getting specialized help. I needed an education, some counseling, help with budgeting, and a supportive environment that would help me get on my feet.

This trip came at a perfect time. Planning for it lit a flame underneath me, making me feel revived and refreshed before we even pulled out of the driveway.

We stayed at a wonderful resort that had a large pool with slides and diving boards where my twelve-year-old son played when we weren't at Disney World. There was also a large playground near the pool that my daughter loved. I found my special place on the porch of an inviting out-building located between the pool and playground.

This building had a huge covered, wraparound porch with wooden rocking chairs all around. You could get fresh towels after swimming or a refreshing drink. Or you could simply sit on the porch out of the sun like I did.

This place was perfect because I could see both of my kids on either side and still talk to them while I sat in a rocker on this huge porch.

This was the first restful time I'd had in so long. I felt safe and at peace. My kids were playing happily. I sat and rocked, enjoying my surroundings, as the burdens I'd been carrying drifted away with the balmy breezes.

While sitting there wishing this moment wouldn't end, I was startled by a vision. I saw a large house with a big wraparound porch and rocking chairs. I can remember to this day saying under my breath, "I wish other single moms who are hurting and in need could feel what I feel right now." Then I thought, "There needs to be a place where struggling single moms can go for a break and receive help getting back on their feet." Every time I'd sit in this spot while my kids played, the vision flooded my mind.

When we got home, life returned to the usual stress level. Months and years passed, and we lived through one crisis after another.

Sometimes I shared my vision, but only with a few people. I prayed often about it, feeling that this vision had come from God. He'd have to be the one to fulfill it because I sure didn't have the means to pursue such a venture.

Then life took over, years passed and the kids grew up. I remarried and started a new life learning how to be a wife again. I always wondered what that initial vision and idea for this type of ministry meant. There were times I thought, "Oh, that was just a silly idea you had because of where you were in life. People won't support it."

Even when I put it on the back burner and tried to forget about it, it would resurface. I'd share it with someone, and they'd say what a tremendous need it would fill. One day I even shared it with my pastor, who agreed it was a good idea. But I'd always get wrapped up in my life again and let it go.

One day when my husband and I came home from out of town, there was a message on our answering machine. A woman's voice explained she'd gotten my number from our pastor. We went to the same church but had never met.

She went on to explain the purpose of her call. She and her husband were purchasing some property with a house on it. They were buying the property to specifically be used for ministry, but weren't sure what yet. She further explained that our pastor had shared with her my vision, and she hoped it was okay that he gave her my number.

When I returned her call, she wanted me to go see the property and let her know what I thought. She gave me the address adding, "It's a big yellow house with a full wraparound covered porch." She had me at "wraparound." I asked God, "Is this You?"

I drove to the property full of anticipation. When I pulled into the driveway and caught a glimpse of the house, my heart fluttered and stomach did flip-flops.

I slowly pulled up, taking it all in. "Wow," was all I could say. I stepped onto the wide covered porch that wrapped all the way around the house.

I slowly walked around the porch, gazing at the woods, peeking through large windows, remembering my vision from eighteen years earlier. Through a rush of emotions, I knew it wasn't a silly dream, but something real and tangible.

The covered porch was massive, and I thought, "Plenty of room for rockers and patio furniture where single moms can rest while planning the course of their lives as their children safely play on the seven-plus acres."

Today, that vision is a 501c3, non-profit ministry to single moms. In early 2015 we hope to take our first four single-mom families into a residential program where they can receive a little help getting back on their feet by going to college, getting better jobs, learning parenting skills, getting counseling, joining support groups and becoming strong family units.

Now I know my nineteen-year, single-mom journey, with its struggles, triumphs, joys and sorrows will not be wasted. This is God's vision, His dream, and it continues to unfold day by day. I can't wait to see what He does next.

~Terri Webster

Chapter
9

Hope
&
Miracles

Mysterious Miracles

Deep Faith

You may ask me for anything in my name, and I will do it.
~John 14:14

In the summer of 1991 our seven-year-old daughter, Patty, waited in gleeful anticipation for her friend Melissa's arrival. Melissa's family planned to spend a day in Nebraska before heading back to their new home in California, and we'd arranged to let the girls enjoy the day together.

Because of the heat, the excited girls begged for a water outing. "But Melissa doesn't know how to swim," I pointed out.

My husband, Jake, came up with a compromise. "Honey, they only have one day together. We can go to the Platte River. It's shallow."

Looking at the girls' hopeful faces, I agreed. We loaded the car with fruit snacks and fishing gear, and headed out.

Nature's symphony welcomed our arrival. Piping birdcalls, the low drone of insects, and the sound of leaves rustling in the breeze mixed with the soft lap of water against the shore. The girls and I declined Jake's offer of fishing. He laid a rod over his shoulder, grabbed his beat-up brown tackle box, and hurried upstream, eager to battle the catfish.

The girls' joy proved infectious, and I joined their exuberant play, chasing iridescent blue dragonflies and tiny sand-colored toads. We drew in deep breaths of the hot, river-scented air and raced into the shallow water. It flowed lazily past our ankles, and we dragged our feet through the smooth golden sand while darting silver minnows tickled our toes.

The heat increased as the early afternoon sun blazed across the cloudless blue sky. In spite of the sunblock we'd slathered on, the intense rays baked our backs. We splashed each other to stay cool, and the girls asked, "Is this as deep as it gets?"

Old timers described the Platte as, "an inch deep and a mile wide," and they seemed to be right. We waded across the wide expanse of slow moving water until it swirled around the girls' knees. Better, but it didn't cool us enough, or satisfy our desire for more river adventure.

We waded in farther and found a pocket that seemed perfect, waist deep on me, chest level for the girls. We splashed each other, refreshed by the cool water.

Laughing, I backed downstream about twenty feet to escape the girls' tag-teamed water barrage, not realizing a deep, swift channel hid in this otherwise sluggish river.

I took another backward step, and the bottom dropped out from under my feet. The current, much stronger here, dragged me in deeper.

I called, "Stay back," but it was too late.

The girls waded closer to see what had happened to me, and the current captured them. They struggled against its pull, but inch by inch it sucked them closer to the swift running channel.

And Melissa couldn't swim.

I yelled to Jake, but he was fishing about a quarter of a mile upstream. Even if he heard me, he'd never reach us in time.

I shouted, "God, help us!"

Both girls screamed. Horrified, I treaded water and watched the current jerk my daughter off her feet. Patty loved swimming in pools, but here she fought to keep the relentless river from sucking her under.

I screamed again, "God, help us," as Melissa succumbed to the river's unyielding pull.

My thoughts raced. I knew I wasn't strong enough to catch both girls and keep them afloat. Just then Jake came around the bend.

Thick interwoven brush blocked the riverbank there, so he fought his way through the shallows. But too great a distance separated us. He couldn't help.

I struggled to keep my head above water. My arm and leg muscles burned as I fought the channel's pull, each stroke more difficult than the last. A sick certainty overwhelmed me—these precious girls would drown, and I could do nothing to save them.

It was hopeless. We needed a miracle.

A sudden, insistent thought overrode all others. "There is power in the name of Jesus."

I'd invited Jesus into my life a few months earlier, and He'd already demonstrated his miraculous power, saving me from a ladder fall that could have killed me.

I spit foul-tasting water from my mouth and screamed, "Jesus, save us!"

Immediately a swell of sand grew beneath my feet. It lifted me as if I was standing on top of an elevator. The sand ridge raised me chest high out of the water at the exact moment the girls swept by.

I reached out and grabbed Patty with my left arm, and Melissa in my right. We clung to each other and inched backwards. Where the drop-off had been moments before, the solid ridge of sand now formed a path for us to escape from the deep channel.

Jake reached us as we staggered into the shallow water we'd spurned such a short time before. "Are you okay?"

Patty jumped up and down. "Jesus saved us, Dad!" She hugged him and grabbed Melissa's hand. They raced through the ankle-depth water to a sandbar, their excited chatter filling the air. They spun in circles, celebrating our miraculous rescue.

Jake held me as I slumped trembling against his side and told him of the divine intervention that occurred the instant I called out Jesus's name.

We stepped closer to watch the girls scoop huge letters in the sand. Their message of gratitude read, "Thank you, Jesus!"

~Jeanie Jacobson

Money from Heaven

When your intentions are pure and clear,
nature will support you in unimaginable ways.
~Sri Sri Ravi Shankar

An angry rain whipped the exposed skin of my face but did not deter me from my mission of finding the perfect honeymoon outfit. Head down, chin tucked in, I trudged up the narrow steps of the boutique on Newbury Street in Boston. Once inside the brightly lit shop, I lingered, purveying the jewelry, the catchy notecards and of course, the summer dresses. Amidst the new arrivals rack, I found a cute gingham dress that not only looked great but also would be perfect for Hawaii. I gave the teenage clerk my credit card and watched her wrap up the dress with bright fuchsia tissue paper, pack it in a monogrammed box, and slip it in a shopping bag.

As I left the store, I noticed a woman standing with a girl of about seven to the side of the green and white striped awning. It took me a moment to realize she was talking to me.

"Can you spare some change?" she asked. "I need to take a train back to Lynne with my niece."

I don't always give to people who ask for money, but this time I paused. The woman's feet were placed squarely on the ground, wide enough to give heft to her stature. She looked to be over fifty, with gray curls and a brown bucket hat. The little girl holding her hand wore a slicker, but still looked uncomfortable and cold. The wind slapped my shopping bag against my thigh.

I took in her wide chocolate brown eyes, and held them for a moment. They were filled with such sincerity and hope, that, in that split second, I decided to help.

She needed to go quite far, and a mere dollar or two probably wouldn't be enough to cover her train fare, so I made a silent commitment to give her a twenty. But when I opened my wallet I was all out of cash.

The rain continued to pour, oblivious to our conversation and her plight, soaking us both. I had already said I would help and I didn't want to go back on my promise.

"Follow me," I said. She hesitated and looked at her niece.

"Come on, there is an ATM machine a few blocks up. We can go there." I had to shout a bit because of the downpour.

She assented and the three of us braced ourselves against the storm until we reached the bank several blocks uptown. I used my card to open the glassed-in ATM foyer. As I walked to the machine, a crisp solitary twenty-dollar bill floated in the air directly in front of me. It must have been caught in a draft, forgotten by the last customer. I quickly checked up and down the street, but no one was around. I plucked the twenty-dollar bill from the air, and in awe, handed it to her.

After she thanked me, I said, "It's not from me, it's from God" and I told her what happened. She broke into a slow astonished grin and her eyes brightened in delight. "I was praying all morning to God to help me get home," she told me, "and then you came right out of that store." We shook our heads in disbelief, both giddy with our good fortune. We parted ways and I stepped back out into the rain. I looked up at the stormy April sky, tipped my head back, and laughed.

~Julia Shepherd Tang

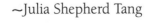

When the Rocks Cried Out

However many blessings we expect from God,
His infinite liberality will always exceed all our wishes and our thoughts.
~John Calvin

The yard of our little fishing cottage was going to disappear if we didn't do something. This was our home but the lapping water of the beautiful lake we lived on was eating away at our shore. To make matters worse, the creek along the side of our property was doing the same thing. Our options were limited. Cement seawalls were very expensive, even if we built one ourselves, and it would take a lot of stone to go such a long way. We were teachers in a small Christian school and our income allowed for very few "extras."

We needed to do something, so we decided to order one truck full of rocks at a time as our budget allowed. It might take a long time, but eventually the job would be complete we would stop the erosion of our property.

As we were discussing the details of placing the rocks with John, who we hired to do the job, we learned that he had recently undergone a bitter divorce. As he shared his story with us, we saw a heartbroken, lonely, bewildered young man. My heart went out to him, and I asked him if he had a church family to help him shoulder his burden. He told us that he used to go to church but had no intention of going back. It was clear that he was quite angry with God. We knew that God was exactly Who John needed at this difficult time in his life, and we prayed that He would reveal Himself to him.

The truckload of rocks arrived, and much to our chagrin, it looked like a very small pile of rocks. The man who delivered a front-end loader to our property looked at the small pile of rocks with John and agreed that it would take many more loads to finish the job. But it was a start, however far it would go.

The next day was a long one for us at work. We taught all day and had to stay for our big annual concert that evening. John was at our home that day building what he could with the first truckload of rocks. When we got home after dark, my husband went out back with a flashlight to see how far the rocks went. After quite a while, he called for me to come outside. We walked all along the lake bank and all along the creek up to the road. The entire bank was thickly covered with white rocks! What on earth? Had John ordered more loads of rock? How would we pay for this?

Back in the house the phone was ringing. It was John. "Mrs. Schumann, did you see your rocks?" He proceeded to tell me what had happened.

He said that every time he went back to the pile to get another scoop of rock, the pile appeared to be as big as it had been in the beginning. After getting halfway across the lake edge, the rented front-end loader broke. The same man delivered the replacement machine and when he saw the pile of rocks he said, "It's too bad it broke down. Looks like you didn't get anything done." John told him how far he had gotten, and neither of them could understand what was going on.

Load after load, the rock pile stayed the same. John said that our neighbor couldn't believe it either, as he watched the amazing day unfold. After finishing the entire bank, there were rocks left over! John surrounded the culvert leading from under the road with the remaining rocks.

"All I could think of was that the Lord is blessing these people for serving Him. It was like the loaves and fishes. Mrs. Schumann, I am going to go back to church!"

All I could think of was, "The rocks cried out to John, today" (Luke 19:28-40).

~Bette Schumann

A Flash of Faith

One machine can do the work of fifty ordinary men.
No machine can do the work of one extraordinary man.
~Elbert Hubbard

Oh no! This couldn't be happening! In an instant, my routine day took a disastrous turn! I sat down in my home office to work, slipped the little flash drive into my computer and clicked to open it. The light on the front blinked on for a second and went out. I clicked a second, third, and then a fourth time... nothing but a blink and then darkness! I pulled out the flash drive and inserted it into a different USB port and clicked... then sat up straighter, now fully awake. Why wasn't the flash drive opening so I could access the data? My whole life was on that flash drive! I took it out and looked at it carefully. The center part that fit into the USB port was loose, and a wire stuck out on the side! I taped around the entire apparatus and inserted it again. The light came on for a couple of seconds and then went out!

In retrospect I realize it was crazy to put everything on that flash drive. I took it back and forth to work, always in too big of a rush to run back-ups.

Sometimes we take technology for granted, and I was scrambling to remember exactly what was on that small bit of metal and plastic—work logs, ideas, and fundraising projects. I had placed all my personal data on that drive including Christmas lists, family photos, and recipes. It held all my personal business documents, writing notes, and speeches. All lost! I felt angry and stupid! Why had I put everything on that small, three-inch drive that wasn't even as big as my finger! It was just so convenient to always have my life right there in the pocket of my purse! But now what?

I took the flash drive into three major computer stores to see if they could extract the data. The light would come on for a second or two and then go out just like it had for me. A clerk at the last store gave me a pamphlet for a data recovery company.

I rushed home to call, and the man who answered was confident. "Just mail it to us. We'll take the case apart, solder the wires, and recover your data."

I felt myself relax at that good news and asked, "About how much will that cost?"

"Oh," he replied, "between $1,000 and $2,700."

I felt my heart sink. There was no way I could afford that! Life went on but every time I started to type something, I realized what I needed was on that ruined flash drive. I had to re-create each document, slowing down every project I worked on.

About a month later I was downloading flash drives of photos onto my computer. (Yes, I was faithfully backing up everything by then.) When I finished, I put the drives into the tray on my desk and noticed my useless flash drive there. I started to toss it into the trash to be rid of the daily reminder of my frustrating failure, but something made me pause.

Realizing that I hadn't asked God to help me, I knelt down with the flash drive in my hand and prayed. I told God that I knew I had been wrong to place my faith in that piece of technology instead of in Him. I had put my trust in something I thought would always be there and it failed me as the things of this world will.

"Lord, from now on I will place my life in Your hands and never take any of my blessings for granted." I got up from my knees and plugged the flash drive into my computer with a hopeful heart. Wait! Was the light on the flash drive on? I couldn't believe it! Was it possible?

My hands were shaking as I opened the drive to view the files. They were all there! I quickly copied everything into my computer.

Once the download completed, the light on the flash drive went out, and nothing I could do would make it come on again! Holding my breath, I checked my hard drive to see what transferred.

Remarkably, everything was there! All the data was perfectly useable! Tears ran down my face. God had extended me grace and a real miracle! I framed that little flash drive, and I keep it on my desk as a reminder to place my trust in God and His power to restore, to never give up hope, and to always believe in miracles.

~Judee Stapp

A Thousand-Dollar Miracle

Ask, and it will be given to you; seek,
and you will find; knock, and it will be opened to you.
~Matthew 7:7

"We're short $1,000 for our school bills—I don't know what we're going to do!" I hated to hear the despair in my husband's voice. Dale and I were both seminary students, newly married and living in a little two-room married-student apartment on campus. Money was very tight. Ever the optimist, I tried to encourage him, saying, "It will be all right, things will work out. Let's pray about it. God will take care of us." In my heart I had no idea how.

In addition to a full course load and a part-time church on the weekends, both Dale and I worked all the hours we could get at part-time jobs on campus. I had an office job; Dale worked for the grounds department. Even I couldn't see how we could possibly make up the shortfall on our tuition bills for the semester. It got so Dale was lying awake nights, worrying about money. When he began carrying a bottle of Pepto-Bismol in his shirt pocket while riding around campus on the tractor mower, I knew we were in trouble. I persisted in trying to reassure him. "It will work out Dale, you'll see. God will provide for us." But inside I wondered what we were going to do if He didn't.

The seminary grounds crew stopped work each day at 4:00 while my office hours went until 4:30—which was nice since Dale usually had supper started by the time I wandered in. But on that particular day I honestly wasn't looking forward to another meal with the dark cloud of our unpaid tuition bill hanging over us. I dawdled on my way down the hill to our apartment building, missing the cheerful man I had married.

As I turned the key and opened the door, Dale greeted me with a huge smile on his face, holding an envelope in his hand. "You won't believe what came in the mail today!" he announced. "What?" I suspiciously asked.

"A check for $500! With a note from my home state's executive minister saying he was thinking about us being newly married and in seminary and all, and figured we could probably use some money from his discretionary fund. Can you believe it? $500!"

I couldn't resist my retort, "See, I told you God would take care of us!"

"You were right—I shouldn't have doubted," he said. And I felt a guilty pang for my self-righteous comment.

Things were a lot more relaxed at our dinner table that evening. The next day I got home early from an afternoon class and was puttering around the kitchen when Dale rushed in all excited. He was waving another envelope in his hand. "You're not going to believe this Laurie! There's another check for $500!"

"Come on, Dale, you're not even funny," I replied.

"No, seriously, it is!" He held the envelope above his head, daring all 5'1" of me to get it out of his hand and see for myself. I had to stand on a kitchen chair, but eventually I got it. Sure enough, there was another check for $500—this one from the widow of Dale's hometown pastor, with a note that said she had received an unexpected bequest and wanted to share a tithe of the money with the newlywed seminarians. This time, even I couldn't believe it. We read and re-read the check and the letter, breathless at the sheer grace of God.

On Day 3, I think Dale was a little nervous about opening the mailbox. It was back to the normal pile of junk mail and bills. But why should there be more? God had met our needs in a truly miraculous way—our tuition bill was paid, and we both learned a lesson in trusting Him to provide our every need.

~Laurie Carnright Edwards

A Message of Hope from the Dragon Lady

The wings of hope carry us, soaring high above the driving winds of life.
~Ana Jacob

My wife, Susan, was three thousand miles away in San Francisco with our daughter, Amy, who was in the hospital recovering from a medical emergency. Amy was recovering, but the whole experience had left me drained and discouraged about the future because of Amy's recurring health issues.

It didn't help my emotional state that Susan's rental car was broken into the first night she was at the hospital. The thief took her GPS and Kindle, and scattered her clothes along the sidewalk.

When Amy left the hospital, Susan decided to stay with her to help in her recovery. Although necessary, Susan's absence increased my discouragement because she was the keystone of my support system.

When my mother had passed away many years before, I had gone on a day trip to the seashore resort of Point Pleasant, New Jersey and found it to be a helpful, soothing experience. I decided to return there, hoping that it would help me feel better during the current crisis.

On the morning I was going to leave, I started to have second thoughts about going. My energy was so low from all that had happened; I just didn't feel like taking a long drive. However, I started thinking about a particular spot I had gone to on a man-made breaker in Point

Pleasant when my mother had passed. I remembered being there for a long time looking out at the ocean and being comforted. There was a pull inside me to go back to that exact spot.

On the drive down, I started thinking about my mother. She was the head waitress at a busy restaurant and because of her rather prickly manner she was called the "Dragon Lady" by her fellow waitresses. They loved her anyway. I know this because a number of them would periodically come over to our house to drink, play cards, and laugh hysterically at life, at themselves, and at a few "not for polite company" jokes.

I got off at my usual exit from the Garden State Parkway for Point Pleasant, but although I had taken this route a number of times before, I somehow got lost. I pulled into a parking lot and asked a man who was carrying a fishing pole for directions. He rolled his eyes and told me I was going exactly the opposite way I was supposed to be going. His directions were somewhat garbled and I got lost again. By this time I felt exhausted and decided to forget the whole thing and just go home. When I saw a sign to get me back to the Garden State Parkway, I went in that direction.

But that spot on the breaker in Point Pleasant kept intruding into my thoughts. As I was approaching a traffic circle, I suddenly recognized the road I was on and realized that if I just went the opposite way it would take me to Point Pleasant. I hesitated, but finally took the traffic circle to turn around.

The parking lot near the boardwalk where I usually parked for free now cost $10, and I almost backed out to look for a free spot somewhere else, but I was tired and decided to just hand over the money.

It was about a mile walk on the boardwalk to the breaker. It was a warm day and I started asking myself, "Why am I doing this?" I kept thinking I should just go home but something made me keep walking.

I finally got to the breaker, but to get to the exact spot where I had gone when my mother passed was tricky because I had to carefully walk out on cement blocks. I balanced carefully as I shuffled toward a cement column. When I got there I grabbed the column for support and looked at the water. At that exact moment a leisure craft was coming into port. On the side of the boat, in large script letters, was its name: Dragon Lady.

The hair on the back of my head stood at attention. For a few seconds I just stared at the spot where the boat had passed, my arms still hugging the cement column. Slowly what had just happened sunk in. With all my delays, my wrong turns, my thoughts of turning back, somehow this boat was there at the exact moment that I could see it. I knew in my heart that things would be okay. The "Dragon Lady," my beloved mother, would make sure of that.

~Edward A. Joseph

Glitter and Glue

Trust in the LORD, and do good;
dwell in the land and feed on His faithfulness.
~Psalm 37:3

A warm breeze wafted through the open doors and windows of the classroom in the small coastal fishing village in Ghana, West Africa. I picked up my scissors and started cutting the first stack of paper for the crowns.

Behind me, ninety children worked with their Vacation Bible School teacher to memorize Psalm 1 and listened to the Bible lesson. I worked with a team of three native teens to cut crowns, apply glue and glitter, and distribute them to each of the children. The only time these children saw glitter (or "shine-shine" as they call it) was when we came for the annual VBS, and each year they looked forward to being crowned sons and daughters of the Most High King.

As the teacher finished the lesson, I began handing out the crowns. I soon realized we hadn't made enough for even half the students. No problem. We had plenty of supplies for more. I turned back to my team and got to work. After we had five or so crowns made, I passed them out while the teens continued to cut and glue. When I had a large stack of crowns, the children were content to wait at their desks, but now that I was only distributing a few at a time, I encountered cries of "Madam, Madam. Me. Me." each time I turned around. The glue was running low and I was starting to get frustrated with all the pushing and shoving. But there were only about twenty children left, so I wasn't worried. I turned back to make more crowns.

The next time I turned around, the number of children without crowns had more than doubled. I sighed but figured we could handle it. But when I looked up again, there must have been at least seventy children crowding around me begging for a crown—and the glue bottles were on empty. I could tell the new children were older, so I asked the teacher why they weren't in their own class. He told me they had run out of supplies so they came to us to get their crowns.

I had reached my limit. Here were these ten- and eleven-year-olds bowling over the tiny tots for a piece of paper with glitter. Then God revealed something to me. These children were used to never having enough. Someone always had to go without. And they were pressing in to make sure they didn't get left out this time. My next thought was, I wonder if this is how Jesus felt with the crowds pressing around Him?

I started praying. "God, this is about more than glitter and glue. This is about your ability to provide. This is about no one being left out. Loaves and fishes, God. Loaves and fishes."

As I prayed, I remembered the words of my pastor: "Jesus does not provide us with everything we need. He IS everything we need. Jesus does not give us sufficient to our need. He IS our sufficiency." I silently started praising God for meeting the needs of these children and proving Himself faithful.

A short time later, I noticed a peculiar thing happening. Whenever I put down a bottle of glue, there would be a mad dash as my helpers dropped their bottles and grabbed for the one I just set down. No problem, next time I picked up one of the others and used it. But when I set it down, everyone dropped theirs and grabbed for the one I just finished with. Then I realized, it didn't matter which glue bottle I picked up, the only one with any amount of glue in it was the one in my hand.

I knew it was time to share my faith, but I was apprehensive. What if there wasn't enough? Then, not only would there be children without crowns, but there would be teens with crushed faith. I decided to have faith, and I handed each teen a glue bottle (we had three—all quite empty by this time) and said, "Jesus will provide. Every child will get a crown." There were still at least fifty children who needed crowns. The teens took the glue bottles and they took the faith I offered them and each time they squeezed a glue bottle I heard, "Jesus will provide." A whole new attitude permeated the room. Not just the workers, but the children themselves, became less desperate as we passed out the completed crowns.

I sent someone to go check the house where we were staying to see if we could get more glue. The door to the supply room was locked and the key was in another village, as I expected. I kept watching the road for the rest of the team to return, hopefully with more supplies. They didn't come, which was what I expected. Someone did go scouring in the other rooms and found two bottles of glitter and a mostly empty bottle of glue. We rejoiced and kept making crowns.

About the time the lids came off the glue bottles and we were sticking our fingers in the bottles to scrape them clean, I asked the teacher to begin praising Jesus with the children.

To the rhythmic beat of African praise, we scraped the bottom of the glue bottles with a stick to get every last drop. But even in that I saw something amazing. One time I'd grab a bottle and there would be nothing left. The next time I scraped it, the stick would come out dripping with glue.

Then it started drying up. We had been using empty glue bottles for over an hour. Finally I had to squeeze the stick to get the last of the glue off it. One of the teens scraped the glue off my fingers to finish that crown. There was nothing left. My heart sank as I looked around the room and saw another dozen empty heads. I took a deep breath, and in faith, picked up the scissors and another piece of paper. Everyone WOULD get a crown.

My helper said, "We are finished."

I pointed to a bareheaded boy standing near me.

"He has one."

"What about them?" I motioned to the group praising in the middle of the room.

"They have theirs."

"And the children outside?"

"Everyone has one. We are finished."

I sank down at the desk and cried.

~Deborah Gatchel

Chapter
10

Hope
&
Miracles

Miraculous Reunions

He's Waiting

If you knew that hope and despair were paths to the same destination,
which would you choose?
~Robert Brault, rbrault.blogspot.com

M y mother stood on the waterfront by New York's Hudson River, searching for a familiar face. It was a warm September evening in 1946 and she was just off the boat, literally, from The Old Country. After a journey that included a six-hour drive to Belgrade, a twelve-hour bus ride to Trieste, and fourteen days on a cargo ship across the Atlantic, a tugboat had finally deposited her, her three sisters, and their mother onto the dock on Manhattan's West Side.

It had only taken them sixteen days—well, eight years and sixteen days, and they'd finally made it to America. And now, they waited on the wharf in the new world with one solitary trunk and no one to greet them.

"Where is he?" my grandmother, Tsena, asked aloud, panicked.

The three younger children—Milka, thirteen, Jovanka, eleven, and Nevena, eight—were mesmerized by the twinkling lights of Manhattan. My mother, Maria, the eldest at fifteen, soothed her mother.

"Don't worry, Mom. He'll be here. We'll find him."

She'd been comforting her mother for eight years—that's how long my grandfather, Elia Christoff, had been separated from the family and living in America. He'd left their hometown of Prilep, Macedonia, in 1938 when the extortion racket, The Black Hand, tried to steal his

American dollars. Elia had been granted American citizenship when he was twenty, after he joined the U.S. Army during World War I (that time, he was fleeing the Turks).

Then, as each daughter and one son, Dimche (who died at two from scarlet fever) was born, Elia registered them as U.S. citizens at the Embassy. One day, he dreamed, they could make America their home.

With her sweet disposition, Maria was her father's favorite. He would take the eight-year-old along with him on daily errands and they'd walk and talk and laugh together.

By 1939, Elia had everything ready for his family to join him in the United States. He'd bought a house in Steelton, Pennsylvania and found a job as an electrician in the Air Force. Just as he was about to arrange passage for them, Germany invaded Poland and World War II had begun.

Elia sent Tsena a telegram:

War. Leave immediately for Trieste for last ship to America. Passage is arranged.

But by the time they got it, it was too late. The ship had left with another family in their place.

For the next six years, as war exploded across Europe, communication was cut off. Without letters, Elia had no idea if his wife and children were alive or dead. He bombarded local politicians with letters, begging for help to get his family out of Europe. He saved every penny and bought U.S. Savings Bonds—so many, that the Air Force awarded him a propeller for his patriotism.

Meanwhile, back in Prilep, the beautiful girls were learning how to dive to the ground at the sound of sirens. One bright afternoon, as German tanks rolled into town, they stood at the side of the road and watched one of their friends dart into the street and get crushed.

Yes, the German soldiers had arrived. And they decided that my mother's home, a two-floor converted schoolhouse, was ideal for their headquarters. They took over the house, leaving the family one bedroom and use of the kitchen.

In the giant atrium on the main level, fifty to sixty soldiers slept lined up in rows on the wooden floor. They were boys, really—seventeen, eighteen, nineteen years old.

As the years and the war raged on, despite lack of food or pretty clothes, Maria blossomed into a beauty by fourteen—she had a heart-shaped face, honey-colored hair, and chestnut eyes. My poor grandmother, I'm sure, didn't sleep a wink. She covered Maria up with scarves and coats, but what about those sultry eyes?

"You are not to make eye contact with the soldiers," Tsena ordered.

Maria tried to obey. But one afternoon when she lay in bed with a high fever, a shy, young soldier knocked on the bedroom door and offered Tsena aspirin from his medical supplies. In those few seconds, Maria turned her flushed face toward him and their eyes met. He was blond and handsome, with gentle eyes. In another world, in another time, the two of them might have walked to school together or shared a first kiss. But not in this world; not in this time.

[Two years later, for a high school class assignment in Steelton, my mother would give a speech about him. "The Germans soldiers were so kind and good," she began. After class, the teacher had to escort her home. Students were waiting outside the classroom to beat her up.]

When the war was finally, thankfully, over, the U.S. Embassy arranged for the family to be on the very first ship leaving Belgrade—a cargo ship, courtesy of the U.S. Marines.

As it pulled into New York Harbor that September afternoon in 1946, the girls and their mother stood on deck as the Statue of Liberty greeted them.

"What's 'liberty'?" one of the girls asked.

Maria took a long, deep breath and smiled. "It means freedom."

She looked toward the shore as they moved closer, knowing her father was standing there.

Suddenly, two hundred feet from land, the ship stopped abruptly. Moments later, a Marine found them to explain:

"The dockworkers are on strike, we can't approach the port," he said, as the anchor splashed into water. "We could be stranded here for days."

This couldn't be! After all those years, they were so close! Close enough to touch their dream.

There was nothing they could do but wait a little longer. They quietly watched the sun set behind the Manhattan skyline and the city light up like a Christmas tree. Six hours later, they were about to go to bed when the Marine returned, excited.

"Mr. Christoff paid a man with a tugboat to come get you! "

The Marine led them to a rope ladder against the ship, and one by one they carefully climbed down into the tugboat. Their father, meanwhile, had been told it would be a few hours still, so he'd gone to get a cup of coffee.

Which is how they ended up on the pier, uncertain, as Maria looked for her father's face.

But it wasn't his face she first recognized.

Off in the shadowy distance, maybe four blocks away and silhouetted against the street lamps, she recognized her father's walk. Maria dropped her mother's hand and ran.

"*Tato!*" she screamed, "Daddy!"

Her sisters ran after her.

"Stop! Maria! Girls!" my grandmother screamed.

As soon as he realized the far away figures were running toward him, Elia began to run, too.

In the middle of a Manhattan street, my mother leapt into her father's arms. A minute or two later, so had her sisters.

The girls sobbed and Elia was in such shock, he couldn't speak. It would be hours before he would utter a word. He held his daughters tightly, and together they made their way toward the dock and his wife.

It was time for the family to go home.

~Natasha Stoynoff

The Season for
Discovery

Family is not an important thing, it's everything.
~Michael J. Fox

The Christmas season often brings wonderful opportunities for renewing old friendships and developing new memories. As the Christmas of 2006 approached I had no idea that a miracle was about to happen to me. It was far more than an occasion to partake in the exchanging of gifts and the celebration of a delicious meal... it was the blending of two hearts joined together as a family.

All my life I had yearned for an older brother. As a small child, every year I asked for an older sibling and every year I was disappointed. It was lonely growing up as an only child. As I got older, and one year melted into the next, I realized that to have the brother I yearned for would remain a dream unfulfilled.

Then, in late fall of 2006—just a few weeks before Christmas—my life suddenly took a profound turn. A telephone call from my cousin, followed by a flurry of breathtaking events, indeed produced a full brother I had no idea I had.

I had only just recently met Fred for the first time, and now my husband Tony and I were about to spend Christmas with my newfound family.

On a night with gently falling snow, we gathered together at my brother's home on Christmas Eve to enjoy this most special of night together for the first time. My heart was lighter than it had been in many years. After the death of my son, I had lived a life of depression and anxiety. Finding a brother and his whole family was most certainly the perfect remedy for my ailing heart.

Fred was as eager to learn as I was to share as many memories as I could about the parents he had never known, but I had grown up with.

"What was Christmas like when you were a child?" he asked.

"It was usually just the three of us," I explained. "Dad loved music and could play the organ and piano really well. When I was a young girl, he entered a contest, and as a result he won an organ. He played all kinds, including Christmas carols, and he was teaching me to play."

"I would have loved to have heard him," commented Fred.

"He also took charge of all the wrapping of gifts," I shared. He would spend hours folding the tissue paper into intricate pleats. He worked so hard on it." Fred listened intently as I continued. "Both Mom and Dad were good cooks and they prepared the Christmas feast together."

"What was Mom like?" he queried.

"Mom loved the Christmas season just as much as I did. She would make special treats for Dad and me, and she was in charge of decorating the tree. It always looked beautiful to me."

"I wish I had known her," sighed Fred. "I only saw her once, when I was about four years old. My dad and I were on a streetcar in Toronto just before Christmas and it was snowing. We had just come from visiting a relative to give them their presents. It was late in the day—suppertime—and I was getting hungry. I sat next to Dad playing with a little toy truck. As I watched, a lady boarded the streetcar. She was pretty, with dark hair; glasses and she wore a tan coloured coat. She seemed to be mesmerized by both of us. She watched me intently as if she was trying to absorb everything there was to know about me. Then I saw her start to cry and she fled the streetcar into the darkness. I asked Dad about the lady, but it was only later that I found out her true identity.

"You know, I never forgot seeing my mother that evening. When I later learned who she was, I wondered what had happened."

I took his hand and gently spoke. "I know our mom, Fred, and I know that giving you up would have broken her heart."

I gently wiped the tears from my eyes and suggested to my brother that we go through photographs. He was anxious to know everyone in the pictures and the role they had played in my life.

"I have pictures too," he said. "Would you like to see them?"

My brother produced photo after photo that he held dear. It was only when he came to one of a lady holding him as a young baby that I was startled. It seemed surreal. Tucked away, lovingly protected against the elements of time, lay the most beautiful picture I had ever seen.

"That's me when I was about four months old with a friend of the family," he explained. "I know I was placed for adoption when I was about six months old."

I sat quietly trying to absorb everything that was happening. I could feel my hands start to shake and my breathing become a bit laboured.

"I really don't know how to say this, Fred," I explained, "but the woman in that photo is more than a family friend... that is you with our mother. And you—you are the brother I spent my childhood longing for."

Christmas of 2006 will always hold a special place in my heart. My brother and I made wonderful discoveries together that year. We continue to grow as a family and I am eternally grateful for Fred, his wonderful wife Janet, and my beautiful nieces and great-nieces. They are truly my ultimate gift.

~Gail Sellers

The Mark of Angels

A person often meets his destiny on the road he took to avoid it.
~Jean de La Fontaine

Many years ago I visited Bern, the charming capital of Switzerland. Feeling liberated from itineraries one evening, I wandered through the medieval streets into the heart of the city. The warm twilight breeze had lured swarms of people into the town square. Old men played checkers at cement tables amid musicians, jugglers and other assorted street performers. I paused to drink in the carnival of sights and sounds.

An American accent rang out above the bustle. "One... Two... Three!"

A burst of laughter erupted from the crowd around a juggler. I moved in closer, drawn in by his act and familiar accent. After a finale of quick-handed magic tricks, his appreciative audience threw coins and moved on.

As the juggler bent down to collect the loose change, I felt compelled to connect. "Excuse me. Uh, I liked your act."

The juggler looked up with a surprised expression, as if he didn't expect anyone to stay around. "Hey thanks! You sound like an American."

I laughed, admitting that I'd been drawn to speak with him partly because of his Yankee accent. As travelers tend to do, I politely asked him what part of the States he was from.

"California," the juggler replied. "And you?"

I responded in the same general way. "Pennsylvania. Outside Philadelphia."

The juggler stopped picking up coins.

"Oh... where outside Philadelphia?"

I was slightly taken aback. Why did the name of the town matter if he was from California? Feeling silly again, but strangely compelled to talk, I answered. "Haverford."

The juggler's jaw dropped and his bearded face softened. He spoke barely above a whisper. "I went to Haverford High School."

"But I thought you said you were from California?"

The juggler got up off his knees and sat on the edge of a concrete flower container. He drew in a breath and poured out a story he'd locked away for a long time.

"I discovered I loved to perform while I was in high school. I wanted to study the arts in college but my stepfather felt I should study a serious subject, like dentistry. I felt I had no choice, so I went to college in California, but I couldn't study what I didn't love. Rather than go home and face my stepfather, I left the States to pursue my dream in Europe." With a quiet sigh he concluded, "I haven't spoken with my mom in seven years."

After further discussion, I learned the juggler's mother lived three minutes from my house. In fact, I drove past her home every day on the way to work. We stood in quiet awe of the "coincidence" of our meeting.

The juggler broke the silence. "If I give you my mom's number, would you call her for me when you get back home? Would you tell her I'm okay?"

As a mother, I ached for a woman who was separated from her son. I nodded a tearful yes and tucked the number away. The juggler and I parted, forever changed by our meeting thousands of miles from home.

On the plane ride back to the States, doubts crept into my thoughts. What if his mother was angry? What if she didn't want to hear from me?

Once back home, I picked up the phone and put it back in the cradle countless times; but I couldn't ignore the strong inner voice that urged me to call. After taking a deep breath, I dialed the number on the crumpled piece of paper. A woman answered the phone. I spoke before I lost my nerve.

"Hello. You don't know me but…" The story of my trip to Bern spilled out, rapidly reaching the part where I met the juggler in the town square. As I relayed her son's greeting, the woman cried, "Oh, thank God!"

In a voice thick with emotion, her questions tumbled out one after another. "How did he look? Is he well? Is he okay?"

I found myself in the peculiar position of describing a son to his mother. I assured her that he was healthy, happy and seemed to be doing well. I described the juggler's hair, his beard and his request that I contact her. The juggler's mom cried even harder.

"My son's last letter said he was thinking of coming home. He wrote that the next time I heard from him would be a sign that all was forgiven and he'd be home soon. This is the sign I was waiting for! Thank you so much for calling!"

After I hung up the phone, I marveled at the odds of meeting the juggler at just the right place, just the right time and just the right moment in his life. I smiled through tears of my own and knew that chance had nothing to do with it.

Destiny, serendipity, sweet forgiveness—all marks of angels at work.

~Teri Goggin-Roberts

The Spoon

Be realistic: Plan for a miracle.
~Bhagwan Shree Rainees

M y life has been full of surprises, but none quite like the surprise that came in the mail on the last day of July in 1999. That was the day my forgotten childhood was returned to me—courtesy of a young stranger blessed with curiosity and intent on doing a good deed.

It arrived in a large manila envelope from the Social Security Administration. I thought it was just another notice about benefits—until I saw the postmark: Batesville, Arkansas. Curious, I thought. I've lived in many places, but never Arkansas. The contents of the envelope were equally puzzling.

There were four enclosures. The first was a cover letter from Arlinda Gardner, Service Representative. "Dear Ms. Fader," she wrote. "We are enclosing a letter which Kim Anderson has asked us to forward to you."

Who in the world was Kim Anderson?

"Because of the circumstances, we agreed to forward the letter. However, we have not revealed your address and cannot disclose whether the letter has been delivered. You are free, therefore, to reply or not as you choose. You need not notify us of your decision."

Now my curiosity was truly piqued. I turned my attention to the first item Ms. Gardner had included: a two-by-three-inch color photograph of a smiling young couple. A notation on the back identified the young blond woman as Kim Anderson, age eighteen, and the dark-haired young man as Kris Holenbeck, age twenty, and noted that this was their engagement picture.

The photograph was attached to a neatly typed letter. In the upper right hand corner was a drawing of a stork holding the traditional bundled baby in its beak. "Strange choice of stationery for a newly engaged couple," I thought.

"Dear Ms. Sonia," the letter began. "My name is Kimberly Roneau Anderson." Kimberly proceeded to tell me about herself. And then this intriguing statement: "About thirty years ago, my mother was on Manasquan Beach and found a baby spoon. You might wonder what this has to do with you. On this beautifully engraved silver spoon were your name, birthplace, birth date and time, and your weight. I am curious," Kimberly wrote, "about how the spoon got lost, and I would like to know more about you."

I slipped the third enclosure out from behind Kimberly's letter. It was a photocopy of the spoon. I had not seen that spoon for more than sixty years. The sight of it triggered something in my head, or perhaps my heart—a surge of extreme joy, inexplicably mixed with a deep sense of sorrow.

I lost both my parents within three years before I was twenty-one, my father to heart disease, my mother to cancer. Their lingering deaths, plus the need to create a safe, stable home for my eleven-year-old brother, triggered a kind of amnesia in me that not only blocked the pain-filled memories connected with my parents' passing, but all the happy memories that came before.

Through my tears, I studied the picture. The spoon handle was molded in the shape of a bespectacled stork poised on a brick chimney, holding a baby in its feathered wings. Engraved in the bowl of the spoon was a grandfather's clock that indicated the time of my birth. My full name was there too, and the date and place of birth, as well as my length and my weight when I entered this world.

I turned my attention back to Kimberly's letter. She wrote that she discovered the spoon in her mother's silverware drawer. Her mother, who thirty years earlier had lived in New Jersey, told Kimberly she found the spoon one day while she was playing with Kimberly's older sister on Manasquan Beach. Charmed by its design, she took it home, polished it, put it in her silverware drawer, and forgot about it. Then Kimberly found it one day when she was rummaging through the drawer for some serving pieces for her future married life.

When I called the number in the letter, Kimberly told me that she got the idea to go to the Social Security office from a movie in which the main character had traced someone that way. But, as Kimberly learned after taking the hour's drive to the closest Social Security office, such things only happen in the movies. In real life, Social Security employees are forbidden by law to give out any information concerning private citizens.

That should have been the end of the story. However, perhaps impressed by Kimberly's resourcefulness, or intrigued by her tale, Ms. Gardner agreed to help her. She told Kimberly if she would write a letter to me and bring it back, she would forward it.

It took Kimberly a month to compose her "perfect letter." It was Arlinda Gardner's idea to include a photocopy of the spoon.

Kim refused any money for returning my spoon, but she had mentioned that she was planning to have daisies, her favorite flower, at her wedding. I sent her a daisy-themed place mat and napkin set, along with a check, as a wedding gift. Her thank you note included an invitation to the wedding, which, unfortunately, I was unable to attend.

Having a stranger return something precious that had been missing more than half a century in itself qualifies as a miracle. What is truly remarkable, however, is the impact Kimberly's curiosity and thoughtfulness has had on my life. That returned spoon unlocked a floodgate to sweet memories I thought I had lost forever.

The spoon and a picture of my mother holding me are now framed in a shadow box that hangs on my bedroom wall. I was about two years old when the picture was taken in front of a house "down the shore" my parents rented one summer. What happy days they were, filled with love and laughter; it was a precious part of my life I had sadly forgotten, until a young woman from Arkansas decided to look for the owner of a lost spoon.

How was the spoon lost? Manasquan Beach is about seventy miles from Atlantic City and Ventnor, where my parents rented their summer homes. It is possible, I suppose, that one day we took a drive up the coast, my mother brought the spoon along, and somehow it got lost. But then what?

Was the spoon buried in the sand all those years until Kimberly's mother happened upon it? And what were the chances that of all the people at Social Security, Kimberly would end up talking to the one-in-a-million who would listen with compassion and help her? Then, there is the timing of her decision to try to return the spoon to its owner.

In the years after my parents' death I was too busy surviving to think about my childhood. But six decades later, I found myself desperately trying to recall those forgotten years. Then, that envelope arrived with a picture of a spoon that opened up the floodgate to those precious lost memories. Every time I look at the spoon, or retell the story of its remarkable journey, my belief in miracles is renewed.

~Sunny Fader

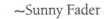

98

Chicken Soup for the Soul

A Family Miracle

Rejoice with your family in the beautiful land of life!
~Albert Einstein

One October, while traveling in Italy, my husband and I were seated at dinner next to a couple from California. During our conversation, I happened to mention my interest in genealogy.

"It's fascinating that you enjoy tracing your family roots," said Annette, a petite blonde with sparkling hazel eyes. "I know nothing about my biological father or his family, including whether he is alive today."

Annette confided that when she was twenty-six she examined her birth certificate and noticed that her father's name was not the father she had grown up with. Tearfully, Annette confronted her mother, who told her there were some things that she didn't want to talk about. "Even when I sat on the end of my mother's bed while she lay dying," said Annette, "I was hoping she would tell me something about my biological father but she never did."

"I was very lucky," Annette continued. "My mother and stepfather loved me very much. They were good parents... but I still wonder about my biological father."

When Annette told me her birth father's name was Virgil Ferren I was sure I could help. Unusual names are a genealogist's dream. When we returned to our hotel room, it took about ten minutes to find the initial information I was seeking.

The next morning I caught up with Annette to tell her that unfortunately, her father had passed away in 1975. He had married in 1947, about ten years after Annette was born.

I explained that I would continue the research after the tour and would order records and his obituary through the mail. It was Annette's gratitude, combined with my own curiosity, that spurred me to dig deeper into this mystery.

When Annette arrived home she sent me a copy of her birth certificate. There it was in bold letters, "FATHER: Virgil Ferren, clerk for the railroad," next to Annette's mother's name. We knew Annette's mother had gone away to school and returned home pregnant. But that's all we knew of the story, other than the fact that she married her husband when Annette was two years old.

The following weeks were busy ones. I researched the Ferren family five generations back and also received some results from my inquiries. Virgil Ferren's obituary revealed that he was survived by his wife, a son, and a daughter. A devoted husband and father, Virgil Ferren was active in both the community and his church.

Virgil's wife had passed away in 1998. But oh, the wonders of the Internet. It took two minutes to find Virgil's son Larry and his daughter Terry on Facebook. Larry's profile revealed he was a college chemistry professor who lived with his wife in Chicago. Terry was married to a pastor and lived in Alabama.

Annette now had answers to questions concerning her biological father and information about her half-siblings. I assumed my genealogy work was coming to an end.

Every once in a while I would ask Annette how she felt about making contact with her brother and sister. "Scared," was her usual reply. "What if they don't like me? Is it morally right to intrude on their lives with information like this?"

"I know what you mean," I replied. I was having similar thoughts as well.

One day I woke up with an idea. "Annette, what if I write a letter on your behalf? I could be the go-between. I won't include your last name, and I'll tell them about how we met in Italy and how your story unfolded. They can contact me if they would like to know you."

Although Annette said she would think about it, I was already composing a letter in my mind. I had decided that my first contact would be with Terry. I wanted to make sure I included everything, especially how special Annette was. I e-mailed the letter to Annette. "This is a beautiful letter," she responded through tears. "But I'm scared."

A week later Annette called and said she would like the letter to be mailed. "I'm seventy-four years old; let's go for it," she said. So I mailed the letter, including Annette's birth certificate and a photo I had taken of her in Venice.

For all the confidence I had that we were doing the right thing, as soon as I mailed the letter I started to have doubts. What if Terry threw the letter in the trash? What if she thought it was some kind of joke or worse, what if it made her angry? I found myself checking e-mail every hour.

Eight days later I logged onto the computer and there it was.... an e-mail from Terry. The subject line was "My Sister!"

Everyone has moments in life when time stands still. Reading Terry's letter was such a moment for me. Her letter was warm and welcoming, sweet and kind. I knew instantly that everything was going to be okay. No, much better than okay. I couldn't wait to call Annette.

Terry wrote that the letter came as a big surprise, but a wonderful one. She did not know the circumstances of Annette's conception and birth. She had always wanted a sister, and she wanted me to convey that to Annette right away. She also wanted to talk with Annette, but first she needed to talk to her brother.

When I read Terry's e-mail to Annette on the telephone we both cried. Annette was so happy she told me later that she slept that night holding a printout of Terry's e-mail.

A few days later I received my first e-mail from Larry. He was as warm and welcoming as Terry had been and wanted to arrange a conference call as soon as possible. He said he couldn't wait to talk to his big sister!

On a beautiful June morning Annette called with exciting news.

She and her husband had been invited to visit Larry and his wife in Chicago. Annette asked if I would be on the cell phone with her when they arrived. "You've been with me all the way through this," she said. I replied that I wouldn't miss it for the world.

A few weeks later Annette and her husband Joe flew from California to Chicago. As they exited the plane and walked up the ramp, Annette described seeing her brother and sister standing together arm in arm. Terry was holding beautiful flowers and Larry held a sign that read, "Welcome to Our Family."

Today Annette and her new brother and sister have a wonderful relationship. They e-mail and talk on the phone regularly. After the initial trip to Chicago, Annette invited everyone to their home in California and last summer they all met in Chicago again. They are making up for lost time and enjoying every minute of it.

Sometimes at night I look up at the stars and say thank you to Virgil Ferren. He must have been a special man to have produced such extraordinary children. Annette's sister Terry believes that God had a hand in placing us next to each other that evening in Rome... and I have to say I agree. Their story is a testament of faith, love, and the irresistible urge we all have for family connections.

~Pamela Chaconas

A Second
Second Chance

To give and not expect return, that is what lies at the heart of love.
~Oscar Wilde

t was early October 2003. I was exhausted, my body filled with excess fluid and my mind focused on worst-case scenarios as we drove past a blur of scenery. Henry gripped the steering wheel, knuckles pale, and turned to gaze at me with a look that—for a moment—washed all my fears and doubts away. I knew by the look in his eyes that his love would see us safely to the hospital despite the twenty-odd staples down his front from the bypass surgery he'd had barely a week earlier. As I touched his forearm, he grinned and stepped on the gas.

In a whirlwind, we arrived at the hospital, an emergency catheter was inserted into a vein in my neck and I started on dialysis. Again.

Henry and I had faced more challenges than most. We'd both grown up with Type 1 diabetes. We'd both experienced kidney failure and had gone on dialysis and the kidney-pancreas waiting list. This was how we met. Only a couple of months apart in 1997, we each had our prayers answered for a second chance at a better future.

And now, here I was, seven years later in need of another kidney transplant. I reached out to family members, a number of whom were tested. None were a match. I reached out to friends. Again, testing was done, but no match was found. My hope dwindled. And the usual sparkle in my spirit faded to barely a flicker.

As always, throughout that winter and spring, Henry stood by me. He drove me to dialysis and eagerly went for any possible type of take-out I thought I might try to eat to keep up my strength. He even helped do chores around the house. He did admit feeling helpless to do anything "to really make a difference." How I wished he knew what a big deal it was.

That summer Henry went on a mission. He recorded a video message at a booth set up by a local news station. With his usual charm, he pleaded into the camera's microphone for someone to come forward to help me.

He phoned the news station and repeatedly left messages. At fifty I lost track but at last he found an editor who would listen. Henry's message appeared on television late one night. My heart swelled as I watched and listened to the man I loved reach out for help. "Consider donating a kidney to my wife," he said through a smile, but on the verge of tears. "She's my world. I need her to be here, healthy, and with me for as long as possible." As he flashed a boyish grin at the end of the clip, tears filled my eyes, although I held onto little hope that it would bring me the kind of help I needed.

Then a news reporter called. She wanted our story. It ran as the second top story of the evening news. The station called us to say that they'd never had such an overwhelming response to a story. Their phones wouldn't stop ringing. By the end of the night, they had compiled a list of over five hundred names of people interested in being tested to see if they were a match to give me a kidney. I couldn't believe it! It was too good to be true.

During a meeting with the transplant co-ordinator, I was told that unless a willing donor was a relative or a close friend prior to my needing a kidney, not one of the thoughtful souls who offered would be allowed to donate one to me. At that time, it was against protocol. Crushed by disappointment, it was all I could do to get up and go through the motions.

In the meantime, our story continued to run for nearly a week.

That Friday the phone rang. Reluctantly I answered it and a voice from my past declared, "Susan? Remember me? It's Tracey…"

Although a grade apart, Tracey and I had gone through public and high school together. During that time, her dad had suffered kidney failure. Unbeknownst to me back then, Tracey had hoped to donate her kidney to him, but wasn't able to do so before he passed away. Because of this, she had vowed — if the opportunity ever arose — to donate one for someone else. By chance her children had left the television on the channel that ran our story. By chance she'd caught one of the broadcasts out of the corner of her eye and recognized me.

She was eager, and determined. "I'm on my way this minute to get tested. Where do I need to go?" And so our journey began.

As we sat side by side in the stalls having our blood drawn, Eric Clapton's "Tears in Heaven" played softly on the radio. "Please," I silently begged the universe. "Please let us be a match." After we left the lab, Tracey pressed the fresh bandage into the crook of her elbow, eyes wide. Flooded with panic that she'd changed her mind and wanted to back out, I asked, "What's wrong?"

"That was the song played at my dad's service," Tracey whispered. "He was there with us, Susan. It'll all work out just fine. I just know it."

The shiver that ran through me left me breathless.

A short while later we received news that "we couldn't have been a better match if we'd been twin sisters," which may or may not have been a slight exaggeration.

And so, in the fall of 2004 — nearly a year to the day after Henry's heart surgery — Tracey and I underwent surgery with the reporter and her cameraman who'd followed my story from the start in tow. Afterward, I awoke feeling strong, filled with energy and somehow "cleansed" from the inside out.

A day or so later, I was told how the cameraman zoomed in on my innards just as the surgeon declared that, "the new kidney produced urine right then and there."

According to Mom, as the family watched the news coverage,

Dad proudly declared to anyone who would listen, "That's my girl! She peed on TV!"

Watching Dad as he stood at the end of my hospital bed recounting his tale again, this time to Henry—who gazed at me with the same look of reassurance as the day he'd first taken me to the hospital to have the dialysis catheter installed—I hoped with all my heart that Tracey's dad would shed no more "Tears in Heaven. I hoped that instead he was grinning with relief and pride for the gift of a better, healthier and longer life his daughter had given to me because of him, and because of a husband whose love was, and is, boundless.

~Susan Blakeney

A Voice from the Past

*We shall draw from the heart of suffering itself
the means of inspiration and survival.*
~Winston Churchill

When I was in my last year of high school, I almost killed my grandmother. I did so not with a gun or a knife, but with a black-and-white postcard from 1918.

I was a salon communist, like most of my other German friends with big egos, big brains and big allowances. We sat together on the floor of my room, legs crossed in carefully torn $200 designer denims, drinking first-flush green tea from China, smoking real Russian cigarettes called Dostoevsky that made me cough for the first few weeks I tried them. We read Lenin and Sartre and talked about revolutions, the ones in the past and the one we would be a part of one day. Needless to say, my family hated it, but they were pragmatic enough to call it "a phase" and just hoped it would pass quickly.

That summer, my friends and I took a trip to Vienna to explore the flea markets and thrift stores. I came back home with a bag full of vintage couture and an envelope of postcards, all dating back to the Russian Revolution and the first years of the Soviet Republic.

When I sat down to frame them, I spent some time trying to read what people wrote. That was when I found it: the postcard that was different from all the others.

It was marked 1918, and the address on the back was that of my great-grandfather's pub. The handwriting was in old German cursive, but I managed to decipher most of the text. A few lines from a German soldier, who seemed to know that this war was lost, writing about the harsh winter and his longing for home. The despair that seeped through the lines was intense enough to make me feel cold and lonely right there in my well-heated room.

Amazingly, this postcard had been sent by my great-uncle August, my grandmother's brother. It was the last the family had heard from him before he was killed in World War I, at eighteen, only three days later. I read it again and again as the realization of my chance discovery set in. Then I went to look for my grandmother.

I gave her the postcard from the brother she had lost when she was still a little girl, the older brother she had adored. My grandmother took the postcard, holding it close to her almost blind eyes with shaky hands. For five long minutes, she stared at it. Then she turned and left for her apartment downstairs, leaning heavily on her cane and walking even slower than usual.

When my mother sent me to fetch my grandmother for dinner that night, I found her in bed, her white rosary running through her fingers in a continuous motion while she cried and prayed. When I called out to her, she looked up, the color of her eyes a faded shade of light blue, and said, "Ich komme bald, August." "I'm coming soon, August."

For the next days, nobody could get her to eat or leave her bedroom. She did not recognize anyone who tried to coax her back into daily life. On the second day, my mother sent for a doctor. On the third day, everybody started to prepare for her to die.

Each day, I dreaded dinner. At 6:30 sharp, my mother, father and I sat down and my grandmother's chair remained empty. And though we talked about our day as we always did, I felt the blame as clearly as if someone had said it out loud: It's your fault if she dies.

I suggested a deal to God: I would give up communism if he let her off the hook once more. Just this once, so that I wouldn't have to live with the guilt. I realized perfectly well that it was a selfish plea, but I was only eighteen and I had a certain confidence that God might understand that this was how teenagers worked. I had plenty of time to become a better person later, I figured.

On day four, I woke up shortly after 6 a.m. from some commotion in the kitchen. I got up and found my grandmother making coffee. She was wearing an elegant brown dress with her mother's little cameo brooch neatly fixed to the lapel and matching coral lipstick. "I need someone to drive me to the hairstylist at eight," she announced, instead of saying good morning. I nodded, not daring to talk about the elephant in the room.

She drank her first coffee quickly, refilled her cup and sat down. From the pocket of her dress, she retrieved the postcard, now folded into a small square. She flattened it on the kitchen table and stroked it with her left hand while sipping her coffee. I sat down across from her, still too stunned to speak.

"Do you know how that postcard got all the way from here to Vienna?" she asked, looking me in the eyes for the first time.

I shook my head. I had thought about that and even asked my parents, but nobody could come up with an explanation.

"Right after World War II," she continued, "your great-grandparents and I moved the pub to the building where it still is today. There were so many people involved in the new construction and the move that nobody was surprised that some things just vanished. But the one theft I could never forgive was that of the drawer in which my father kept all the postcards people from the village had sent to the pub. And this one," she held her brother's postcard up as if I hadn't seen it before, "this one I could never forget. Just imagine, by the time we got it, we had already been told that he was dead." A single tear rolled slowly down her cheek. She didn't wipe it away.

"You know, I have been so worried about you getting involved with these communists. But now I understand that there has been a purpose to it. God sent you to recover this card for me." Her tears now fell freely.

I didn't know what to say, so I just held her hand for a while. But later that afternoon, I threw away all the communist cards and pamphlets I had collected. I was done with that.

We found August's postcard in my grandmother's purse, again folded into the small square when we went through her things after she died—more than fifteen years later. I reclaimed it and moved it to my wallet. It is still there.

Only recently did I realize that there was something else I took from this episode, something much more important than that old piece of cardboard: Whenever life throws me a curve, I give myself three days to sulk. Three days spent in bed, without showering or eating. Then I get up again and go on with my life. Just like my grandmother did.

~Olivia de Winter

It's Never Too Late
for Miracles

Life is a series of thousands of tiny miracles.
~Mike Greenberg

Once upon a time, during those crazy years between the two World Wars, there arrived in England two South African students. The young man, Francis Nelson, was from Johannesburg while the girl, Constance Murrell, was from Port Elizabeth.

Young and eager, they embraced with enthusiasm their new life at college, where they met and fell in love. However, love has a way of manifesting itself. I arrived unplanned and unwanted. A marriage was hastily arranged but my parents decided to give me to an older and wiser family to foster. They returned to their carefree student life.

Three years later another unwanted baby arrived. My brother, Ian, was sent to an orphanage.

Just before I turned five my mother and foster family quarrelled, so my mother took me off to a small, private boarding school. However, my holidays were often spent at the orphanage with my brother so we bonded and grew close, depending on each other for love and companionship.

Those years remain a dim memory for me, with no understanding of quite why I was removed from my foster parents. All I remember about my family is that my father had vanished and I only saw my mother and brother occasionally. My physical needs were well catered for but I felt I was somehow responsible for myself. Alone.

When Ian turned five, a couple arrived from South Africa looking for a child to adopt. They went to the orphanage where the children were lined up for them to inspect. They chose Ian. He dearly wanted them to adopt me too, but although they searched everywhere they said that I was nowhere to be found. So they took Ian to South Africa without me.

Come September 1939 and war with Germany was declared. After a year of war my mother decided to return to South Africa and take me with her. We arrived home in Port Elizabeth in August 1940.

Both my parents died young carrying their secrets to the grave with them. I put my past behind me and went on with my life.

Fast-forward to the twenty-first century, the digital age and the Internet.

A friend of Ian's named Annette decided to play sleuth and see if she could find me after hearing Ian's story about his childhood. All she knew were my parents' names and my mother's maiden name: Murrell. She looked for me in England since that was where Ian believed I lived. After months of following up on hundreds of Nelsons with no results, Annette decided that just maybe I had returned home to South Africa. She perused the Castle Liner passenger lists where a record is kept of every passenger who ever sailed on their ships. Miraculously, she found my mother's name and mine. In August 1940 we had left Southampton on the Capetown Castle, which was serving as a refugee ship bound for Port Elizabeth. She decided to contact the Africana Library in Port Elizabeth to see if they had any information on the Murrells. She e-mailed the head librarian.

Coincidentally, on that same day, Neville Murrell, a distant cousin of mine, was busy in the library doing research on our family's genealogy. To add to this synchronistic event was the fact that the librarian, Carol, knew me personally. The timing was miraculous. She printed the e-mail and handed it to Neville.

What to do? Carol decided to phone me and invite me to tea at the library in order to meet Neville and discuss family research. Always keen to meet family, I complied with pleasure.

Meanwhile, my two guardian angels, Neville and Annette corresponded in secret until another divine intervention occurred. Annette's husband John, an author, had a new book out that was being distributed in South Africa. John and Annette decided to fly over and spend time with their friend, my brother Ian, while publizicing the book. They planned that Ian and I should be told about each other on the same day. Timing was all-important.

One afternoon Neville visited me at home, bringing with him vast pages of information on our family history. After circling around distant relatives for a while he dropped the bombshell. My brother, Ian, was alive and well and living just a two-hour plane ride away.

I was stunned. Frozen with shock. My emotions were in turmoil. After all these years my brother was alive and here, so close. Dare I reach out? Would he want me in his life? I needed time to think.

Neville told me that Annette had spoken to Ian that same day. What did he think? Did he want to see me? The "what if's" crept into my thoughts. Maybe I should just let the dreams remain. Reality might be a disappointment.

I waited. Two days went by. A short e-mail arrived from Ian. Tentatively I replied. I kept my emotions in check. This safe exchange went on for a few weeks until Providence fast-tracked events.

Ian's son, Michael, who is a Master Mariner for Greenpeace, was given instructions to travel to South Africa to collect certain legal documents. He arrived, heard his father's story and acted immediately. A couple of phone calls later and their flight to Port Elizabeth and accommodations were booked for the following weekend. I waited nervously.

The plane arrived early. My husband and I rushed to the arrival entrance. I saw two tall, long-limbed men stride through the arrivals hall and knew immediately it was my brother and his son.

Ian said nothing. He just swept me up and held me close. Time stopped for us as we stood in the middle of the crowds embracing each other.

The words would flow later, through the e-mails, phone calls and visits that fill our lives as we play "catch up."

My brother and I, separated so young, were united after seventy-five years apart. Sometimes the synchronicity of events defies all logic. Mysterious helpers combined to create a miracle.

~Ann Hoffman

Hope
&
Miracles

Meet Our
Contributors

Dale Amend is a retired Air Force pilot, a well decorated Vietnam combat veteran. His life revolves around five "G"s: grandkids, gardening, golf, gladioli, and good fitness. The flowers are used for visiting at the church where he and his wife of six decades are active. He is humbled by God's greatness and goodness. He is grateful each day for life.

Sharon Babineau is an advocate, author of *The Girl Who Gave Her Wish Away*, speaker, and founder of not-for-profit, Maddie's Everlasting Wish. Recognized for her work at home and in Africa, Sharon is the recipient of the Queen Elizabeth II Diamond Jubilee Medal and YWCA Women of Distinction 2013. Contact her at www.mindbreak.ca.

Cathy Baker is an award-winning poet who delights in observing God at work in the nuances of life and sharing those observations through writing, journaling, and blogging. She and her husband Brian live in South Carolina with their answer to the empty nest syndrome—a pampered pooch named Rupert.

Roopa Banerjee is a freelance writer and editor, mum of two feisty kids, an avid reader and a coffee addict. She loves living in a world filled with the joy of words. Roopa loves to procrastinate by filling the bird feeder and tweeting at @roopabanerjee. She believes in making each day a little nicer, a little happier.

Barbara Beaird was born and raised in New England where she developed a love of animals, music, photography and writing. She currently lives in Northwest Louisiana with two rescue dogs and five rescue cats.

Rob Berry is a graduate of California State University, Bakersfield. He lives in Bakersfield with his wife and best friend, Amy.

Ghanshyam Singh Birla has dedicated his life to teaching the ancient science of Vedic Palmistry. He is founder of Montreal's famous Birla Center, where he practices and teaches the college-level Palmistry Diploma Program. Ghanshyam has published two acclaimed palmistry books and is writing his autobiography. Visit birlacenter.com for more information.

Susan Blakeney is a writer of fiction for children and young adults with several novels on the go at various stages of development. Her works include historical fiction as well as speculative fiction/fantasy. Susan enjoys cooking and baking, and time with her "hairy boys" — Rudy and Barrett — and her supportive husband, Henry.

Trish Bonsall is a wife, mother and nanny. She is surrounded by her four sons, three daughters-in-law and three grandsons. Her life is a bit hectic but she is happiest when she is encircled with the loving chaos she calls life. Besides writing poetry and short stories, she enjoys cooking for family and friends, entertaining and reading.

Valaree Brough received her Bachelor of Arts degree in Elementary Education, with a dual minor in English and French, from Utah State University in 1971. She has four children and twelve grandchildren. Valaree enjoys writing, reading, playing the piano, teaching, and family history.

Judy Buch is the author of a nonfiction book, *Mastering & Marketing Your Performance*, two inspirational fiction short stories, "Wrapped in Love" and "Covered." Her first mystery novel, *Snapping Point*, will be available mid-2015. Judy lives in South Carolina with her husband Ken. E-mail Judy at judy@judybuch.com.

Maureen Buckley lives in Eugene, OR with her two dogs. Her greatest pleasures come from her family and friends. She has a blast exploring Eugene and the Northwest by foot, bike and kayak. She writes short stories, essays and poetry (which she reads aloud at a weekly poetry group), often focusing on women in transition.

Sally Willard Burbank practices medicine in Nashville. Her book, *Patients I Will Never Forget*, is a collection of hilarious and inspiring stories about her most memorable patients in twenty-five years. Visit her website at www.sallywillardburbank.com or read her blog at patientswewillneverforget.wordpress.com. E-mail her at salburbank@comcast.net.

Christy Caballero lives a couple of deer trails off the beaten path in Northwest Oregon. She has earned four Maxwell Awards from the Dog Writers Association of America, along with national awards from the National Federation of Press Women. Her focus now is on more personal writing.

Leona Campbell lives in Meridian, ID with her family and a Pug named Rocky. She has written and published her memoir with a twist on humor. Leona's articles have been featured in numerous magazines and she's written countless short stories for publication. Currently she's a student at Life Bible College in Meridian, ID.

Barbara Canale has been published in thirteen Chicken Soup for the Soul books. She is the author of *Prayers, Papers, & Play: Devotions for Every College Student*, and *To Have and To Hold: A Daily Marriage Devotional*. She has a new devotional for parents of teenagers available in the spring of 2015 from Liguori Publications.

Danny Carpenter is pastor of a nondenominational church in Texas.

He loves golf, playing the ukulele, and anything to do with family trips and getaways! He and his wife Sandi proudly admit to spoiling their three grandchildren whom they cherish!

Mary Carroll-Hackett earned an MFA from Bennington College. She is the author of four poetry collections: *The Real Politics of Lipstick*, *Animal Soul*, *If We Could Know Our Bones*, and the forthcoming *The Night I Heard Everything*. She teaches writing at Longwood University and West Virginia Wesleyan, and is working on a memoir.

This is **Eva Carter's** second story published by Chicken Soup for the Soul. Eva had several winning entries in Hallmark greeting cards contests. She enjoys photography, travelling and dining out with her husband of twenty-nine years, Larry. Squeaky, the cat, is an important member of their family. E-mail her at evacarter@sbcglobal.net.

Pamela Chaconas graduated from the University of Maryland with a degree in education. She was an elementary school teacher and later the education director for a symphony orchestra. Pam and her husband have two grown sons and two beautiful grandchildren. She enjoys travel, writing, and genealogy. E-mail her at pamelachaconas@gmail.com.

A.B. Chesler is a writer, educator, mommy, and wife from sunny Southern California. She enjoys reading, writing, traveling, and finding happiness in the simple things. Feel free to contact her at achesler24@gmail.com or follow her blog at http://thishouseoflove.net.

Lola Di Giulio De Maci contributes regularly to Chicken Soup for the Soul. She also enjoys writing children's stories (several in the *Los Angeles Times*). Lola is a retired teacher with a Master of Arts degree in education and English. She writes from her loft overlooking the San Bernardino Mountains. E-mail her at LDeMaci@aol.com.

Olivia de Winter received her MA degree in literature, history and communications from the University of Munich, Germany in 1994. She is a writer, blogger, translator and life coach. In her free time, she reads mysteries and trains for her first marathon. Originally from Frankfurt, Germany, Olivia lives in Seattle, WA.

Shirley Dilley worked as a critical care nurse over twenty-six years after the child-rearing nest emptied. A late blooming passion for writing has her pushing the pencil rapidly to catch up with frontrunners. Most days are spent traveling with her husband, capturing thoughts and visions with pen and camera.

Beulah Dobson, a retired real estate agent, is quite active after her remarkable recovery from three broken vertebrae. She enjoys life by going shopping, savoring the outdoors, crocheting and visiting her friends and family.

Bob Dreizler is a Chartered Financial Consultant who specialized in green investing. He is also a writer, artist, and photgrapher. He has two adult children, Sonya and Ross, and a grandchild named Pax. In 1998 he published *Tending Your Money Garden*, a humorous money management book.

Laurie Carnright Edwards is a writer, substitute teacher, and ministry partner with her pastor husband Dale. In addition to Chicken Soup for the Soul, she has been published on Leadership Journal's website. Laurie is the proud mom of two adult children and a graduate of Berkshire Christian College and Gordon-Conwell Seminary.

Diana Creel Elarde, BA, MA, teaches psychology for Maricopa Community Colleges. Her husband Vincent encourages her quest to become a successful writer. Amanda and Zdravko, her children, are her great sources of inspiration. She is a featured writer for *Thrive Detroit*. E-mail her at Diana@astarinmyhand.com.

Nancy Engler lives in the Arizona desert. Her work has been published in *Chicken Soup for the New Mom's Soul, Chicken Soup for the Soul: Family Caregivers, The Ultimate Teacher, Boys' Quest* and *Fun for Kidz* magazines. In her spare time, Nancy paints, draws, and tends her drought-resistant garden. E-mail her at nanenglerwrites@gmail.com.

Steve Erwin is an award-winning journalist and wrote the New York Times bestseller, *Left to Tell: Discovering God Amidst the Rwandan Genocide* with Immaculée Ilibagiza. He was an NYC correspondent for the Canadian Broadcasting Corporation and writer for *People* magazine. He's written seven nonfiction books and is finishing his second novel.

Sunny Fader is a nonfiction author and writing coach, the latest iteration of a long career that has included television writing, documentary writing/field producing and teaching broadcast writing and screen writing at the University of Florida and Pepperdine University in California. Learn more at www.sunnyfader.com.

Donna Fawcett is a retired creative writing instructor for Fanshawe College in Ontario, Canada. Donna writes in the freelance magazine market and has two award-winning novels. Her final song on her debut CD won best song lyrics. Learn more at www.donnafawcett.com.

Claire Fullerton is the author of *A Portal in Time* and *Dancing to an Irish Reel*. She hails from Memphis, TN, and now lives in Malibu, CA with her husband, two German Shepherds, and one black cat.

Deborah Gatchel is a certified teacher with a heart for missions. She and her husband have four girls, whom they homeschool. She has worked with Grace Community Outreach since 2006. The Gatchels plan to move to Ghana in the near future to open a school and work with the GCO libraries.

James A. Gemmell spent most of his working life in industrial settings. Possibly as a result of this, he now spends as much time as possible outdoors—hiking, fishing, snowshoeing and walking continental camino routes. To date, he has racked up more than four thousand kilometers hiking in Spain and France.

Rita Gigante dedicates her life to healing people spiritually, emotionally, and physically using energy therapy, intuitive healing, and angel readings at her practices in New York and New Jersey. Her autobiography, *The Godfather's Daughter: An Unlikely Story of Love, Healing, and Redemption*, was published by Hay House in 2012.

Teri Goggin-Roberts fell in love with writing after receiving a baby blue typewriter for her ninth birthday. Her first efforts were rough (as was her typing). Thankfully, both have improved. Teri's writing has appeared in many outlets and she recently wrote her first novel, *The Charm Academy*. Teri lives in the San Francisco Bay Area.

Halia Grace is a writer, hiker, psychotherapist, and crazy dog lady. She lives in a one-room shack in the Catskills with five rescued dogs and her long-suffering husband.

Darla S. Grieco holds a bachelor's degree in psychology with a minor in writing and a master's degree in school psychology from Duquesne University. She is married with four children and resides near Pittsburgh, PA. Darla shares lessons she has learned along life's journey at dsgrieco. wordpress.com.

Bonnie Compton Hanson, artist and speaker, is author of thirty-seven books for adults and children, plus hundreds of articles, stories, and poems (including thirty-four for Chicken Soup for the Soul). A former editor, she has taught writing at colleges and writers conferences—plus loves cats! Learn more at www.BonnieComptonHanson.com.

Carol Goodman Heizer, M.Ed., resides in Louisville, KY. She is an eight-time published author whose books have sold in the U.S. and overseas. Her work has appeared on several occasions in Chicken Soup for the Soul and *Christian Communicator*. Her works may be purchased through Amazon.com, CreateSpace, and at bookstores.

Ann Hoffman is a retired university lecturer of English and music. Her hobbies are choral singing, patchwork quilting and writing. She has five children and eleven grandchildren, and lives with her husband in the small coastal town of Port Elizabeth in Nelson Mandela Bay in South Africa.

Immaculée Ilibagiza is the author, with Steve Erwin, of several books including the New York Times bestseller *Left to Tell: Discovering God Amidst the Rwandan Holocaust*. A recipient of the Mahatma Gandhi International Award for Peace and Reconciliation, she travels the world speaking about forgiveness. Please visit her website: www.immaculee. com.

Jeanie Jacobson is on the leadership team of Wordsowers Christian Writers in Omaha, NE. She's published in four Chicken Soup for the Soul books, and is writing a Christian-slanted young adult fantasy series. Jeanie loves visiting family and friends, reading, hiking, praise dancing, and gardening. E-mail her at jeaniej@cox.net.

Mary Pat Johns is currently a Bible teacher at Faith Family mega-church in Victoria, TX. Her teaching venues include assignments for Ladies Bible Study and instructing for Destiny Bible Institute. A mother and grandmother, she lives with her husband and their miniature Dachshund Ike, who runs the show.

Since retiring as an educator, **Edward A. Joseph** has been working as a freelance writer. His work has appeared in regional newspapers and magazines, as well as national publications. His memoir, *The Loneliness of the Long Distance Teacher*, is available at Amazon.com. E-mail him at edwardajoseph@optonline.net.

Janet Sheppard Kelleher, graduate of Sweet Briar College, authored

Big C, little ta-ta: Kicking Breast Cancer's Butt in 7 Humorous Stories, the first of an inspirational gift book series based on how she used humor to whip cancer. *Big C, Bosom Buddies* and *Big C, Big Difference* debut in March and September. E-mail her at gop53her@gmail.com.

Deborah J. Kinsinger is a life coach, writer, traveller, and mom. She has a private practice in Canada. Deborah believes in the power of positive thinking, in listening to one's own inner intuition and in the magic inherent in everyday life.

Mary Ann Klein received her Bachelor of Science and two Master of Science degrees, with honors, from Adelphi University, NY. She was a resource room teacher for twenty-eight years and now privately tutors and teaches piano and religion. She loves spending time with family and friends and hopes to write inspirational children's books.

Elizabeth S. Kline earned her B.A. degree with honors from Vanderbilt University in 1977. A medical biller by day, she continues to write and is delighted to have her second story published by Chicken Soup for the Soul. She enjoys metal detecting, crafting and keeping up with her two kids, two cats and a dog named Linus.

Joyce Laird is a freelance writer living in Southern California with her menagerie of animal companions. Her features have been published in many magazines, including *Cat Fancy*, *Grit*, *Mature Living*, *I Love Cats* and *Vibrant Life*. She contributes regularly to *Woman's World* and to the Chicken Soup for the Soul anthology.

Cathi LaMarche is a novelist, essayist, poet, and educator. Her work appears in over two dozen books. Residing in Missouri with her husband, two children, and three dogs, she is currently working on her second novel.

Stephen Lautens is a writer and lawyer who has written a weekly column for a number of major Canadian newspapers including the

National Post, Toronto Sun, Calgary Sun and *The London Free Press*. He also appears on TV and radio. When not writing he can be found on Twitter. E-amil him at stephen@lautens.com.

Scarlett Lewis is the mother of Jesse Lewis, who was killed in his first grade classroom during the tragedy at Sandy Hook Elementary School. She founded the Jesse Lewis Choose Love Foundation and wrote the book *Nurturing Healing Love* based on a prophetic message her son wrote on their kitchen chalkboard.

Dana Liesegang is a certified life coach, expert in spinal cord injury recovery, and 2014 Hero of Forgiveness Award recipient given by the Worldwide Forgiveness Alliance. Her memoir, *Falling Up: My Wild Ride from Victim to Kick-Ass Victor*, will be published in fall 2015 by Hay House Publishing. Learn more at Danaliesegangbook.com.

Julia Lucas has always loved ghost stories, and dreams of being an author. But for now, she designs needlework projects for magazines. She has been married for thirty-seven years, has two stepsons and two grandchildren.

Jesse Malarsie is a stay-at-home mom with three young children and works as a child photographer in the Great Salt Lake City area. She also helps manage her husband's business endeavors and is a fan of traveling. Jesse likes to read, craft, be outdoors and is an avid NHL and college football fan.

Kristen Margetson is passionate about education and travel. She was a high school social studies teacher for fourteen years and spent many summers traveling to other nations in an effort to inform her students about the global community. Her favorite writing companion is her neurotic Jack Russell mix, Bosley.

Tina Wagner Mattern is a Portland, OR writer who has been blessed with more miracles in her life than she can ever count: She has a wonderful husband, two awesome kids, and is a fifteen-year cancer survivor, to name only a few. This will be her eighth story in the Chicken Soup for the Soul series. E-mail her at tinamattern@earthlink.net.

Claudia McCants calls herself a survivor, and she believes God guides her life. She encourages people through her writing, showing them that even the worst circumstances can be survived when you trust in God. Her latest novel, *Broken Angel*, was published in 2013. She is currently working on a book about prayer.

Though her career is in music, **Cynthia McGarity** has an international following for her blog, *God's Daily Message... for the terminally dense.* She's a Master Teaching Artist for The Young Americans and The Walt Disney Company. Her latest project, the *Branching Out in Faith* app, is available through iTunes. God is the greatest!

Kathy McGovern is a founding member of the Christian music group Ekklesia, and the composer of the popular Christmas song, "Mary Had a Baby." Kathy writes a weekly scripture column, "The Story and You," which appears in parish bulletins around the country. Visit her website at www.thestoryandyou.com.

Curt Melliger grew up in the middle of America and left at age seventeen to see the rest of it. During his travels, he worked a variety of jobs before beginning his writing career. Since then, over seventy of his articles have been published. He currently writes a column for the *Four Corners Free Press*, and lives near Cortez, CO.

Jan Penton Miller graduated with honors from the University of Southern Mississippi. She is the mother of three wonderful children and grandmother to two beautiful grands. Jan is a remarried widow whose heart's desire is to honor God and encourage others with her writing. E-mail her at lilsisjan@yahoo.com.

Marie-Therese Miller is the author of nonfiction books for children and teens, including the Dog Tales series, *Managing Responsibilities*, and *Rachel Carson*. Eight of her stories appear in Chicken Soup for the Soul books. She is completing her doctorate in English at St. John's University. Learn more at www.marie-theresemiller.com.

Jackie Minniti is a former teacher and the award-winning author of *Project June Bug*, a novel about a teacher's efforts to help a student with ADHD. She is a columnist for *The Island Reporter* in St. Petersburg, FL, and is a previous contributor to Chicken Soup for the Soul. Learn more at www.jackieminniti.com.

Linda Newton is an Empowerment Educator, helping people find healing and strength for a better life. See her blog at youtube.com/user/answersfrommomanddad. She has written three books, including *12 Ways to Turn Your Pain into Praise*. Learn more at www.LindaNewtonSpeaks.com.

Sandy Novotny is a dedicated wife and homeschooling mother with a passion for writing. Describing her life as "joyfully rooted in our Creator," she prioritizes her time in pursuit of His truth. She is currently working on a new blog project and eBook series at www.beconvicted.com.

Cheryl Bland Oliver has been blessed to be a stay-at-home mom for twenty years to daughters Anna, Kathleen and Lauren. She is co-creator of the Lauren and Kathleen Oliver Scholarship Fund (see Facebook page for details) and is currently writing an inspirational memoir about grief, love, and hope.

Beth Huettner Olsen is a wife, mom, daughter, sister, and aunt. She taught school for thirty years, most all of them at Immanuel Lutheran School in Columbus, NE. Beth retired at the end of the 2013-2014 school year, and is now substitute teaching. She loves nature, quilting, cooking, and spending time with family and friends.

Nancy Emmick Panko is a retired RN who loves to write. She belongs to The Light of Carolina Christian Writers group and the Cary Senior Writing Circle. Her story "A Journey of Healing" appeared in *Chicken Soup for the Soul: Find Your Inner Strength*. She and her husband, George, live in North Carolina.

Kathleen Pellicano is a transplant from a cool, crisp North Shore, Long Island town to the dramatic, steamy city of Savannah. She likes to use her writing to share her experience and observation of the world around her. She doesn't claim to pursue mystical or spiritual topics but finds they present themselves to her unbidden.

Laura Lee Perkins is a writer, educator and musician (flutist — ten CDs). She has earned five Artist-in-Residencies, eleven grants and third place in the 80th Writer's Digest Awards (Inspirational category). Her book, *Lighting Your Spiritual Passion*, was recently published. E-mail her at spiritualquest@earthlink.net or learn more at www.LauraLeePerkinsAuthor.com.

Connie Pombo is a freelance writer, author and speaker. Her stories have appeared in numerous publications and compilations, including the Chicken Soup for the Soul series. Connie enjoys traveling, running and swimming. She is working on her first fiction novel based in Sicily. Learn more at www.conniepombo.com.

Beckie Pruder is a married mom of two girls and has worked as a financial services manager in Canada for forty years. Beckie also loves gardening, spending time with family and friends and is an avid hockey fan. This is her first published story!

Heather Rodin is a freelance writer and author of *Prince of Vodou-Breaking the Chains* being released later this year. She serves as Executive Director for Hope Grows Haiti, and lives with her husband Gord on an acreage near Peterborough, Ontario, Canada.

Beth Saadati is an English teacher and has invested her time and heart into the lives of hundreds of teenagers. She is currently teaching writing classes, homeschooling her son and daughter, drafting two books, and sharing a message of hope in the aftermath of her beloved firstborn's suicide. E-mail her at bethsaadati@gmail.com.

Theresa Sanders is honored to be a frequent Chicken Soup for the Soul contributor. She lives with her husband near St. Louis, MO, and has four grown children. Theresa loves connecting with readers. Stop by and chat with her on Facebook at www.facebook.com/pages/Theresa-Sanders-Author/208490939276032.

Eloise Elaine Ernst Schneider is a writer and artist. She has published several books, including *Taking Hearing Impairment to School* and *Jesus is Born*. EloiseArt can be found in several physical and online galleries. Her most popular renderings are located at http://fineartamerica.com/profiles/eloise-elaine-schneider.html.

Bette Schumann teaches sixth grade and is a school nurse in a small Christian school in Georgia. After her five children and fourteen grandchildren were grown, she has returned to writing and oil painting. Some day she hopes to write and illustrate a book for tweens. Learn more at bschumannartist.com.

Gail Sellers enjoys writing, in particular inspirational, animal (cat), and children's stories. She enjoys spending relaxing days at the cottage with her husband Tony. E-mail her at gailsellers2011@gmail.com.

Marti Davidson Sichel graduated *cum laude* from the University of Connecticut with a BA degree in English. In the constant pursuit of knowledge (and trivia fodder), she loves to travel and read, takes in a ton of film and theater, adores a good podcast, is always looking for her next best recipe and totally geeks out on science.

For twenty years **Sandra Sladkey** wrote and produced an internationally syndicated Christian children's radio program. Since the mid-1980s, she has presented live Bible-based children's programs at churches, conferences, and retreats. Her passions are writing, acting, and directing plays. Read her blog at heaven-headed.blogspot.com.

Reverend Jim Solomon, a former businessman, has helped over 1,000 families and individuals across the nation experience life-change through counsel and care. He lives with his wife and two children in Newtown, CT, serving as Pastor of New Hope Community Church and chaplain to the Newtown Police Department.

Judee Stapp has written stories and poems all her life. She lives with her husband John of twenty-three years, and has three children, two sons-in-law, and three grandchildren. She loves Angels baseball, reading and travel. Judee plans to continue to inspire adults and children with her writing about hope and miracles.

Diane Stark is a former teacher turned stay-at-home mom and freelance writer. She loves to write about the important things in life: her family and her faith. She lives with her husband and their five children in southern Indiana. E-mail her at DianeStark19@yahoo.com.

Jolene Starr, M.D., worked as a psychiatrist for over twenty-five years, but is now a writer and a poet. Her soon-to-be published memoir is entitled *Thirteen Days: Psychedelics and Self-Discovery in the Mexican Jungle*. She has three daughters and one granddaughter, and enjoys traveling, hiking and skiing.

Cathy Stenquist is a mother of three who loves to write about everyday connections with God and with each other. You can follow her creative explorations on her blog: cathystenquist.tumblr.com, where she shares her love of writing, painting and cooking. She is currently writing her first inspirational children's book.

Dani Stone is an author from the flatlands of Kansas. When she's not writing marketing copy for Lee Media Group or romantic comedy stories, she's probably lost in a book. Dani is proud to be founder of VOGMParents.org, an organization created after her daughter battled a rare brain disorder, vein of Galen malformation.

Julia Shepherd Tang is a grant writer and teacher of the Art of Living Happiness Program. She received her masters in education from Harvard University in 2003. She enjoys hiking, sailing, traveling and meditating. She lives in the San Francisco Bay Area with her husband Jonathan and her two beautiful girls.

Since 2006, **Carol Marsden Taylor** has lived in beautiful Sedona, AZ with her husband Steve. Carol has always been interested in the afterlife, and feels a close connection to her friends and family members who now live in that realm.

Leslie Tierney lives in New Jersey and is a dance teacher/choreographer for children and adults. For over twenty years, she's found joy by encouraging and inspiring women in their faith through Bible study and prayer. Her latest endeavors include writing and speaking at women's conferences. Learn more at www.leslietierney.com.

Deborah Voigt is one of the world's leading dramatic sopranos, revered for her performances in the operas of Richard Wagner and Richard Strauss, and for her portrayals of iconic heroines in Italian opera. Her memoir, *Call Me Debbie: True Confessions of a Down-to-Earth Diva*, was published by HarperCollins in January 2015.

Pat Wahler is a grant writer by day and award-winning writer of essays and short stories by night. She is proud to be a contributor to six previous Chicken Soup for the Soul titles. A lifelong animal lover, Pat ponders critters, writing, and life's little mysteries at critteralley.blogspot.com.

Beverly Walker loves her time with grandchildren when she isn't writing,

Facebooking, scrapbooking or being caregiver for her husband who is battling cancer. She and their cat Maya take good care of him.

Nick Walker is a TV meteorologist with The Weather Channel in Atlanta, GA, and a songwriter/author of *Sing Along with the Weather Dude*, a CD/book teaching children weather basics, and *Don't Get Scared, Just Get Prepared*, a CD of songs teaching storm preparedness. Contact Nick at his "Weather Dude" website at www.wxdude.com.

Terri Webster wrote *Markers for Single Moms: Finding God's Direction in the Chaos*, available on Amazon.com. She's working on two more to complete a series. Her single, "When All Seems Lost," featuring Sara Oliver, is available on iTunes and Google Play. She founded Spring Ministries, a 501c3 ministry to single parents in 2011.

Elizabeth Adinolfi West is a full-time English instructor at Central Piedmont Community College. She is married to her husband Mark and has two children, John and Colleen. She enjoys reading, traveling and most of all teaching her students how to love writing. She contributes to a weekly blog shared with her sister.

Helen Wilder, a former kindergarten/first grade teacher in southeastern Kentucky, is married with one daughter, a son-in-law, and one grand puppy, Paco. Helen is passionate about teaching young children, storytelling, journaling, scrapbooking, reading, and writing inspirational articles.

Cynthia Zayn lives in the Atlanta area, and is the author of *Narcissistic Lovers: How to Cope, Recover and Move On*. She has taught in public and private schools throughout the United States and Mexico City, and now works as a freelance editor for community magazines as she pursues a full-time career as an author.

Karen Vincent Zizzo, MA, is an author and inspirational speaker whose passion is to inspire people to overcome obstacles in their lives. She generously shares very personal messages of faith, hope, love and the power of prayer through her Ask and You Shall Receive series of books, CDs and workbooks at karenzizzo.com.

406 Meet Our Contributors : Hope & Miracles

Meet Our Authors

Amy Newmark was a writer, speaker, Wall Street analyst and business executive in the worlds of finance and telecommunications for more than thirty years. Today she is publisher, editor-in-chief and coauthor of the Chicken Soup for the Soul book series. By curating and editing inspirational true stories from ordinary people who have had extraordinary experiences, Amy has kept the twenty-one-year-old Chicken Soup for the Soul brand fresh and relevant, and still part of the social zeitgeist.

Amy graduated *magna cum laude* from Harvard University where she majored in Portuguese and minored in French. She wrote her thesis about popular, spoken-word poetry in Brazil, which involved traveling throughout Brazil and meeting with poets and writers to collect their stories. She is delighted to have come full circle in her writing career — from collecting poetry "from the people" in Brazil as a twenty-year-old to, three decades later, collecting stories and poems "from the people" for Chicken Soup for the Soul.

Amy has a national syndicated newspaper column and is a frequent radio and TV guest, passing along the real-life lessons and useful tips she has picked up from reading and editing thousands of Chicken Soup for the Soul stories.

She and her husband are the proud parents of four grown children and in her limited spare time, Amy enjoys visiting them, hiking, and reading books that she did not have to edit.

Natasha Stoynoff began her career as a teenaged entertainment sleuth in her hometown of Toronto, nabbing interviews and photos of elusive celebrities like Bruce Springsteen, Marlon Brando, and Madonna for the local dailies.

After earning a B.A. in English and Psychology at York University and studying Journalism, she worked as a two-way news reporter/photographer at the *Toronto Star* and created her own Showbiz column, "Celebrity Bytes," at the *Toronto Sun*.

While still in Canada, Natasha became a correspondent for *People* and *Time* magazines, covering the Cannes International Film Festival and writing cover stories on sports, politics, and human interest. Before the turn of the century, she moved to New York City to join *People* on staff, where she remained for more than a decade interviewing top film and music icons including Meryl Streep, Paul McCartney, and Lauren Bacall.

Currently the author of ten books (with more in the works) including two New York Times bestsellers, Natasha lives in New York City where she is writing a screenplay that involves a lot of hope and a few good miracles.

Thank You

We owe huge thanks to all of our contributors. We know that you poured your hearts and souls into the thousands of stories that you shared with us, and ultimately with each other. As we read and edited these stories, we were truly amazed by your miraculous experiences and your stories of hope. We appreciate your willingness to share these inspiring and encouraging stories with our readers.

We could only publish a small percentage of the stories that were submitted, but we read every single one and even the ones that do not appear in the book had an influence on us and on the final manuscript. We owe special thanks to our editor Susan Heim, who read all the stories submitted for this book and helped us narrow the field down to the finalists. After we chose the 101 stories, managing editor Kristiana Pastir put together the initial manuscript and chose most of the inspirational quotations that start off each story. Our assistant publisher D'ette Corona worked with all the contributors to make sure they approved our edits, and she and senior editor Barbara LoMonaco performed their normal masterful proofreading job.

We also owe a very special thanks to our creative director and book producer, Brian Taylor at Pneuma Books, for his brilliant vision for our covers and interiors.

~Amy Newmark and Natasha Stoynoff

Sharing Happiness, Inspiration, and Wellness

Real people sharing real stories, every day, all over the world. In 2007, *USA Today* named *Chicken Soup for the Soul* one of the five most memorable books in the last quarter-century. With over 100 million books sold to date in the U.S. and Canada alone, more than 200 titles in print, and translations into more than forty languages, "chicken soup for the soul" is one of the world's best-known phrases.

Today, twenty-two years after we first began sharing happiness, inspiration and wellness through our books, we continue to delight our readers with new titles, but have also evolved beyond the bookstore, with wholesome and balanced pet food, delicious nutritious comfort food, and a major motion picture in development. As a socially conscious company, we use the sales of our products to give back, supporting numerous non-profits in the U.S. and across the globe. Whatever you're doing, wherever you are, Chicken Soup for the Soul is "always there for you™." Thanks for reading!

Share with Us

We all have had Chicken Soup for the Soul moments in our lives. If you would like to share your story or poem with millions of people around the world, go to chickensoup.com and click on "Submit Your Story." You may be able to help another reader, and become a published author at the same time. Some of our past contributors have launched writing and speaking careers from the publication of their stories in our books!

We only accept story submissions via our website. They are no longer accepted via mail or fax.

To contact us regarding other matters, please send us an e-mail through webmaster@chickensoupforthesoul.com, or fax or write us at:

Chicken Soup for the Soul
P.O. Box 700
Cos Cob, CT 06807-0700
Fax: 203-861-7194

One more note from your friends at Chicken Soup for the Soul: Occasionally, we receive an unsolicited book manuscript from one of our readers, and we would like to respectfully inform you that we do not accept unsolicited manuscripts and we must discard the ones that appear.

Miracles happen every day! And these 101 true stories of divine intervention, answered prayers, healing, and extraordinary connections prove that miracles can happen to anyone at any time. You will be awed and uplifted by these personal stories of faith, prayer, and healing that show a higher power at work in our lives.

978-1-61159-932-9

When good things

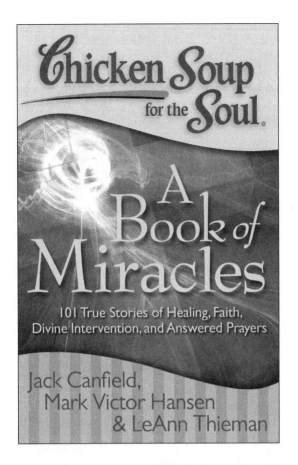

Everyone loves a good miracle story, and this book provides 101 true stories of healing, divine intervention, and answered prayers. These amazing, personal stories prove that God is alive and active in the world today, working miracles on our behalf. The incredible accounts show His love and involvement in our lives. This book of miracles will encourage, uplift, and recharge the faith of all Christian readers.

978-1-935096-51-1

happen to good people

When our loved ones leave this world, our connection with them does not end. Sometimes when we see or hear from them, they give us signs and messages. Sometimes they speak to us in dreams or they appear in different forms. The stories in this book, both religious and secular, will amaze you, giving you new knowledge, insight and awareness about the connection and communication we have with those who have passed on or those who have experienced dying and coming back.

978-1-935096-91-7

More hope & miracles

Chicken Soup for the Soul

for the Soul.

Touched by an Angel

101 Miraculous Stories of Faith, Divine Intervention, and Answered Prayers

Amy Newmark
Foreword by Gabrielle Bernstein

Seen or unseen, angels are in our midst! These divine guides, guardian angels, and heavenly messengers help and guide us when we need it most. In this collection of 101 miraculous stories, real people share real stories about their incredible, personal angel experiences of faith, divine intervention, and answered prayers. You will be awed and inspired by these true personal stories, from religious and non-religious, about hope, healing, and help from angels.

978-1-61159-941-1

to deepen your faith!

Every cloud has a silver lining. Readers will be inspired by these 101 real-life stories from people just like them, taking a positive attitude to the ups and downs of life, and remembering to be grateful and count their blessings. This book continues Chicken Soup for the Soul's focus on inspiration and hope, and its stories of optimism and faith will encourage readers to stay positive during challenging times and in their everyday lives.

978-1-935096-56-6

Change your life with

Chicken Soup for the Soul

Count Your Blessings

101 Stories of Gratitude, Fortitude, and Silver Linings

Jack Canfield,
Mark Victor Hansen, Amy Newmark,
Laura Robinson & Elizabeth Bryan

This uplifting book reminds readers of the blessings in their lives, despite financial stress, natural disasters, health scares and illnesses, housing challenges and family worries. This feel-good book is a great gift for New Year's or Easter, for someone going through a difficult time, or for Christmas. These stories of optimism, faith, and strength remind us of the simple pleasures of family, home, health, and inexpensive good times.

978-1-935096-42-9

positive thinking & gratitude

Chicken Soup for the Soul

Changing lives one story at a time™
www.chickensoup.com